THE GOSPEL HISTORY AND ITS TRANSMISSION

THE GOSPEL HISTORY AND ITS TRANSMISSION

BY

F. CRAWFORD BURKITT, M.A., D.D.

NORRISIAN PROFESSOR OF DIVINITY IN THE
UNIVERSITY OF CAMBRIDGE

Wipf and Stock Publishers
150 West Broadway • Eugene OR 97401
2001

The Gospel History and its Transmission

By Burkitt, F. Crawford
ISBN: 1-57910-759-1

Reprinted by *Wipf and Stock Publishers*
150 West Broadway • Eugene OR 97401

Previously published by T & T Clark, 1925.

PREFACE

The ten Lectures contained in this volume were delivered in the spring of this year at the Passmore Edwards Settlement in London as the Jowett Lectures for 1906. I repeated them with very little change for my inaugural course at Cambridge as Norrisian Professor of Divinity, so that it seemed advisable to keep them in lecture form when they came to be printed.

It is sometimes supposed that the result of modern historical criticism is to diminish the historical value of the Gospels. My own researches have made me believe that there is a much larger element of genuine history in the Canonical Gospels, than a general view of the tendencies which influenced Christendom during the first century and a half of its existence might have led one to anticipate. The general aim, therefore, of the last three Lectures, those on the Gospel Canon, on Marcion, and on the Apocryphal Gospels, is to elucidate this to me somewhat remarkable fact, to examine the reasons why the tradition by which the Catholic Church came to hold fast is on the whole so much truer to the actual course of events than the theories of the Heretics.

While the volume was passing through the press, I read Professor Harnack's new book *Lukas der Arzt.* After some consideration I thought it best to leave my Lectures as they were, without attempting to review this brilliant vindication of the Lucan authorship of the Third Gospel and the Acts. With the greater part of Harnack's thesis I find myself in thorough agreement, though I still hold that S. Luke had read Josephus (or at least part of the *Antiquities*), and that both Gospel and Acts were the work of the author's old age. But whatever view may be taken, there can be no doubt that Harnack has said in this monograph the true and necessary word on many a vexed question connected with the subject; especially I must here single out the admirable remarks on the 'Paulinism' of S. Luke. 'Wo ist denn der Paulinismus, ausser bei Marcion, geblieben?' asks Harnack (p. 101). He himself says something in answer to this pregnant question, but the fact that he asks it at all may serve to shew that my Lecture on Marcion was not out of place in this book.

F. C. BURKITT.

CAMBRIDGE, *October* 1906.

PREFACE TO SECOND EDITION

This new Edition of my Lectures is an almost unchanged reprint of the former Edition. I have added a Note on de Bruyne's discovery of the Marcionite Prologues to the Pauline Epistles, and I have corrected a few minor errors. But I cannot say that the criticism, to which parts of my book has been subjected, has caused me to regret the line I took. The criticism has been exceedingly kindly; but in a good many cases it has seemed to me that the writers have not quite understood what I was aiming at, or what were the rocks ahead which I had perceived. To judge by most of the criticisms one would suppose that I had been the first person to deny the historical value of the Fourth Gospel for determining the course of events in the public life of our Lord, or the first to have rejected the historicity of the Raising of Lazarus! As a rule the critics limit themselves to bringing forward reasons why the Synoptic Gospels are silent about the Raising of Lazarus: what they have not done is to explain how and where the tale as told in the Fourth

Gospel can possibly be inserted into the framework given by S. Mark. The 'argument from silence' in this case is not merely that the Raising of Lazarus is ignored by S. Mark, but that his narrative appears to leave no room to fit it in.

What I have had in view in writing these Lectures on the Gospel History and its transmission to us is something very different from an attack upon the much assaulted Fourth Gospel. I was not anxious to prove that the narrative books of the New Testament are not all historical: that was a conclusion only too likely to be arrived at in the case of the Sacred Writings of an obscure Jewish sect that was destined in the end to dominate the Roman world. If there is one thing more than another that clearly issues from A. Schweitzer's admirable history of the attempts to write a Life of Jesus (*Von Reimarus zu Wrede*, 1906) it is this, that the complete historical scepticism of Bruno Bauer was not a mere individual eccentricity, but the expression of serious difficulties in an excessively complicated historical problem. The rise of Christianity is such an extraordinary event, that we must be prepared to find again and again that those who study it find themselves bewildered, and that then they begin to doubt whether the traditional accounts of the process have any historical foundation at all.

PREFACE TO SECOND EDITION

The more we investigate the early history of the Christian Church with open and unprejudiced eyes, the more we find ourselves in a strange world, dominated by fixed ideas that are not our fixed ideas and permeated by an intellectual atmosphere quite different from ours. We come to ourselves, and we rub our eyes and wonder if what we have been gazing upon ever had any reality. It was for the student in this state of mind that my book was written. What I have attempted to shew is, that at least the Gospel according to S. Mark is in touch with the actual condition of Palestine in the times of the Herods; and, further, that the course of events in the second century enables us to understand some of the reasons which led the Church to cherish on the whole a historical, as distinct from an ideal, account of the foundation of Christianity.

F. C. BURKITT.

CAMBRIDGE, *May*, 1907.

PREFACE TO THIRD EDITION

In the interval between the second and the third editions of this book, English readers have been effectively introduced to what is called the Eschatological view of the Gospel History, most prominently associated with the name of Dr. Schweitzer, of Strassburg, and the question arises how far modifications should be introduced dealing directly with the problems now under discussion. After consideration it seems to me better not to make any great changes in the text as originally written. I have altered a phrase here and there, and rewritten a paragraph in order to bring Chapter IV. more definitely into line with the conclusions so eloquently set forth by Dr. Verrall in his *Christ before Herod*.[1] But even Dr. Verrall's Essay raises some objections to the point of view from which the public career of Jesus Christ is looked at in part of Chapter III., and certainly if this part of the book be left unchanged some indications of its relation to Dr. Schweitzer's view will not be out of place.

[1] See p. 138.

Put in a single phrase, the question is whether I ought to retain the Map facing p. 92. One of the most curious features of the Gospel History as told in S. Mark is the long absence from Galilee indicated in Mk vii 24, 31. The small amount of tradition connected with this period, which very likely took up more than half the time included in the Ministry, is easily explicable, for we are expressly told in vii 24 that Jesus had sought retirement; but the question remains why He sought it.

The object of the Map is to point out the fact that, according to Mark, during this period of retirement Jesus had avoided the dominions of Herod Antipas. But Dr. Schweitzer does not connect this retirement with Herod at all: Jesus, he says (*Quest*, p. 362), 'really does flee; not, however, from hostile Scribes, but from the people, who dog His footsteps in order to await in His company the appearing of the Kingdom of God and of the Son of Man—to await it in vain.' And while Dr. Schweitzer seems to exclude Herod from one point of view, Dr. Verrall from another reminds us that 'the "hostility of Antipas," "the designs of Antipas," "the danger from Antipas," are phrases easily found, as one may say, anywhere except in the Evangelists.' Perhaps this is a little over-stated, unless we are careful to understand it exclusively of the personal attitude of the Tetrarch; but it may serve to warn a reconstructor of the Gospel history against unduly magnifying the political prominence of our Lord and His disciples, or of the danger in which they stood from the government of Galilee.

Nevertheless I retain the Map, and with it most of the theory which the Map is intended to illustrate. In the first place, it really does exhibit the places named in our only source, and the order in which they are named. Gennesaret, Tyre, Sidon, Decapolis, 'Dalmanutha'-Tiberias, Bethsaida, Cæsarea Philippi, a journey through Galilee, 'the borders of Judæa,' Jericho, Jerusalem,—these are the stations named in Mark; and even if it be no true itinerary, it is well that we should clearly realise what kind of route our document puts before us. On an uncoloured sheet of paper the route is indeed odd; with the territory of Antipas indicated it becomes, I venture to think, more intelligible, and I have suggested in the Note to p. 92 that the enduring physical features of Palestine supply some reasons for the most northerly angle of it.

Very possibly I may have exaggerated 'the danger from Antipas'; in any case the parts avoided are the Tetrarch's territories and also (till the last journey) the land of Judæa. Possibly if I were to plan the whole section over again I might lay more stress on the idea of retirement, of waiting for the Kingdom of God, rather than that of exile; but whatever may have been the cause the long cessation of public work still remains—*αὐτομάτη ἡ γῆ καρποφορεῖ*, and the Sower was letting the wheat and tares grow unchecked to the Harvest. Absence from Herod's territory was also absence from the districts where Jewish life and religion were predominant; it involved a cessation of most of the features which we commonly associate with our Lord's Ministry. We do not even know how many of the Disciples followed Jesus to the borders of Tyre.

It still seems to me that the idea of retirement and passive waiting for the Kingdom is not quite enough to explain all the data given by S. Mark. Especially, it is not enough to explain the passage through Galilee *incognito* (Mk ix 30); this, if nothing else does, points to the avoidance of definite political dangers, or rather the definite choice of one danger rather than another. Jesus goes to Jerusalem to die, because a Prophet must perish at Jerusalem—there and not elsewhere. The Gospels show us Jesus not only going forward to His Death, but also choosing the time of it and the place: it is one of the special merits of the Gospel according to Mark that it gives us some indications of the means whereby Jesus preserved His freedom until the time for the Passion arrived.

I have attempted elsewhere to set forth my reasons for regarding the picture of the Gospel History given in Mark as being in its main features historical.[1] The scope of this book never included a discussion of this fundamental question. What I specially have had in view has been a consideration of the reasons that led the Church to preserve so historical a tradition of its origins, and to contrast the Church's theory with a non-historical theory like Marcion's. It might have been thought in England a few years ago that such a consideration was unnecessary. Now we are confronted with the movement in which Professor Arthur Drews, of Karlsruhe, is the chief figure, the movement which preaches in the name of modern Comparative Religion that Jesus is not a historical personage at all, but the rendering into history of a primitive religious myth. In words notably orthodox in sound, Professor Drews declares that 'the Jesus of the Gospels is to be understood only as a God made man' (*The Christ Myth*, Eng. tr., p. 265), while his book ends by

[1] Besides what I have said in the little book called *The Earliest Sources for the Life of Jesus*, I have attempted to give my reasons for dissent from the historical scepticism of Wrede in the *American Journal of Theology* for the current year (1911).

saying that the 'chief obstacle to a monistic religion and attitude is the belief, irreconcilable with reason or history, in the historical reality of a "unique," ideal, and unsurpassable Redeemer' (p. 300). This book has reached a third edition in Germany. It is, in my opinion, as unsatisfactory as Marcion's Gospel; but the whole movement shows that the question of the existence of the merely historical, nationalistic, Jewish element in Christianity is still as living a question as it was in Marcion's day. It is the question whether human ideas or the one non-recurring Course of Events constitute the true reality. I cannot but believe that the Church was right when it included the Course of Events in the Christian Creed.

F. C. BURKITT.

CAMBRIDGE, *February*, 1911.

CONTENTS

1

CONTENTS

THE GOSPEL HISTORY AND ITS TRANSMISSION

I.

INTRODUCTORY.

Lo, in Four Volumes hath our Sun shone forth.
S. EPHRAIM, *Lamy* iv 659.

THE Gospel History and its transmission is a wide subject, and it is not to be supposed that any one could exhaust it in ten Lectures. At the same time, it is impossible to talk profitably for ten hours on a single subject, however wide, without going into details; and details are apt to be dry and tiresome. I am very glad, therefore, that my subject is one of such importance and interest to every thoughtful man who is born in a Christian land, that I can appeal to its general importance and interest when I claim your attention in the discussion of dry and tiresome details.

We are all agreed, I suppose, as to the importance of the Gospel History, whatever our religious views may be. The brief and tragic career of Jesus of Nazareth, put to a shameful death by the rulers of Jerusalem though He taught love to God and kindness to men, would in any case have been a moving and pathetic incident. But when we remember that this tragic incident was the immediate starting-point and source of all the varied manifestations of Christianity, we are compelled, whether we be orthodox or unorthodox, believers or agnostics, to acknowledge that the study of it has a transcendent interest, and we shall be prepared to admit beforehand that no pains and no attention can be too great to bestow on its investigation.

Nevertheless it is easy, nay inevitable, that we should sometimes lose sight of the greatness of the subject—inevitable, that is, if we give the several parts of our task the attention which they need. Indeed, the parts and the details are so interesting and absorbing to the investigator, that it is often easy for him to forget the whole. I shall therefore ask your pardon beforehand if I sometimes seem to be shewing you the trees, when you want a view of the wood. Before, then, we enter the wood together let us look at some of the reasons which make detailed examination of the trees necessary; or, to drop the metaphor, let us explain why we need to attack critical and literary questions about the Gospels, before busying ourselves with the real problems of the Gospel History.

The first thing that an unsophisticated little child asks about a story is, 'Is it true?' It is indeed the most vital and important question to ask, but the answer cannot generally be contained in a simple 'yes' or 'no.' And the child gradually learns, as he grows up, that 'Is it true?' must often be the last and not the first question to be asked. Undoubtedly this is the case in the study of the Gospel History. There is no dispute as to the object of our study. We want a true portrait of our Lord and of His work among men. But there is more than one kind of truth in portraiture. There is the truth of the photographer and the truth of the impressionist artist. A complete set of working drawings for S. Paul's might very well fail to reveal the true architectural relation of the Cathedral to the great City, which can be suggested by a picture, faulty and inaccurate as it may be in many a detail. It is not fair to blame the architectural drawing for failing to give the general impression, or to blame the picture which aims at giving a certain impression for being unreliable in details. And one of the problems before us is whether our Gospels are to be classed with architectural drawings or with impressionist pictures, or with some other kind of portraiture.

Besides this, we have to a great extent to reconstruct the Portrait for ourselves. As I have said, it is not fair to blame our documents for not giving us more than they profess to give; but at the same time we may legitimately try to learn from them more than the writers directly aimed to tell us. We have to learn not only to hear our witnesses, but also to cross-examine them.

To reconstruct the Portrait of Jesus Christ for ourselves—this is a task which is incumbent not only upon all Christians, but also upon all those who are concerned with religion and the aspirations of the human race. And to make this reconstruction we must study the Gospels. It will be one of the conclusions which I shall bring before you, that the study of all Four Canonical Gospels, even the Fourth Gospel, is necessary. Neither of them is entirely superseded by the others. Each one of them contains an exceedingly valuable element which is not represented in the others. I am not saying, I am very far from saying, that each of our Gospels is equal to the others in historical value or in philosophical value. The contrary is the case. But each of them does singly preserve portions and aspects of the Gospel History which we cannot afford to lose.

I have spoken of 'reconstructing the Portrait of Jesus Christ for ourselves.' Some of you may perhaps reply that this is not a work for everybody, and that it is not to be expected that the ordinary Christian, who has his own work and his own studies to attend to, should go through the critical investigations that occupy learned men. You will expect me, perhaps, to tell you of this brilliant Monograph, or that epoch-making Article, which will really explain the origin of Christianity, or the relations of the Gospels to one another and to history. This is, of course, part of my business, but it is the least important part. Naturally there are some branches of Gospel study which must be left in the hands of specialists, and in regard to these branches our chief duty is loyally to accept the specialists' matured conclusions. To begin with, there are questions of language. The Gospels are written in Greek, and they deal for the most part with the sayings and doings of persons who spoke a language akin to Hebrew, known to modern scholars as Jewish Aramaic. Now it is eminently desirable that those who make a study of the Gospels should know Greek and Aramaic. You have only to read Professor Wellhausen's short commentaries on the Synoptic Gospels to see how many things are immediately clear to one who has a thorough command of Aramaic, which are only half-perceived by less fully equipped scholars. And it is obvious that minute investigation of the style of the several Gospels, of the use the Evangelists made of their sources and of the Old Testament, can only be satisfactorily carried out in the original Greek.

Yet the fact remains that an intelligent use of the English Bible brings us face to face with the most important Gospel problems, and even suggests their solution. It is one of the great attractions of Biblical study that the chief document is in everybody's hands in an available form, so that all the main results and many of the processes of learned critical study can be at once made plain to those who will read the English Bible carefully for themselves. Far be it from me to undervalue the help that erudition gives, or to seem to assert even for one moment that the investigator can do without it. Again and again the amateur in Biblical study, as in other subjects, falls into errors and pitfalls from which a little more solid learning might have saved him. But if the ordinary Bible reader—I will not say 'the man in the street,' for that phrase has a certain connotation of heedlessness, which disqualifies the class to whom it is applied from the right to sit in judgement—but if the ordinary Bible reader must be shy of trying to blaze out a path for others to follow, he has every right to demand that the steps which others cut for him shall be made quite plain. There is nothing in the nature of the subject to prevent him from understanding every step of the way that his guide is taking him, and sometimes he may claim the right of refusing to follow any further in a new path, at least till cause be shewn that it is the right one.

What I have said about questions of language is true also of textual criticism. The scholar really familiar with the ancient manuscripts and versions of the New Testament has a great critical instrument at his command. He sees before his eyes the process by which many a characteristic phrase has become obliterated in the course of the transmission of the Gospels down to modern times. He can read the Gospels in a form appreciably nearer the originals than it was possible for Erasmus or Bentley to do. But after all, the problems raised by the MSS only touch the fringe of the subject; the great difficulties are not obliterated in the purest text, or in the most corrupt.

The only things of quite capital importance that the textual criticism of the Gospels tells the ordinary, non-specialist student is—(i) that the paragraph known as the last twelve verses of S. Mark [xvi 9–20] is a later addition, made to complete a work which (as we have it) is mutilated and incomplete at the end; and (ii) that there was circulated in the West of Europe, about the middle of the second century, an edition of the Four Gospels which contained a number of noteworthy interpolations, some of which present claims to be regarded as materials for history intrinsically as strong as can be urged for much of what is found in the genuine and authentic text of the Gospels. The story of the woman taken in adultery is certainly not a genuine portion of the Fourth Gospel, and the story of the man working on the Sabbath, found in Codex Bezæ, is certainly not a genuine portion of the Third Gospel (see p. 9). We cannot trace back the literary history of these tales with any assurance, but they do not read like the invention of an annotator.

But—and this is the point which I wish to emphasise here—suppose that a student had no knowledge of MSS and versions beyond what he finds in the margin of the Authorized and the Revised English versions. In this case he will

MATT xii 3–8.	MK ii 25–28.	LK vi 3–5.
. . he said unto them,	. . . he said unto them,	. . . Jesus answering them said,
Have ye not read	Did ye never read	Have ye not read even this,
what David did, when	what David did, when	what David did, when
he was	he had need, and was	he was
an hungred, and	an hungred, he, and	an hungred, he, and
they that were with him ;	they that were with him ;	they that were with him ;
how he entered	how he entered	how he entered
into the house of God,	into the house of God	into the house of God ;
	when Abiathar was high priest,	
and did eat	and did eat	and did take and eat
the shewbread,	the shewbread,	the shewbread,
which it was not lawful	which it is not lawful	and gave also to them
for him to eat, neither	to eat save for the priests,	that were with him ;
for them that were with him,	and gave also to them	which it is not lawful to
but only for the priests?	that were with him?	eat save for the priests alone?
Or have ye not read		[On the same day
in the law, how that on		seeing a certain man
the sabbath day		working on the sabbath,
the priests in the temple		he said to him,
profane the sabbath,		Man, if indeed thou know
and are guiltless?		what thou doest,
But I say unto you,	And he said	thou art blessed ;
that something greater	unto them,	but if thou know not,
than the temple is here.	The sabbath	thou art cursed
But if ye had known	was made	and a transgressor
what this meaneth,	for man,	of the law.]
'I desire mercy, and not	and not man	*So Codex Bezæ* (D).
sacrifice,' ye would not	for the sabbath :	*All other authorities have*
have condemned the guiltless.	so that	And he said unto them,
For the Son of Man is	the Son of Man is	The Son of Man is
lord of the sabbath.	lord also of the sabbath.	lord also of the sabbath.

not have heard of the story of the man working on the Sabbath, for there is no note about it in the margin of Lk vi 5. Consequently he will not be troubled to explain how the story was transmitted if it be genuine, or how it came to be invented if it be altogether unhistorical. Such a student will merely observe that in this whole section of stories about Sabbath observance S. Luke is content to follow S. Mark, as he does elsewhere. But when our student comes to investigate the corresponding section of S. Matthew he will find, even if he confines himself to the Authorized Version, that he has to face very much the same problem that he left in S. Luke to the professed textual critic. He will find that the First Evangelist bases his narrative on S. Mark, just as S. Luke did, but that he adds to the words of our Lord about David and the shewbread, 'Have ye not read in the law, how that on the sabbath day the priests in the temple profane the sabbath, and are guiltless? I say unto you, that something greater than the temple is here, but if ye had known what is meant by "I desire mercy, and not sacrifice," ye would not have condemned the guiltless.' Whence did our Evangelist get these words? Have they the same claim on our acceptance as those narratives which are related by all three Synoptic Evangelists? Have they any better claim on our acceptance than the precisely similar story of the man working on the Sabbath, found only in a single ancient MS?

Thus the attentive reader of the Gospels in English has forced upon him the same problems that occupy the technically learned textual critic. Moreover, the textual critic brings but little towards the direct solution of the problems, except what is afforded by the very existence of these important variants and interpolations. I mean, that the mere fact of their occurrence is enough to shew us that the text of the Gospels, the actual wording, and even to some extent the contents, were not treated during the second century with particular scrupulosity by the Christians who preserved and canonized them. There is nothing in the way which Christians treated the books of the New Testament during the first four centuries that corresponds with the care bestowed by the Jews upon the Hebrew Scriptures from the time of Aqiba onwards.

All this, of course, is sufficiently well known, and I am not bringing it forward now to discredit antiquated theories of verbal inspiration, or to justify us in making extensive and drastic changes in the transmitted text. What I have rather in mind is the danger of applying to the criticism of the Gospels a method which has been found suitable enough in the case of the Pentateuch, but is far too mechanical for the free and unofficial literary habits of the early Christian writers. We all know something about the 'higher criticism' of the Pentateuch. We know that the general structure of that venerable compilation has been divined, and the several documents of which it is composed marked off. The separation of these documents has been effected by internal evidence only, but there is such a general consensus of agreement in the final results that the outsider, the non-specialist, cannot but acquiesce in the verdict. I should be the last person in the world to say anything to disturb the assured results of Pentateuchal criticism. I firmly believe in the three main strata of legislation, viz. the books of Prophetic story (JE), the Deuteronomic literature (D), the Priestly Code (P). I believe that these three documents, or rather literatures, came into existence separately one after the other, and that they have been combined together to make our Pentateuch, as the critics say. But I have my private doubts whether we can trust some of the minor and minuter pieces of analysis, an analysis which descends to the confident assignment of every single fragment of the Massoretic Text to its proper source. I am pretty sure that we cannot reconstruct the earlier documents with anything like completeness, except perhaps the Priestly Code, which as a literary whole is the latest of them all. And I am absolutely certain that the analogy of the Pentateuch will not help us much when we try to investigate the sources of our Gospels.[1]

It is one thing to demonstrate that the Gospels were compiled from previously existing sources; it is quite another thing to attempt to reconstruct these sources. In the case of the Pentateuch there is some justification for the reconstructors. To begin with, the Pentateuch is essentially a codifying of legislation, and a code to be useful must in some respects be complete. Moreover, the compiler of the Pentateuch was dealing with an ancient and venerable literature. The later stratum (P) was already statute law; the earlier portion (JE, D) was a legacy from the old times, from the pre-exilic state. The main business of the compiler was incorporation; earlier documents and codes were to be superseded by the new Pandect. Something, of course, is left out in such a procedure, but most of what is important

[1] 'In den Erzählungsbüchern des Alten Testaments liegt die Sache ganz anders [als bei den Synoptikern], und auch dort kann die literarische Analyse zum Kinderspiel ausarten' (Wellhausen, *Einl. in die drei ersten Evangelien*, p. 57).

is retained. Indeed, one of the really striking features about the narrative in Genesis, to take the obvious instance, is the number of Doublets, *i.e.* stories told twice over. We have two stories of Creation, two stories of the Flood, two stories about the destruction of Sodom, two stories about the Patriarch's wife and the heathen monarch. The critical explanation, no doubt correct, is that in all cases these Doublets are parallel stories taken from the separate documents or literatures out of which the Pentateuch is compiled.

Now in the Gospels we do occasionally meet with the same sort of thing, but far less frequently, and the same explanation does not always seem to apply. The true analogy to the criticism of the Pentateuch in New Testament literature would have been afforded by the Diatessaron, if unfortunately the Gospels were no longer extant and we were reduced to extracting the Gospel history from Tatian's famous Harmony. The Diatessaron, like the Pentateuch, is a compilation. If we had only the Diatessaron to go upon, I think it very likely that critics might have identified the Fourth Gospel, and reconstructed it almost entire: this would correspond to the Priestly Code in the Pentateuch. It would further have been recognised that there were other earlier documents of superior historical value besides the Johannine Gospel, and some of the characteristics of some of these documents might have been discovered. We should probably also have distinguished the two Nativity stories of Matthew and Luke, and recognised the Jewish-Palestinian character of some sections of Matthew. But I do not think the Synoptic Gospels as wholes would have been successfully reconstructed; we should have had to remain content with passing historical judgement on single narratives and sayings.

Now, if we should fail when we attempt to reconstruct the Gospels out of the Diatessaron, supposing we had no independent knowledge of the Gospels themselves, how much more shall we fail if we attempt to reconstruct the sources of the Gospels out of the Gospels? Such an attempt assumes what may be called literary piety on the part of the surviving writer whose works we try to use as a quarry, and literary piety is a quality—I will not go so far as to call it an absolute virtue—which hardly makes its appearance in Christendom before 150 A.D. Indeed, there is not much of it to be found even then. I am not quite sure if I have made my meaning clear. What I mean can be illustrated by considering the same passage to which reference has already been made. I hope subsequently to shew you that our first Gospel, the Gospel according to Matthew, was directly based on our Gospel according to Mark; and, further, that this is the case with respect to the passage Matt xii 3–8, which has been already quoted. On this view, Matt xii 3–8 is simply rewritten from Mk ii 25–28, with another saying of our Lord, drawn from another source, worked into the narrative. As I say, I hope to give you some reasons for believing this in a subsequent Lecture; I must ask you now to take it more or less upon trust, merely premising that it is a generally accepted conclusion, not a private fad of my own. But the reason why it has been possible to formulate this conclusion is that the Gospel of Mark is actually before us. I venture to assert that if we had only had Matt xii 3–8 and Lk vi 3–5, we could never have reconstructed Mk ii 25–28, their common source. We should never have known that the common source contained a curious, and chronologically a rather inaccurate, reference to Abiathar, nor should we have guessed of the existence of the characteristic saying, 'The sabbath was made for man, and not man for the sabbath.' Being, as we are, in possession of the common source, we can give a fairly intelligible account of the manner in which the later Evangelists treated it, when adapting it for their own narratives; but we could not reconstruct the source from these later narratives alone.

The Gospel according to S. Mark is not the only source used by Matthew and Luke, but it is the only source which has survived. We see, clearly enough, that we could not have reconstructed the Gospel according to S. Mark out of the other two Synoptic Gospels, although between them nearly all Mark has been incorporated by Matthew and Luke. How futile, therefore, it is to attempt to reconstruct those other literary sources which seem to have been used by Matthew and Luke, but have not been independently preserved.

Another instance of the literary procedure of an Evangelist has been well characterised by my predecessor in the Norrisian Chair. He is writing of what he calls the 'moulding influence of the editor's hand,' and goes on to say: 'S. Mark's record of the opening words of the dialogue between our Lord and the rich young man is as follows (x 17 f):—"Good Master, what shall I do that I may inherit eternal life? . . . Why callest thou me good? None is good save one, even God." With this S. Luke's account (xviii 18 f) coincides. But in S. Matthew (xix 16 f) a significant variation confronts us. The word "good" reappears indeed, but its reference is wholly changed—"Master, what *good thing* shall I do that I may have eternal life? . . . Why askest thou me *concerning that which is good*? . . . One there is who is *good*." Here it is clear that the wording of the dialogue has been altered to avoid the appearance of our Lord's calling in question His own goodness, and of His refusing to accept the attribution to Himself of what is Divine.'[1]

So far Dr. Chase. It is quite evident that if we only had had the narrative of S. Matthew we should never have guessed how the dialogue stood in his source. We might have said that something was wrong in the report, and that our Lord was not generally accustomed to discuss the Meaning of Good, but we should have been unable to reconstruct the original form of the conversation. The chances would be that the most ingenious restoration would have been rather further from historical truth than the narrative as told in S. Matthew.

It may perhaps seem a melancholy doctrine, to teach that the Evangelists whose works we possess altered freely the earlier sources which they used as the basis of their narratives, and yet that we can do little towards reconstructing these earlier sources. Of course, it would be indeed unsatisfactory if we had reason to believe that the accounts of Jesus Christ on which we rely were

[1] *Cambridge Theological Essays*, p. 387.

misleading. If, for instance, it should be proved that the Gospel according to Mark, or according to John, gave a thoroughly false notion of the life or personality of our Lord, even when we looked at these documents from the proper point of view, then indeed we should be in a melancholy position. But as a matter of fact, this is far from being the case. Every picture demands that we shall look at it from the proper point of view, whether our object be to learn from the picture, or to pass judgement upon it. And when we come to examine the Fourth Gospel, the Gospel according to John, we shall find that it is necessary to look at it from a quite peculiar point of view. This we might expect beforehand to be the case with any work of exceptional character. But this does not prove it to be valueless, or that we could do better without it.

Let us admit at the outset that there are many things in the Gospel History, about which we most of us feel much excusable curiosity, which nevertheless we must be content to leave undefined. When a great man leaves this earth, we have begun to feel that all is not satisfactory unless we have the 'Life and Letters of Mr. Z.' in two volumes, written by one of his nearest friends, to be followed at an appropriate interval by 'The real Mr. Z.,' a work compiled by a more or less discriminating critic. If there be any dark or mysterious episodes in Mr. Z.'s career, we want the searchlight turned on to explain the matter from all points, and from the standpoint, if possible, of all the actors in the drama.

We cannot get that out of our materials for the Life of our Lord. On the very shortest estimate the length of the Ministry must have extended to about 400 days, and I doubt if our Gospels contain stories from 40 separate days. So that nine-tenths at least of the public life of Jesus remains to us a blank, even if we were to take every recorded incident as historical and accurately reported. And all the recorded sayings of Christ, how long would they take to pronounce? With due gravity and emphasis they might take six hours,—hardly, perhaps, so much. In other words, they would take no more than two great political speeches, and a considerably less time than this present course of Lectures.

Even apart from the results of the 'higher criticism,' we do not possess enough information to enable us to write a biography of our Lord after the modern pattern. But this is not all loss. The real question is not whether we have as much as we should like, but whether we have as much as we need. The craving for elaboration is really a kind of covetousness; and a man's life, as our

Lord Himself tells us, does not consist in the abundance and superfluity of things connected with him. How often it is one story, one letter, one illuminative saying or judgement of the subject of a bulky modern biography, which tells us more than all the rest what the real meaning of the life was. The part of Lady Macbeth is just 250 lines long; how many a biography in two large volumes tells us less of what is really essential about its hero!

To come back to the Evangelists, we have quite enough in mere bulk to obtain an intelligible picture of the Gospel History, if our materials are fairly trustworthy. We have admitted that it is to some extent and from some points of view regrettable that our sources are not more extensive. But I should like here to say a few words in passing upon another side of the question. I have said that our Evangelists altered freely the earlier sources which they used. They changed, added, omitted. This sounds, no doubt, very terrible and dangerous. Let us put the statement, then, in another form, a form quite as legitimate, but less shocking. Let us say that the Evangelists were historians, and not chroniclers. This does not assert that they were trustworthy or even truthful. There are plenty of people who do not agree with Macaulay or with

Froude, who would be eager to deny the quality of trustworthiness to these distinguished historians. 'Well,' you may say, 'this is worse than ever. Is it not a misfortune that our knowledge of Christ should come to us only through writers, of whom you assert that they are not less partisan than Macaulay, and not more trustworthy than Froude?'

Waiving the question for the present whether the Evangelists are, as a matter of fact, suitably compared with Macaulay and Froude, I still think there is something to be said in reply.

Put very shortly, I think we may say that a true impression is on the whole and for most people better conveyed by a friend than by an observer wholly dispassionate. What is the real reason for the modern demand for documents? Is it not because we believe in our hearts that we, the modern historian, have a better right than those who have gone before us to sit in judgement on the evidence? This conviction is justified in certain departments of thought, and it is not to be denied that some of these departments of thought concern Gospel study very nearly. One of them, of course, is the question of what is commonly called 'miracle'; no doubt, we are better qualified than the Christians at the end of the first century of our era to decide what is, and what is not, a likely contravention of the uniformity of nature. I am not so sure that we are better qualified to judge ethical questions, to choose the good and reject the evil. In all seriousness I am not prepared to maintain that Professor Schmiedel's Christ, or Professor Harnack's Christ, or Count Tolstoi's Christ, is in essentials any nearer the historical truth than the Christ as conceived by S. Luke or the compiler of the Gospel according to S. Matthew. All kinds of science are valid in their own province: this is the great critical principle of which M. Loisy is the prophet, and for which he is the symbol. The chronicling of events is one thing, and the characterisation of a personality is another. The course of events is a fixed objective series; things happen once for all, and the determination of the course of past events is a wholly definite task, difficult indeed, yet perfectly mechanical. In this sense, a Cambridge audience does not need again to be reminded that 'History is a science, no more and no less.'

But the appreciation of a living personality is not entirely a mechanical task, for it describes the effect of the personality on the writer or speaker: one man may be the subject of many adequate portraits. And from this point of view we shall do well to approach the Gospels in the spirit of those who are as ready to be taught as to sit in judgement. 'Matthew' took the narrative of 'Mark'; he set the Sermon on the Mount at the beginning of the public ministry of Jesus, and he added, at the end of the final warnings concerning the approaching destruction of Jerusalem, the parable or discourse about the Sheep and the Goats. By doing this, says the objective historian, the narrator of facts, 'Matthew' has entirely disturbed the balance of the story. The progress of the narrative is destroyed; we cannot trace in 'Matthew' the development of hostility in our Lord's opponents, the disciples appear from the very beginning as an organised body distinct from the unbelieving Jews, and so the march of events becomes incomprehensible. Furthermore, we shall be told that the Sermon on the Mount itself is not a true discourse at all; it is a cento of more or less detached sayings, grouped under heads, and many of these sayings, even if they be genuine, belong to the later stages of the Ministry. We shall find also that many critics are inclined to assign the parable of the Sheep and the Goats to the latest cycle of the Synoptic period, and to say that in any case it has no historical claim to be considered a part of the discourse traditionally ascribed to Christ upon the Mount of Olives. All this is more or less justifiable historical criticism. The story of Jesus Christ's life on earth, it cannot be too often repeated, happened in one way, and one way only. And when our object, a noble and worthy object, is to trace out to the best of our power the story of that life regarded as an outward chain of events, it is our first duty to weigh these historical considerations, to choose the probable course of events on which to believe, and resolutely to reject a presentation of the course of events, which careful consideration shews to be historically improbable.

But this is not all. The course of events is important, but the effect produced upon us by the course of events is still more important. What was the effect which the course of events, the Life of Jesus Christ on earth, produced on our First Evangelist? Was it not this, that it made him arrange his Gospel as it stands for us to read? When we take as our aim and object to consider what was the real effect of Jesus Christ's Ministry, in other words, to consider what manner of man He was, it is not for nothing that we find these dislocations and rearrangements which so seriously disturb the historical order of the First Gospel. It is not for nothing that the Evangelist would not describe the preaching of Jesus, not even for a chapter, without telling his readers at length that what Jesus preached was the blessedness of those who hungered and thirsted after righteousness, that anger was like murder and lust like adultery, and that miracles and prophesyings even in His own name were nothing without simplicity and sincerity of life. It is not for nothing that the Evangelist considered it appropriate to make Jesus conclude His discourse on the Coming of the Son of Man and the consummation of all things by a description of the End in which the *King of the Day of Judgement* appears not as the *Merciful* and *Compassionate* towards His followers and the avenger of their sufferings, but as one that pronounces His highest blessing on those who, being in no sense His disciples, and without looking for His reward, had yet been kind to the unfortunate and the wretched. Interesting indeed is the question, but after all of secondary importance, whether the words which describe this scene are a literal Greek translation of words once upon a time spoken by Jesus of Nazareth; what is of real moment, a fact certainly of objective history, is that the total impression of the life and words of Jesus of Nazareth made the Evangelist write in this manner, and made the Society for which he wrote accept the portrait he has drawn. The more a rigorously objective criticism impels us to regard this and that traditional Saying of Christ as a later accretion into the Gospel legend, how much more wonderful, how much more forceful, must He have been, round whose Personality grew up not only the stories of the Nativity and the Temptation, but also the parables of the Prodigal Son and of the Pharisee and the Publican? I hope I may not be misunderstood: we have not discussed these stories and parables yet at close quarters, and for aught our investigation may show, we may yet find that they are authentic reminiscences. What I want to urge here, now that we stand on the threshold, is the witness borne by the Evangelists to the moral impression produced by Jesus Christ upon His followers. The Evangelists are not mechanical chroniclers, they are not afraid to treat the material before them with great literary freedom, and here and there we actually see unhistorical legends growing as it were before our eyes. Under these circumstances, the real miracle, which only escapes our notice because it is so familiar, is the irresistible vitality of the ethical teaching of the Gospel. The Fire has been laid on the earth, and we see it kindling on every side. The Christian has hardly need to claim more from the scientific historian than that the life of Jesus Christ on earth inspired the canonical Gospels, made the Evangelists write as they did, made the Gospels what they are.

We might perhaps stop here, and say that further investigation is superfluous. But this would be, I am sure, a wrong conclusion. I shall therefore say a few words upon the reasons which make minute and searching investigation of the details of the Gospel History a profitable as well as a fascinating study. As I said at the beginning of this Lecture, we lose ourselves so often and for so long in the details that we sometimes forget the general reasons for our occupation. For this cause we shall do well to consider why we are thus occupied, and what we may hope to find.

And here I may take as my text two contrasted sentences from the *Cambridge Theological Essays*, which together express what I wish to say better than I could have put it myself. The first is from Dr. Cunningham, who reminds us that we must not expect to attain to fuller appreciation of religious truth merely by studying the details of the Synoptic Problem. "The most complete success," he says, "in the reproduction of the past would still show us the crowds who stoned the prophets, or from whom the Lord turned because of their unbelief."[1]

This is expressed with as much truth as

[1] *Camb. Theol. Essays*, p. 39.

picturesqueness. We shall only be disappointed if we expect orthodoxy to be the natural result of a competent knowledge of the history of Dogma, or if we expect to understand the nature of conscious life by a study of the process of Evolution. What such study will give us is not the vital truth, but the removal of errors. Historical criticism does not create, it clears away; clears away everything but the objective fact of the course of events. But the course of events remains. Dr. Cunningham does not deny that the crowds who stoned the prophets were really there. They are a part, and a real part, of the whole truth; and perhaps, but for historical criticism, we might forget their existence. Nevertheless we shall do well to master Dr. Cunningham's warning at the outset, lest we be disappointed later on with the results of our inquiries. We must be prepared to find the unbelieving crowds and the other less obviously edifying parts of the scene loom larger and more important the nearer we get to them. We must be prepared to find the whole drama of the rise of Christianity more confused, more complex, more secular, in a word, more appropriate to the limitations of its own age, than we should gather from the epic selectiveness of the Creeds and the theological manuals.

Why then, you may say, should we proceed at

all? What is the ultimate use of this destructive historical criticism? The answer lies, I am sure, in that other sentence from the *Cambridge Theological Essays* to which I referred above. It comes at the end of a footnote in Dr. Foakes Jackson's admirable Essay on 'Christ in History,' coming, in fact, rather as a *caveat* or necessary reservation than as part of the author's special thesis. Dr. Foakes Jackson has been speaking of the evolutionary standpoint from which we now rightly treat Church History. He points out the impossibility of resuscitating the past, that is, the impossibility of resuscitating the practices and the standpoint of past ages as actual rules for our own conduct, and his whole Essay is an attempt to portray our Lord as one who is constantly revealing Himself with increasing clearness to the conscience of men (p. 524). Yet he feels himself constrained to add: "At the same time, since in every age the Church is tempted to regard her interpretation of her Lord as final and complete, a return to the historic Christ is a constant necessity, and the only cause of progress."[1]

It is not to get new ideas of religion or of philosophy that we need a minute and searching historical criticism; rather do we need to test

[1] *Camb. Theol. Essays*, p. 476 note.

the ideas we already have by the historical facts, and we cannot get at the facts without the criticism. Not that it is always or generally an easy task to exercise a true historical criticism upon a great subject, and it is only too easy to fall into error. But of this, at least, we may be confident, that our errors will not long escape detection: if not by our own generation, then by the next. And the attempt to 'return to the historic Christ' is the only way by which we can escape from the tyranny of the last generation's theories about Christ.

I ventured at the beginning of this Lecture to speak of the task incumbent upon us all as the reconstructing of the Portrait of Jesus Christ. Perhaps it would better express my meaning if I said the painting of the Portrait on the retina of our minds. We have to answer for ourselves the old question, 'What think ye of Christ?' and the answer varies for various ages and various degrees of intelligence. But that the retina of our minds may take an impression of Christ, it is necessary that Christ be brought before them; and this I understand to be the work of the historical critic and investigator.

The events of the first century are imperfectly known to us; it may turn out on investigation that some things happened differently from what we thought, or what our fathers thought. But there is one thing at least which we know before we start. We know that the events of the first century produced the second and succeeding centuries. There is no need for the most timid to be afraid of the results of historical investigation. We know the result of the events beforehand; the investigations of the critics cannot alter the events of past history. We have no reason to be afraid of the unbelieving crowds that Dr. Cunningham has called up from the past: they were really there and really dangerous, but the Christian Church came through somehow in spite of them.

II.

THE GOSPEL OF MARK: ITS LITERARY ORIGINALITY.

Marcus . . . Euangelium . . . scripsit, ostendens in eo quid et generi suo deberit et Christo.

ANY estimate of the effect of the Gospels upon the early Church and upon later ages must almost inevitably begin with a statement about the date, literary origin, and historical value of the Gospels; and these are questions of such importance and complexity that a statement of conclusions alone would not carry sufficient weight. It will be necessary, therefore, first to consider the Gospels at some length as literary and historical documents, and afterwards, with the help of the results thus attained, to examine their influence upon the Church and their place in the development of the Christian religion.

The four Gospels are not by any means four independent literary works. The Fourth Gospel is most conveniently treated apart. But the three

Gospels according to Matthew, Mark, and Luke, obviously have something in common: they must either copy one another or make use of a common source. The first question is whether this source or sources be written or oral. All kinds of answers have been given in the past, but I have no doubt at all which answer is correct. I am fully convinced that the main common source of the Synoptic Gospels was a single written document.

In the first place, the common matter is not mere floating tradition, the property of all the Christian community. Had it been this, I cannot but think that the incidents identically related by Matthew, Mark, and Luke, would have been to a larger extent the critical points of the Ministry, and not a capricious selection of anecdotes. The story of the Resurrection, the words from the Cross, the narrative of the Last Supper,—in these we might have expected all our authorities to agree, even in detail; but they do not agree. On the other hand, the parenthesis which explains that Jesus turned from addressing the Pharisees to say to the sick of the palsy, 'Arise,' is found in all three Synoptic Gospels; all three insert the statement concerning Herod's alarm about Jesus at the same point, and Matthew and Mark go on to relate, so to speak in a footnote, the circumstances of John the Baptist's murder; all three inform us that the Pharisees, when they asked about the tribute-money, began by assuring our Lord that He taught the way of God in truth. These points are matters of secondary detail; an oral teaching or a catechetical tradition which contained them must be held to have had singular consistency. And if our Evangelists had worked upon a fixed oral tradition of this definite sort, I cannot imagine how they dared to take such liberties with it. An oral tradition which is definite is authoritative: can we conceive of an oral tradition which accurately distinguishes between the *baskets* (κόφινοι) of fragments taken up after the feeding of the 5000, and the *creels* (σφυρίδες) taken up after feeding the 4000, but which left the details of the Crucifixion and the Resurrection vague?

A written source, on the other hand, is perfectly definite, but not necessarily authoritative. When the Evangelists simply copy their common source they agree, whether the point of agreement be important or unimportant, while at the same time the existence of the written document did not prevent the use of other documents or of any oral information which might come to hand. There was nothing in the nature of things to compel either of our Evangelists to reproduce the whole of the documents upon which they worked, or to follow them exactly: if they had had such respect for their predecessors' work as never to alter it, they would never have dared to supersede these documents or traditions by their own new Gospels. They would have been mere scribes or, at the most, harmonists like Tatian.

Our Synoptic Gospels, then, resemble one another because they are based on common written documents. But we can go one step further. In the parts common to Mark, Matthew, and Luke there is a good deal in which all three verbally agree; there is also much common to Mark and Matthew, and much common to Mark and Luke, but hardly anything common to Matthew and Luke which Mark does not share also. There is very little of Mark which is not more or less adequately represented either in Matthew or in Luke. Moreover, the common order is Mark's order; Matthew and Luke never agree against Mark in transposing a narrative. Luke sometimes deserts the order of Mark, and Matthew often does so; but in these cases Mark is always supported by the remaining Gospel.

Now what is the deduction to be drawn from

these facts? There is only one answer. We are bound to conclude that Mark contains the whole of a document which Matthew and Luke have independently used, and, further, that Mark contains very little else beside.

This conclusion is extremely important; it is the one solid contribution made by the scholarship of the nineteenth century toward the solution of the Synoptic Problem. And I think it will not be out of place to pause for a moment to pay a tribute to the memory of the great scholar Lachmann, who was the first clearly to formulate it as long ago as 1835. Lachmann started from the central fact that the common order of the three Synoptic Gospels is Mark's order. "There is not so much diversity," he says, "in the order of the Gospel tales as most people imagine. It is indeed very great if you compare the Synoptic Gospels indiscriminately together, or compare Luke with Matthew; but if you compare Mark with both the others separately the diversity is inconsiderable."[1] And he goes on to draw the conclusion that the order of the narrative, as we

[1] *Sed narrationum evangelicarum ordinis non tanta est quanta plerisque videtur diversitas; maxima sane si aut hos scriptores eadem complexione omnes aut Lucan cum Matthæo composueris, exigua si Marcum cum utroque seorsum* (Lachmann in *Studien und Kritiken* for 1835, p. 574, quoted by Wellhausen, *Einleitung*, p. 43).

read it in Mark, is presupposed by and underlies the narratives in Luke and Matthew.[1]

Until Lachmann's time the prevailing opinion had been that S. Matthew's Gospel was the earliest, or at least that it offered the most primitive arrangement. The priority of Matthew was upheld by critics of such different opinions as S. Augustine and Ferdinand Christian Baur, the founder of the Tübingen School. I am not going to give a history of the ebb and flow of modern criticism; it will be enough to say that the relative priority of Mark is now accepted almost as an axiom by the great majority of scholars who occupy themselves with Gospel problems. But I should like to observe that this great change of opinion is a result of the change of method used in studying the question. From Augustine to Baur, and indeed often at the present day, attempts have been made to determine the relation of the Synoptic Gospels to one another by beginning with historical and dogmatic considerations; Lachmann, as you see, treated it mainly as a question of literary criticism. Far be it from me to disparage the high studies of history and philosophy in favour of literary criticism; but

[1] *Quid superest nisi ut illum quem omnes velut sibi præscriptum sequuntur ordinem, prius quam ipsi scriberent, auctoritate ac traditione quadam evangelica constitutum et confirmatum fuisse dicamus?* (Lachmann, p. 582.)

as the wise man said, 'To everything there is a season,' and in the particular study before us the season of literary criticism comes logically first. As long as those who studied the Synoptic Problem attacked it by considering mainly the actual contents of the Gospels, they seemed to be unable to shake off a certain confusion between the earliest Synoptic Gospel and the primitive preaching of Christianity. It has always seemed to me, though from the nature of things it would be very difficult to prove, that this was the master cause which made Baur and his followers proclaim the priority, at least the relative priority, of S. Matthew's Gospel. What they really cared about was the Sermon on the Mount. S. Matthew's Gospel contains the Sermon on the Mount, and S. Mark's does not; they concluded, therefore, that S. Matthew's Gospel is earlier than S. Mark's. This is, of course, a very crude way of putting the matter, but I believe it to be near enough. At least it expresses the truth that Baur had a much firmer hold on primitive Christian Ethics than primitive Christian History, and it is the History we are now investigating—the History and the way that History is told in our documents.

Let us come back again to our examination of the three Synoptic Gospels and see whether we cannot advance yet another step. We have seen that the marked agreement of Matthew, Mark, and Luke in many minor points, taken together with their frequent difference in many important points, indicates the use of a common written source rather than a common tradition. And further, the fact that Matthew and Luke never agree in order, and hardly ever in wording, against Mark indicates that Mark contains the whole of a document which Matthew and Luke have independently used. Now let us go on and see whether there is any reason to suppose that the document thus used by Matthew and Luke is any other than the Gospel according to S. Mark itself.

Suppose for a moment that the common source was not S. Mark, but some earlier document, the greater part of which has been incorporated in our S. Mark,—a document, in fact, such as the Germans call *Ur-Marcus*. Well, then, we have Matthew, Mark, and Luke all basing their work upon this *Ur-Marcus*. What will be the result? As long as they all copy *Ur-Marcus* exactly, they will all agree. That is, indeed, what we often find. Sometimes one of the three, say Matthew, will not copy exactly: either he will drop something out, or add something fresh, or make some change or correction. In that case, if Mark and

Luke still go on copying exactly, they will still agree, but Matthew will be different. That also is what we find, and the same is true if it was Luke who did not copy exactly. But if it was Mark that did not copy exactly when Matthew and Luke did, we should find Matthew and Luke agreeing against Mark; and this we do not find. Either, therefore, Mark always copied this hypothetical *Ur-Marcus* exactly, or we must suppose that wherever he did not copy exactly, Matthew and Luke also did not copy exactly.

Again, it will naturally happen that at a given point both Matthew and Luke will be unwilling simply to copy the *Ur-Marcus*. If they have no acquaintance with each other's work, the result of their ceasing to copy out their exemplar will be that they will produce something different from it and from each other. In such a case Mark, Matthew, and Luke will all differ from each other, a state of things often found. But it will equally be the case whether Mark copies *Ur-Marcus* exactly or not, *i.e.* whether the common original was identical with our Mark, or different from it. Instances, therefore, in which all three Synoptic Gospels differ from each other, tell us nothing about the existence of an *Ur-Marcus*.

What, then, are the conditions which call for the hypothesis of an *Ur-Marcus*, or, in other words, which make it unreasonable for us to believe that Matthew and Luke actually used not our Mark, but an earlier edition of that Gospel?

A moment's consideration will tell us that the hypothesis of an *Ur-Marcus* can only be required by those places where Matthew and Luke agree against Mark; or where, all three Synoptists being different, the differences cannot be explained from the text of Mark as it stands. We must therefore pass in review the very few places where Matthew and Luke may be said to agree against Mark. These have often been collected together; the clearest arrangement is to be found in Sir John Hawkins's *Horae Synopticae*, pp. 174, 175 (2nd ed., pp. 210, 211). Sir John reckons 20 or 21 places in all, some of them concerned with very small points indeed: in others the agreement between Matthew and Luke is best explained as due to special and fairly obvious causes.

1. Mk ii 22 = Matt ix 17 = Lk v 37, 38.

Mark—And no man putteth new wine into old wine-skins: else the wine will burst the skins, and the wine perisheth, and the skins: but new wine into fresh wine-skins.

Matthew—Neither do men put new wine into old wine-skins: else the skins burst, and the wine is spilled, and the skins perish: but they put new wine into fresh wine-skins, and both are preserved.

Luke—And no man putteth new wine into old wine-skins; else the new wine will burst the skins, and itself will be spilled, and the skins will perish. But new wine must be put into fresh wine-skins.

Here Matthew and Luke agree in stating directly that the wine will be *spilled* (ἐκχεῖται Matt, ἐκχυθήσεται Lk), while in Mark the verb ἀπόλλυται applies to the wine as well as to the wine-skins.

2. Mk iv 11 = Matt xiii 11 = Lk viii 10.

Mark—And He was saying to them, 'Unto you is given the mystery of the kingdom of God.'

Matthew—And He answered and said to them, 'Unto you it is given **to know** the mysteries of the kingdom of heaven.'

Luke—And He said, 'Unto you it is given **to know** the mysteries of the kingdom of God.'

Matthew and Luke agree in inserting the verb 'to know,' in explanation of what Sir John Hawkins calls the more difficult expression, viz. 'Unto you the mystery is given.' 'To give the mystery of (a rite)' is simply 'to initiate into (a rite).'[1] Mark preserves the Aramaic expression; Matthew and Luke give a paraphrase of Mark which is so natural that it is not necessary to explain it by having recourse to a documentary source. It should be added that 'mystery' (τὸ μυστήριον) is probably the original reading in Matt xiii 11 as well as in Mk iv 11.

3. Mk v 25–27 = Matt ix 20 = Lk viii 43, 44[a].

Mark—And a woman, who had an issue of blood twelve years, and had suffered many things of many physicians, and had

[1] *E.g.* Aphraates (p. 21) speaks of our Lord *giving the mystery* of baptism to the apostles.

spent all that she had, and was nothing bettered, but rather grew worse, having heard the things concerning Jesus, came in the crowd behind, and touched His garment.

Matthew—And behold, a woman, who had hemorrhage for twelve years, came up behind, and touched **the border of** His garment.

Luke—And a woman who had an issue of blood for twelve years, which could not be healed of any,[1] came **up** behind, **and** touched **the border of** His garment.

I have quoted the introduction to the story of the Woman with an Issue rather fully, although the only point that Matthew and Luke have in common against Mark is that they say she 'came up behind, and touched the border of his garment,' while Mark has 'came in the crowd behind, and touched His garment.'[2] Apart from this one point, the passage very well illustrates the normal characteristics of the three Synoptic Evangelists. Mark is the fullest, the most graphic; Matthew the shortest, and the least interested in subsidiary detail. It is surely not necessary to suppose that Matthew and Luke were obliged to have recourse to something different from Mark in order to account for the mention of 'the border.' In Mk vi 56 we read that the sick who touched the border

[1] This is the true text, attested by the Sinai Palimpsest as well as by B D and the Sahidic.

[2] Mk has *ἐλθοῦσα ἐν τῷ ὄχλῳ ὄπισθεν ἥψατο τοῦ ἱματίου αὐτοῦ*; Matt and Lk have *προσελθοῦσα ὄπισθεν ἥψατο τοῦ κρασπέδου τοῦ ἱματίου αὐτοῦ*.

of Christ's garment were healed:[1] if we are to look for a literary source from which to derive the word in Matt ix 20, Lk viii 44, this is the most probable one.

It should be added that it is not quite certain that 'the border' really belongs to the text of Luke. In Matt ix 20, *τοῦ κρασπέδου* is omitted by the best Old Latin MSS, but it is found in all Greek and Syriac texts. But in Lk viii 44, *τοῦ κρασπέδου* is not only omitted by D and the best extant Old Latin texts; the Old Syriac version also paraphrases, having 'laid hold of the skirt of His garment' for *ἥψατο* [*τοῦ κρασπέδου*] *τοῦ ἱματίου αὐτοῦ*. In the other Gospels *ἥψατο* is not paraphrased, so that perhaps *τοῦ κρασπέδου* *may* have been absent from the Greek text that underlies the Old Syriac.

4. Mk vi 14 = Matt xiv 1 = Lk ix 7.

Mark—And King Herod heard. . . .
Matthew—At that season Herod **the Tetrarch** heard the report concerning Jesus. . . .
Luke—Now Herod **the Tetrarch** heard all that was done. . . .

Mark here calls Herod Antipas incorrectly a 'king'; Matthew and Luke give the correct title. But he is called 'king' in Matt xiv 9, following Mk vi 26.

[1] The phrase is confirmed by the parallel Matt xiv 36.

5. Mk vi 30–34 = Matt xiv 13, 14 = Lk ix 10, 11.

Mark—And the apostles gather themselves together unto Jesus; and they told him all things, whatsoever they had done, and whatsoever they had taught. And He saith unto them, 'Come ye yourselves apart into a desert place and rest awhile.' For there were many coming and going, and they had no leisure so much as to eat. And they went away in the boat to a desert place apart. And many saw them going, and knew, and on foot from all the cities they ran together there, and outwent them. And He came out and saw a great multitude, and He had compassion on them, because they were as sheep not having a shepherd, and He began to teach them many things.

Matthew—Now when Jesus heard, He **withdrew** from thence in a boat to a desert place apart; and when **the multitudes** heard, they **followed Him** on foot from the cities. And He came out, and saw a great multitude, and He had compassion on them, and healed their sick.

Luke—And the apostles, when they were returned, declared unto Him what things they had done. And He took them, and **withdrew** apart to a city called Bethsaida. But **the multitudes** knowing it **followed Him**: and He welcomed them, and was speaking to them of the kingdom of God, and them that had need of healing he cured.

The introduction to the story of the Feeding of the Five Thousand exhibits very well the characteristic differences of the three Gospels. I cannot see that there is any need to suppose that any other source underlies Matthew and Luke here, except the text of Mark as we have it. It is true that there are some points shared by Matthew and Luke which are not found in Mark. They have *withdrew* (ἀνεχώρησεν Matt, ὑπεχώρησεν Lk), where Mark has *went away* (ἀπῆλθον), all three words being quite common, and ἀναχωρεῖν being specially characteristic of Matthew. The curious wording of Mark, where it says that 'many went round by land and arrived beforehand at the point of disembarkation,'[1] becomes in Matthew and Luke the commonplace statement that 'the multitudes followed Him.' Finally, where Mark speaks of our Lord beginning to teach them, Matthew and Luke both speak of healings, but not at all in the same words. This introduction of general healings without details is characteristic both of Matthew and of Luke; *e.g.* Matt ix 35, xix 2, xxi 14; Lk v 15, vii 21. The mention of such healings here is surely due to the general tendencies of the Evangelists rather than to the following of a special documentary source.

When we compare these trifling agreements of Matthew and Luke against Mark with those of Matthew and Mark alone, or Mark and Luke alone, we cannot but feel that they belong to a different order and demand a different explanation. Matthew and Mark both tell us about the journey by boat, and the uninvited arrival of the multitude by land (πεζῇ), and they verbally agree all through the phrase, 'and he came out and saw a

[1] In Mk vi 34, I cannot but think that ἐξελθών means 'when Jesus had got out of the boat,' otherwise 'outwent them' has no meaning. This also is the view of the passage taken by Dr. Swete in opposition to Hort, who thought it meant 'when Jesus had come forth from some sequestered nook in the desert.'

great multitude, and He had compassion on them.' Mark and Luke agree in beginning with the return of the apostles from their missionary tour, and in mentioning that Jesus preached to the waiting multitudes. Moreover, the common omission by Matthew and Luke of the circumstance that our Lord and the apostles were so busy that they had no time for meals is explicable enough: such a detail, vivid and interesting as it is to us, is not obviously edifying. To omit it would be the natural course for a later Evangelist, especially to writers such as Matthew and Luke, who have so much fresh matter to add, which is not represented in Mark at all.

6. Mk viii 29 = Matt xvi 16 = Lk ix 20.

Mark—'Thou art the Christ.'
Matthew—'Thou art the Christ, the Son **of** the living **God.**'
Luke—'The Christ **of God.**'

No argument for the use of a common document by Matthew and Luke can be based on the addition of 'of God,' because of the difference of expression.

7. Mk ix 7 = Matt xvii 5 = Lk ix 34.

Mark—And there came a cloud overshadowing them. . . .
Matthew—**While He** was yet speaking, behold, a bright cloud overshadowed them. . . .
Luke—And **while He** said these things, there came a cloud and overshadowed them. . . .

It is fairly obvious that no conclusion can be drawn from this; any more than from the fact that in Mk ix 4 = Matt xvii 3 = Lk ix 30, Matthew and Luke agree in having the commonplace order 'Moses and Elijah,' while Mark has 'Elijah with Moses.'

8. Mk ix 19 = Matt xvii 17 = Lk ix 41.

Mark—And He answereth them and saith, 'O faithless generation, how long shall I be by you? how long shall I bear with you? carry him unto Me.'

Matthew—And **Jesus** answered and **said**, 'O faithless **and perverse** generation, how long shall I be with you? how long shall I bear with you? carry him **hither** to Me.'

Luke—And **Jesus** answered and **said**, 'O faithless **and perverse** generation, how long shall I be by you, and bear with you? bring **hither** thy son.'

Here, as elsewhere, I have made some slight changes in the familiar diction of the English in order to emphasise some of the slighter verbal agreements and disagreements. The agreement of Matthew and Luke in adding *perverse* to *faithless* does indeed shew that they have a common literary source at this point; but that source is Deut xxxii 5, where the LXX has *γενεὰ σκολιὰ καὶ διεστραμμένη*, 'a crooked *and perverse* generation.' That this phrase came readily to the pens of early Greek-speaking Christians is illustrated by its occurrence in Phil ii 15.

9. Mk x 30 = Matt xix 29 = Lk xviii 30.

Mark—'A hundredfold.'
Matthew—'Manifold.'
Luke—'Manifold.'

Westcott and Hort read 'manifold' in Matt xix 29, but very many ancient authorities have 'a hundredfold,' like Mk x 30. But what makes the agreement of Matthew and Luke of no significance in either case is that it is probable that in Lk xviii 30 we ought to read 'sevenfold' with D and the Old Latin MSS.

10. Mk xi 19 = Matt xxi 17 = Lk xxi 37.

Mark—And every evening He went forth out of the city.
Matthew—And He left them, and went forth out of the city to Bethany, **and lodged** there.
Luke—And every day He was teaching in the temple; and every night He went out, **and lodged** in the mount that is called the mount of Olives.

11. Mk xi 27[b] = Matt xxi 23[a] = Lk xx 1.

Mark—And as He was walking in the temple, there come to Him the chief priests, and the scribes, and the elders. . . .
Matthew—And when He was come into the temple, the chief priests and the elders of the people came unto Him as He was **teaching**. . . .
Luke—And it came to pass, on one of the days, as He was **teaching** the people in the temple, and preaching the gospel, there came upon Him the chief priests and the scribes with the elders. . . .

I only include these two passages, because they occur in Sir John Hawkins's List.

12. Mk xiv 45 f. = Matt xxvi 49 f. = Lk xxii 47 f.

Here Matthew and Luke agree in recording that Jesus spoke to Judas at the moment of the Arrest, but as they do not agree at all as to the words spoken, this passage cannot supply an argument for the use of a common literary source other than Mark.

13. Mk xiv 72^{b} = Matt xxvi 75^{b} = Lk xxii 62.

Mark—And when he thought thereon, he wept.
Matthew—And **he went out, and wept bitterly.**
Luke—[And **he went out, and wept bitterly.**]

The resemblance between Matthew and Luke is too close here to be the result of independent interpretation of Mark's obscure phrase *καὶ ἐπιβαλὼν ἔκλαιεν.* But Lk xxii 62 is omitted by all the MSS of the Old Latin version. It is impossible to supply any cogent reason for this on the supposition that the words are genuine; it is therefore probable that the verse in Luke is an early harmonistic addition derived from Matt xxvi 72 itself.

14. Mk xiv 65 = Matt xxvi 67, 68 = Lk xxii 63–65.

Mark—And some began to spit on Him, and to cover His face and to buffet Him, and to say unto Him, 'Prophesy': and the officers received Him with blows of their hands.

Matthew—Then did they spit in His face and buffet Him: and some smote Him with the palms of their hands, **saying,** 'Prophesy unto us, thou Christ: **who is he that struck Thee?**'

Luke—And the men that held Him mocked him, and beat Him. And they covered Him up, and were asking Him, **saying,** 'Prophesy: **who is he that struck Thee?** And many other things spake they against Him, reviling Him.

This passage undoubtedly supplies more support than any other to those who believe that Matthew and Luke used Mark in a form different from that in which it is known to us. It is true that a number of Greek MSS add in Mark the missing words after 'Prophesy,' in agreement with Matt xxvi 68, but they are not the best MSS, nor are they supported by the Latin and the Syriac. It is wholly contrary to analogy that these MSS should have inherited the true text in a passage where our better MSS have a corruption. Of course, it is possible that we have here a primitive lacuna in the text, and that the ancestor of all our MSS, a copy which was (as we know) mutilated at the end and had several blunders elsewhere, had here lost a line after *Προφήτευσον*.

I do not think we are in a position entirely to solve this problem, but it stands practically alone. If two or three other instances of equal cogency occurred, we should be obliged to conclude that Matthew and Luke used a form of Mark different from what we know, and the question would arise whether this was a better or a worse text than that which we have. For though the longer text here is appropriate enough in Luke, according to whose narrative our Lord is rudely treated by the guards as they are whiling away the night hours till it shall be time for Caiaphas to get up and try the Prisoner, it is not so appropriate in Mark and Matthew, where the ill-treatment comes after the trial by Caiaphas, a trial which ended by taking Jesus away 'straightway' to Pilate, according to Mk xv 1. I cannot help thinking that *τίς ἐστιν ὁ παίσας σε*, in Matt xxvi 68, is after all a mistaken addition by the Evangelist, and that the real meaning of the covering of our Lord's face, in Mk xiv 65, is that the Jewish Court regarded Him as a condemned criminal, like Haman of old.[1]

15. Mk xv 30 = Matt xxvii 40^{b} = Lk xxiii 35^{b} and 37.

Mark—Save Thyself, and come down from the cross.
Matthew—Save Thyself: if Thou art the Son of God, come down from the cross.
Luke—Let Him save Himself, if this is the Christ of God, His chosen.
(the soldiers saying) If thou art the King of the Jews, save Thyself.

These passages in Matthew and Luke can hardly be held to shew literary connexion; I give

[1] Esth vii 8.

them merely because like Nos. 10 and 11 they figure in Sir John Hawkins's List.

16. Mk xv 39 = Matt xxvii 54 = Lk xxiii 47.

Mark—And when the centurion who stood by over against Him saw that He so gave up the ghost, he said, 'Truly this man was a son of God.'

Matthew—Now the **centurion**, and they that were with him watching Jesus, when they saw the earthquake, and the things **that were done**, feared exceedingly, saying, 'Truly a son of God was this man.'

Luke—And when the **centurion** saw **what was done**, he glorified God, saying, 'Certainly this was a righteous man.'

I do not think there is any indication here that Matthew and Luke have here any common source, though Matthew mentions τὰ γινόμενα and Luke τὸ γενόμενον. The word for 'centurion' is κεντυρίων in Mark, ἑκατόνταρχος in Matthew, and ἑκατοντάρχης in Luke.

17. Mk xv 42–46 = Matt xxvii 57–60 = Lk xxiii 50–54.

Mark—And when even was now come, because it was the Preparation, that is, the day before the Sabbath, there came Joseph from Arimathæa, a worthy councillor, who also himself was looking for the kingdom of God; and he boldly went in unto Pilate, and asked for the corpse of Jesus. And Pilate marvelled . . . and granted the corpse to Joseph. And having bought a linen cloth, he took Him down, and wound Him in the linen cloth, and laid Him in a tomb which had been hewn out of a rock; and he rolled a stone against the door of the tomb.

Matthew—And when even was come, there came **a** rich man from Arimathæa, **named** Joseph, who also himself was

Jesus' disciple: **this man** went **to** Pilate, and asked for the **body** of Jesus. Then Pilate commanded it to be given up. And Joseph took the body, and **wrapped it** in a clean linen cloth, and laid it in his own new tomb, which he had hewn out in the rock: and having rolled a great stone to the door of the tomb, he departed.

Luke—And behold, **a** man by **name** Joseph, who was a councillor, a good man and righteous (he had not consented to their counsel and deed) from Arimathæa, a city of the Jews, who was looking for the kingdom of God: **this man** went **to** Pilate, and asked for the **body** of Jesus. And he took it down, and **wrapped it** in a linen cloth, and laid Him in a tomb that was hewn in stone, where never man had yet lain. And it was the day of the Preparation, and the Sabbath drew on.

I have quoted the passages which have to do with Joseph of Arimathæa in full, because they seem to me to be very instructive for our purpose. The points which Matthew and Luke have in common are emphasised as before in thick type. The only one of importance is the word used for enshrouding our Lord's body. Matthew and Luke say that Joseph ἐνετύλιξεν αὐτό, while Mark has αὐτὸν ἐνείλησεν, both Greek words being quite common. Matthew and Luke also agree in refusing to speak of the dead body of Jesus as a corpse (πτῶμα), but Mark, according to the true text, has no such scruple. It should further be noticed that Matthew and Luke agree in the form of the sentence, 'this man went to Pilate.' Against these comparatively slight coincidences we may notice that Mark and Matthew have in common the mention of the evening at the beginning, and the description of the tomb and the rolled stone at the end; while Mark and Luke have in common the mention of the Preparation, the term 'councillor' (βουλευτής, *i.e. decurio*) applied to Joseph, and the description of him as 'looking for the kingdom of God.' Furthermore, it should be noticed that Mark calls Joseph of Arimathæa εὐσχήμων βουλευτής. Now εὐσχήμων is a word exactly like our 'worthy' or 'respectable'; εὐσχήμων βουλευτής means 'a worthy alderman,' where 'worthy' means of good standing either morally or financially. And, as a matter of fact, Matthew interprets it by πλούσιος, 'rich'; while Luke interprets it by ἀγαθὸς καὶ δίκαιος, 'good and righteous'; and, further, he supposes that the 'council' to which Joseph belonged must have been the Sanhedrin of chief priests and elders which condemned our Lord. Thus the phrase actually used by Mark explains some of the characteristic differences of Matthew and Luke.

18. (Mk xvi 1) = Matt xxviii 1 = Lk xxiii 54[b].

Sir John Hawkins here notices that Matthew and Luke, but not Mark, make use of a rare word, ἐπιφώσκειν, to express the 'dawning' of a new day, not however of the same day, for in Luke it is used of the 'dawning' of the Sabbath, in Matthew of the day after the Sabbath. The peculiarity of the expression consists in this, that whereas the Greek word means 'to grow light,' the Jewish Sabbath begins at dusk on what we call Friday evening. But as the word does not come in the same context in Luke and Matthew, it cannot prove that they are making use of the same special literary source. In the Gospel of Peter, § 2, ἐπιφώσκει may come direct from Lk xxiii 54, but its occurrence in that document, again in another context, may serve to shew that the word did not seem particularly odd to Christians about the end of the first century AD.

19. Mk xvi 5 = Matt xxviii 2, 3 = Lk xxiv 4.

Mark— . . . A young man . . . arrayed in a white robe.
Matthew— . . . An angel of the Lord . . . his appearance was like lightning, and his raiment white as snow.
Luke— . . . Two men stood by them in dazzling apparel.

Here in the Greek 'dazzling' is ἀστραπτούσῃ, lit. 'flashing like lightning'—a very natural enhancement of the simple 'white,' given by Mark.

20. Mk xvi 8 = Matt xxviii 8 = Lk xxiv 9.

[Not included, because we do not know the conclusion of the incomplete sentence in the middle of which Mk xvi 8 breaks off.]

These twenty passages contain all the instances which Sir John Hawkins gives, as to which he says it seems almost impossible that Matthew and Luke could have accidentally concurred in their additions to the narrative of Mark.[1] In other words, these passages afford the strongest evidence that can be found against the supposition that Matthew and Luke used our Mark much as it has come down to us. It appears to me that the evidence is extremely weak, and that we are not compelled by it to imagine a hypothetical *Ur-Marcus*, a Gospel very much like our Mark, only slightly different here and there, differing, in fact, very much as a first edition of a modern book may differ from the second or subsequent editions.

We have lingered to-day among details. In the Introductory Lecture I said that I might be obliged to ask you to look at the trees, when you wanted rather a view of the wood as a whole, and now I fear you will think that I have taken you into a thicket. We have for the moment lost sight of the religious and historical value of the

[1] Yet another instance is given by Sir John (*Horae Synopticae*, p. 175), viz. the omission of Bethphage in Mk xi 1, according to D and the Latin texts, whereby this place would be named by Matthew and Luke only. But the subsequent discovery of the Sinai Palimpsest has told us that the Old Syriac version did not omit Bethphage in Mk xi 1, so doubtless it really has a place in the genuine text of Mark, and therefore does not come in our list.

Gospels in a preliminary literary question, and even the literary question is confused by subsidiary detail. But we really have got through the thicket at last, and we shall be free to study our documents from a more general and historical point of view. I do not mean that we have settled all the questions connected with the literary genesis of the Second Gospel. Far from it: all that we have done is to explore a particular nook, an obscure corner out of which might conceivably have issued a fatal objection to our considering the Gospel according to S. Mark as a primary source for the Gospel History.

We have looked well over this corner, and found no irresistible argument for an *Ur-Marcus*, for an earlier edition of our Mark. If there were time we might go over the ground so admirably covered by Sir John Hawkins, and consider the parts of Mark not represented in Matthew or Luke. These peculiarities of Mark are divided by him into passages seeming to limit the power of Jesus Christ, or to be otherwise derogatory to or unworthy of him;[1] passages seeming to disparage the attainments or character of the Apostles;[2] other passages which might cause offence or difficulty;[3] minor enlargements of the narrative, such as later adaptors would omit in

[1] *Horae Synopticae*, p. 96. [2] *Ibid.* p. 98. [3] *Ibid.* p. 99.

works primarily intended for edification, including some Aramaic phrases and unimportant proper names.[1] These are followed by a long list of rude, harsh, obscure or unusual words or expressions, which may therefore have been omitted or replaced by others.[2] All these peculiarities of Mark may be summed up as exhibiting unecclesiastical unconventionality, a characteristic which we might expect to find in a primitive document coming from the circle of the earliest Christians and written before it had been considered what style of writing was appropriate for telling the story of our Lord's Ministry.

All these things tend to demonstrate the originality of our Mark, and therefore to shew that 'Ur-Marcus' either never existed or was almost indistinguishable from the Mark we possess. But the most convincing argument against postulating a literary source behind our Mark remains to be noticed. It is this—that the hypothesis of an 'Ur-Marcus' presupposes an interest in the biographical details of the public life of Jesus Christ, of which there is little trace elsewhere. In the extant remains of very early Christian literature we find the doctrines of the Crucifixion and the Resurrection; we find the arguments from prophecy; we find the ethical

[1] *Horae Synopticae*, pp. 100–105. [2] *Ibid.* 106–110.

teaching of the Sermon on the Mount; and as early as the middle of the 2nd century we find copious references to the stories of the Nativity. In other words, we find what corresponds to the rudiments of the Creed, together with a real and vivid interest in Christian morality. But the details of the Galilean Ministry of Jesus Christ are hardly mentioned. It is not a mere chance that the fragments of non-canonical Gospels discovered in recent years—the Oxyrhynchus *Logia* (so-called) and the Gospel of Peter—concern themselves the one with detached Sayings of Jesus, the other with the Passion. It is the peculiar merit of S. Mark's Gospel, from the point of view of the historical investigator, that it deals mainly with a cycle of events foreign to the life and interests of the growing Christian communities.

The Gospels according to Matthew and Luke represent far more nearly than the Gospel according to Mark the temper and the preferences of the early Churches: one of the unsolved problems of the New Testament literature is to supply the reasons why Mark became part of the Church's Canon. I therefore think it most improbable that this Gospel was one of a series of successive revisions of what was fundamentally the same work. Both the merits and the defects of the Gospel according to Mark seem to me to shew that we are dealing with what is, from a literary point of view, an original document and not an adaptation of something else.

This is not the same thing as asserting that Mark is either a faithful or an intelligent transcript of the events with which it deals, or that some of the sayings and tales which are related in it had not already passed from mouth to mouth and acquired thereby a more or less fixed form. What I think to be essentially new in Mark is the general cast of the whole narrative, the story of our Lord's Ministry told from the beginning to the end. It is our main historical source, and it is not itself based on older literary sources, but the single narratives represent the way in which the disciples of the disciples of Jesus told to one another such stories of the earthly Ministry of their Lord as they remembered in the light of all that had happened during the momentous thirty or forty years which succeeded the Crucifixion.

In one instance it is possible that a written source may underlie the words of the Second Gospel, viz. in the Eschatological Discourse (Mk xiii 3–37). It was antecedently not improbable that what professed to be words of the Lord about the Last Times should be independently circulated, especially during the agony of Jerusalem in AD 70, and our Evangelist may very well have incorporated such an independent fly-sheet into his work, with or without alteration. Whether the substance of this chapter be authentic reminiscence can only be determined by the same general tests of internal evidence that we apply to other parts of the Gospel; its external attestation is the same as the rest of the work—that is to say, it comes to us on the authority of the Evangelist who incorporated it. Both the general purport of the discourse and most of the single sayings seem to me, if I may venture to give an opinion, perfectly to harmonise with what we otherwise know of the teaching of Jesus. But the literary form is different from the rest of Mark; it is much the longest uninterrupted speech in the Second Gospel, and the several sentences are articulated together with *δέ* and *γάρ* and the other appropriate particles. One has only to compare it with the string of loosely connected Parables and Sayings in Mk iv 3–32 to feel the difference.

The hypothesis that the Eschatological Discourse in Mk xiii once circulated, very much in its present form, as a separate fly-sheet, explains the allusion to 'him that readeth' in Mk xiii 14. And I venture to suggest that this fly-sheet, rather than our Gospels themselves, may have been the ultimate historical source from which the eschatological chapter at the end of the Didache was derived. But however this may be, there is no doubt that this one Discourse stands alone in S. Mark's Gospel. Nowhere else is there any sign that I can see of the use of previously existing written sources. On the other hand, I believe with Wellhausen that 'Mark was known to both the other Synoptists in the same form and with the same contents as we have it now.'[1] It is, I repeat, our main source for the Gospel History. In the next Lecture we shall examine it as a whole, with the object of inquiring to what extent the picture which it presents of the outward life of Jesus Christ is to be taken as a credible historical view.

[1] Wellhausen, *Einleitung*, p. 57.

III.

THE GOSPEL OF MARK: ITS HISTORICAL VALUE.

Μετὰ τῶν μαθητῶν τῇδε κἀκεῖσε ἀποδιδράσκεις.
CELSUS, *ap. Origen*, I 380.

S. MARK'S Gospel being the main source of information we possess for the general course of our Lord's Ministry, it is most important to determine its trustworthiness as a historical document. The problem before us, therefore, is still one of objective external history, and the general aim of this present Lecture will perhaps best be understood if I put it in the form of a question: Does the story of Jesus Christ, as given in S. Mark, approve itself as an adequately historical outline of the main events? We shall be ready perhaps to admit that this or that detail is inaccurately told or too cursorily treated, but we want to discover whether the work as a whole gives a faithful view. Above all, are we dealing with a piece of history, however popular and unscientific; or is the work mainly mythical, a fancy picture cast in an historical form?

It is obvious that no guarantees of age or authorship can give us the assurance we need, and that we must ultimately rely on internal evidence. If the picture presented in S. Mark's Gospel be in essentials true, it will give an essentially reasonable account of the Ministry. I do not mean it will contain no stories of what are called 'miracles,' or that we should at once be able without misgiving to accept every incident as having actually occurred in the way related. But if this Gospel be in the main historical, it will have two characteristics; it will be generally self-consistent, and it will fit in with the known political and social history of the time. We know from non-Christian historians, notably from Josephus, something of the general history and condition of Palestine about AD 30; and we know from Jewish sources, both Talmudic and pseud-epigraphic, something of the culture and the hopes and fears of the Jewish population in the first century. If S. Mark's Gospel be an historical work, it will fit into this framework. Furthermore, if it be in the main historical, it will not lend itself easily to attempts which seek to explain the Gospel as a work designed to set forth particular doctrines or theories about Jesus and the Church.

All these conditions I venture to think satisfied. Let us consider for a moment what are the contents of the Gospel according to S. Mark. Let us approach as outsiders, as persons desirous of a preliminary general view. We read in Mark that the public ministry of Jesus, the carpenter of Nazareth in Galilee, took its rise from the preaching of John the Baptizer. The preaching of John had chiefly attracted the people of Judæa, but Jesus had gone down from Galilee and had been baptized. At the moment of Baptism He hears a voice from Heaven calling Him the beloved Son of God, but His public career does not begin until John was cast into prison by Herod Antipas. Then Jesus comes to Galilee announcing the Kingdom of God to be at hand, and exhorting men to repent and believe the message. How long the first period lasted we have no means of judging, for it is not until Simon and his companions join the new Prophet that the narrative becomes detailed. At first Jesus teaches in the Synagogues, and His commanding personality produces a great effect. But the very success of the announcement of the Gospel brings interruptions to the work which are far more clearly brought out as such in Mark than elsewhere, viz. the intrusion of invalids in season and out of season, seeking for cures and acquiring for Jesus a kind of popularity which He definitely tries to avoid; and the growing opposition of the official Jewish world, both religious and secular. These points afford a very remarkable testimony to the historical value of Mark, as they are features which can hardly have been supplied by later reflexion, and therefore must have been derived from real historical reminiscence. The way in which the story of the leper is told—the cure importuned and the man sent away with almost fierce injunctions of silence, and then the man's disobedient and unseasonable publication of his cure, so that Jesus is obliged to keep in the open country for privacy—goes far to shew that cures of this kind actually took place. Naturally we do not know enough about the details to found any medical doctrine on the cures. As Dr. Sanday says: 'We may be sure that if the miracles of the first century had been wrought before trained spectators of the nineteenth, the version of them would be quite different.'[1] I doubt if the evidence suffices for us to go very much beyond this admirably cautious statement. What does appear certain is this, that the final rupture of Jesus with the religious authorities in Galilee arose out of the healing of the man with

[1] *Dictionary of the Bible*, ii 625, art. 'Jesus Christ.'

the withered hand in the Synagogue on the Sabbath.

This event, according to Mark, was the parting of the ways. The religious leaders decide to get rid of Jesus by the help of the friends of the Herodian government; while Jesus, on the other hand, begins to organise His followers into what was destined to develop into the Christian Church. He no longer preaches in the Synagogues, save once (and that unsuccessfully) in His own home,[1] and for the remainder of His ministry His main efforts are directed towards preparing His disciples for the trials in store for Him and them. For this purpose, and for present safety, Jesus more and more avoids appearing in public, much of the remaining time being spent out of Galilee, away from the jurisdiction of Herod Antipas, or else in the open country far from the main routes. Shortly before the breach with the Scribes and Pharisees it had been early spring.[2] In the following year Jesus determines to go up to Jerusalem for the Passover, though fully aware that it can lead to no earthly victory. While still in the territory of Antipas He remains as much concealed as possible, but in the Roman province of Judæa He resumes public teaching, and enters

[1] Mk vi 1 *εἰς τὴν πατρίδα αὐτοῦ*: the name *Nazareth* is only mentioned by Mark in i 9.

[2] Mk ii 23.

Jerusalem openly amid His followers. He does not sleep inside the walls, but at Bethany, where He has friends. The next day after His first entry He comes in to the city and drives out from the Temple courts those whom He finds buying and selling there. The people in general are friendly, and when the priests and elders demand on the following day to know by what right He thus acts, He is able to silence them by raising the question of the authority of John the Baptist.

Various attempts are made on this day to entangle Jesus in some pronouncement which will discredit Him with the people; but they all fail, and the priests and elders decide that they must get Him out of the way as quietly as possible before the Feast begins. This plan is duly accomplished through the treachery of Judas, one of the Twelve apostles of Jesus. On the Thursday evening Jesus had gone in to Jerusalem to eat the Passover; at least that seems to have been what Mark intends, but several considerations derived from the Synoptic narratives themselves (cf. Mk xv 21; Lk xxii 15, 16) conspire to shew that the 'Last Supper' was not the legal Paschal feast, though it may have been regarded by some of the disciples as a more or less irregular equivalent for it. The place for the meal had been previously arranged with some secrecy, but afterwards Jesus was discovered with the disciples in a garden and carried off almost without resistance. A hasty trial followed; for a long time Jesus keeps silence, but at last avows Himself to be the Messiah and the Son of the Ineffable God of Israel. This is considered blasphemy, and the next morning the chief priests persuade Pilate, the Roman Governor of Judæa, to let Jesus be crucified. Pilate is at first unwilling, but seeing that it will satisfy the chief priests and their friends, and that no voice is raised for the prisoner, he consents. Before 10 AM on the Friday morning Jesus has been conveyed outside Jerusalem and crucified. His disciples had fled at the moment of the arrest, and His disheartened and disorganised followers made no demonstration even of sympathy. Before the tribunal of Pilate Jesus had practically kept silence, and on the cross His only utterance had been a cry which the Evangelist understood to have been in the words of the most despairing verse of the Psalms.

About 3 PM He expires on the cross in the sight of a few faithful women friends who look on from a distance. Somewhat later a certain Joseph obtained from Pilate permission to bury the corpse, and just before the Jewish Sabbath began, at dusk, it was taken down and laid in a rock-hewn tomb, with the intention of completing the burial as soon as the Sabbath was over. But when the women came early on the Sunday morning, they find a young man sitting in the tomb, who announces to them that Jesus had been raised; that He was not there, but was going to meet the disciples in Galilee. At this point the text, as we have it, breaks off, but we can hardly doubt that it went on to tell how the Lord was seen by the apostles and others in Galilee.

The above outline is not an adequate picture of Jesus Christ, even if we confine ourselves to the Gospel according to Mark. I have not attempted even to indicate the doctrines taught by Him as there related, and I have intentionally passed over miraculous details, as far as it was possible to do so, without altering the framework of the narrative. My aim was not to construct a Life of Christ as it really was, as seen from the inside, but to draw up a plain narrative of the outward career of Jesus the Nazarene, as it might have appeared to a rather unsympathetic observer. That it is possible to do this at all from the details furnished by the Second Gospel is a very strong argument for regarding that Gospel to be a trustworthy historical record. A wholly unhistorical myth cannot be rationalised without becoming absurd.

This is perhaps the best point to say a few

words about the Gospel miracles. Whatever our own judgement may be with regard to what is commonly called the 'supernatural,' it is evident that the occurrences related in the Gospels were not things which impressed the adversaries of Jesus. He gave them no 'sign'; in fact, He refused to give them one when they asked for it. Nay more, occurrences which are certainly narrated as 'miracles' by the Evangelist did not greatly impress even the disciples themselves. That on at least two occasions Jesus and His disciples had found themselves far away in the open country in the presence of large crowds without means of feeding them, and that nevertheless, when they made them sit down as for a meal, there was more than enough and to spare, is attested by the narrative in Mk viii 11–21, a narrative which it is impossible not to regard as derived from genuine historical reminiscence. Yet the same passage shews us that the apostles had not been influenced by the events of these two meals, a circumstance which would be indeed incredible if these events had come to pass in the way generally supposed. What actually happened is of course quite beyond our power to ascertain: we only know that the same document that tells us of the wonderful meals, tells us also of the distress of the apostles when shortly afterwards they found that they were running short of provisions.

That the Gospel according to Mark contained the story of the Resurrection of Jesus Christ is surely no reason for questioning its right to rank as an historical document. Here again we cannot reconstruct the details of the history with any confidence, whatever our beliefs may be. The believer is confronted with details that do not harmonise, and the unbeliever has to explain away the triumphant progress of the new sect. There is no doubt that the Church of the apostles believed in the resurrection of their Lord. They may have been mistaken, but "there is satisfactory evidence, that many professing to be original witnesses"—I will not say with Paley, "of the Christian miracles": that claims too much, but certainly that Jesus had been raised from the dead,—"passed their lives in labours, dangers, and sufferings, voluntarily undergone in attestation of the accounts which they delivered, and solely in consequence of their belief of those accounts; and that they also submitted, from the same motives, to new rules of conduct." Let us add, what Paley omitted, the abiding personal influence of Jesus in the memories of the first disciples, and let us concede that like all other men they may have been mistaken: with these amendments, Paley's famous allegation still stands. Yet no considerations of this kind explain the vitality of the Christian Religion: we do not know why it lived and lives, any more than we know why we ourselves are alive.

To return to the Gospel of Mark, we cannot but be struck by the sobriety of tone in the fragmentary narrative at the end. There is no earthquake, as in Matthew, and no Theophany, as in the apocryphal Gospel of Peter; what is dwelt upon, as compared with other Christian accounts, is the talk of the Women and their dazed emotion on hearing the news. Whatever interpretation we may put on the narrative, it does not read like a myth written in the form of history.

I have attempted to shew you that the Gospel according to Mark presents a reasonably consistent account of the public life of our Lord; and I have tried to indicate to you some general grounds for thinking that its treatment of the miraculous is what might be expected in an historical, as distinct from a mythical, document coming from Christian sources in the first century. But these are in a sense negative tests of historicity; we have done little more than raise a plea that the work is not inconsistent with history. If this Gospel is really to rank as an historical work it must be something more; it must reasonably answer some of the main questions which lie at the very root of the Gospel history. These questions are four in number. Two, as I believe, are answered in the Gospel of Mark; a third it answers adequately, but less fully than the other Gospels; the fourth is insoluble.

The first question is, *How does the story of Jesus Christ fit into general history?* If He really lived on this earth, His earthly life must fill a certain place, however small, in the great Pageant of events. What position did He occupy with regard to the politics of His age, to the general course of affairs?

The second question concerns the Christian Church. However unhistorical the life of Jesus may be declared to be by advanced criticism, the Christian Society is a present fact. Before Jesus began to preach it did not exist; after His death on the cross it is found to be actually existing. And so the question arises, *How did the Christian Society come into being?*

The third question is, *What did Jesus Christ teach?* This is the question which is answered more fully by other Gospels, and will be best considered later. But it is obvious that if S. Mark's Gospel provides a satisfactory answer to the first two questions, it will have given enough of the teaching of Jesus to vindicate its claim to give an historical picture of Him.

The fourth question, which I have called insoluble, is, *How did Jesus of Nazareth become what He was?* I think the approved modern formula is, 'The Messianic Self-consciousness of Jesus—how was it evolved?' or something of that kind. Well, I do not know, and I do not think it very profitable to inquire. What is certain is that our Gospels are very far from being a sort of psychological novel with Jesus Christ for the Hero. From the moment that He came forth in public, He spoke with authority, and His ascendancy over His disciples was from the first unquestioned. He had been, as we have been, an infant in arms with an unawakened, undeveloped mind; He increased in due course in wisdom and stature, and the story of the Temptation may be taken to describe symbolically and parabolically the mental struggles through which He came into possession of Himself. But it is idle to attempt to trace any inner development after the Ministry has begun. We may, it is true, note a difference between His methods and actions when He first delivers His Message and after He has been rejected by the spokesmen of the official religion of His own countrymen. But all the information we possess consists of some of the impressions of His followers; and for them, as for us, He remains a fixed centre of authority. It was the attitude of the Scribes and Pharisees that changed, not the teaching of Jesus Christ.

Yet, though our Lord throughout His public Ministry remains essentially unchanged for us, there is one thing which happened during that period, about which (as I said just now) we may reasonably expect to be informed. The history of our Lord's Ministry is the history of the birth of the Christian Church. When Jesus was baptized by John, the Church did not exist, even in germ. A short time elapses, a time to be measured rather in months than in years, and we find the Church existing as a society in Judaism, and yet distinct from it. This Society was founded by Jesus Christ Himself, for whatever view the historian may take about the Resurrection, it is impossible to believe that the appearances of the Risen Christ could alone have sufficed to knit together the Christian community. The belief that the Lord was risen indeed, raised also the spirits of the followers of the Crucified Prophet and animated their faith; but that any group of followers at all survived the shock of the Crucifixion shews us that the Christian community was already formed.

The Church came into being in the period between the Baptism and the Crucifixion, and if the Gospel of Mark be really an historical document, it will give an intelligible account of the beginning of the separate Christian Society.

I believe that the Gospel of Mark gives an intelligible and credible account; and, further, that it is the only one of the Gospels, canonical or uncanonical, which does give an intelligible account of the process by which Jesus Christ broke with the Synagogue, or rather, the process by which the Synagogue — that is, the official embodiment of Jewish religion—broke with Jesus Christ and forced Him to withdraw from their system.

Let us consider a little more closely the story of the earlier Galilean Ministry, as told in Mark. First of all we hear of a period during which our Lord has not yet come to any breach with the ordinary ecclesiastical system. During this period, which may have lasted for some months, Jesus teaches in the Synagogues. His personal friends gather round Him at His call, but they have no special organisation. The religious world of the Galilean Jews, on the other hand, has not yet made up its mind. In the light of history we may very well see it was inevitable that the new wine should burst the old wineskins; nevertheless, the rent had not yet been made. Objections to various unconventional acts of the new Teacher are made from time to time, but some answer is always forthcoming. This state of things could not last. According to S. Mark the crucial dispute broke out over a matter of Sabbath observance, as to whether the healing of the man with a withered hand was lawful or not. As I said just now, the evidence is hardly sufficient for us to found any medical doctrine about the cure, but I think it clear that the general description of the event comes from real historical reminiscence. It is totally unlike what a Christian would have produced, if he had been obliged to rely on his imagination alone. There was evidently a scene of great excitement. Jesus, says S. Mark, looked round upon the Pharisees with anger at their crassness (Mk iii 5); and they on their part quitted the building to concert measures with the 'Herodians,' *i.e.* with what we should now call 'Government circles' or 'the Bureaucracy,' to plan how they might get rid of this impossible personage. Here, in Mark iii 6, as I read the Gospel, we have our Lord's definite breach with official Judaism. He left the Synagogue, never to return again, save once in His own town.[1]

[1] The date of the events recorded in Mk iii 5 ff. cannot be accurately determined, but it is reasonable to suppose that it

After Mark iii 6 a new era in the Ministry is opened. From that moment begins the separate existence of the embryo Church. From that moment the aim of Jesus is not the rousing of the multitudes, as it had been hitherto, but the instruction and training of His own disciples. True, a crowd still follows Him on occasions, and sometimes He is willing still to teach. But if He does so it is by way of an exception, because they have come to Him from a distance and He will not send them away without a word.[1]

On the present occasion the circumstances were different. It was a time for preparation and organisation, not for an appeal to the crowd; for choosing men and training them, not for precipitating an outbreak. After the scene in the Synagogue, Jesus withdraws to the seashore, but He is followed by an enthusiastic and uninstructed multitude (Mk iii 7–10). He cannot

was shortly after the occasion on which the disciples had plucked the ears of corn on the Sabbath (Mk ii 23 ff). This story, placed as it is somewhere near the shore of the Sea of Galilee, implies a date somewhere in April or May. Lk vi 1 does not tell us any more than the parallel in Mark. The textual evidence makes it certain that the δευτεροπρώτῳ of the Byzantine and some Western texts is not genuine, and even if it were accepted it does not seem to correspond to any known Jewish expression. Probably an ancient Western Scribe wrote ΕΝϹΑΒΒΑΤΩΒΆΤΏ by dittography, and Β̄ Λ̄ΤΩ was erroneously expanded into δευτερο-πρώτῳ.

[1] See Mk vi 31–34, also viii 34. How large is an ὄχλος?

escape from their importunities, even by remaining in a friend's boat. So He goes away altogether to the hills, and only those whom He summons to Him are allowed to invade His retreat. There He appoints Twelve of them to be with Him, and to undertake what we may call the revival ministry, the announcement in places which had not yet been visited of the coming of the Kingdom of God, and the accompanying summons to repentance. Our Lord's own time henceforth is reserved for other work.

I may pause here for a moment and remind you how differently this whole scene is told in Matthew and Luke. Their information is simply derived from Mark, but the general historical setting is so altered that we could not restore the proportions of the original, if the Gospel of Mark had not itself survived. I am not saying that the First and Third Evangelists may not have been justified from their own point of view in making their alterations. But their narratives can make no claim to set forth the march of events.

Having told us of the appointment of the Twelve, S. Mark goes on to describe how Jesus came down from the hillside to the shore, in order to go over with a few of His disciples to the country opposite (Mk iv 35, 36). On His way down He passes through Capernaum (Mk iii 19[b], 20). The place is still agitated by His recent quarrel with the religious world. The Clergy—for so we may call the Scribes—have now definitely made up their mind that He is a magician working by the aid of the prince of the devils, and His own family think Him mad (Mk iii 22 ff, 21, 31 ff). Hastily leaving the town without even having had a meal there, He spends the day on the shore of the Lake (Mk iii 20, iv 1, 35). Those who now form His audience are composed of His own party, both those who are more instructed and those who are less so, together with a multitude of outsiders.

Just at this point comes the Parable of the Sower and the two other Parables that have to do with the early growth of the Kingdom of God. It seems to me that they are extraordinarily appropriate in the setting given them by S. Mark. As a matter of fact the seed had been sown, the first harvest of disciples had just been reaped. The preaching of Jesus had gone on in Galilee for some months at least, and now, although much of what had been said had fallen on deaf or forgetful ears, yet a body of disciples had been formed, some of whom were ready to go wherever their Master led. The first season was over, and now a new sowing was about to begin. The Kingdom of God had really been inaugurated on earth (Mk iii 26, cf. Matt xii 28), and it was time that those who were to inherit the Kingdom should be conscious of their position, even though as yet the Mustard Plant, with which Jesus compared it, was in no sense a 'tree,' but only a tiny shoot, just visible above the ground.

Moreover, the position of these Parables, placed immediately after the breach with the Synagogue and the appointment of the Twelve, explains the language used when the Parable of the Sower is interpreted. Naturally we are not bound to hold that the Parable of the Sower (Mk iv 2–9), the explanation (*vv.* 10–20), and the other Parables (*vv.* 21–25, 26–32), all follow one another in strict chronological sequence. We learn, in any case, that the explanation of the Parable of the Sower, which in the Gospel immediately follows the Parable itself, was not given till Jesus and His more intimate companions were alone (*v.* 10).

It was when they were alone, according to S. Mark, that they that were about Him with the Twelve asked of Him the Parables. He said unto them: 'To you has been given the secret of the Kingdom of God: but to the outsiders it must all come in a Parable, that, as Isaiah said, they may see, and yet not see' (Mk iv 10–12).

These words are an old difficulty. Readers of *Encyclopædia Biblica* will perhaps remember that Prof. Schmiedel, in his elaborate article on the Gospels (col. 1866), tells us that they are 'impossible in the mouth of Jesus,' and that it is 'utterly futile' to make out a connexion in the words as given by S. Mark. 'What pleasure,' says Prof. Schmiedel, 'could he have had in his teaching if he had to believe his God-given task to be that of hiding from the people the truths of salvation?' And so we are told that Mark iv rests upon a composite source A + B*a* + B*b* + C, not to mention the subsidiary interpolator who inserted the Parable of the Leaven (col. 1867), who seems to have been later than the canonical Mark! It is all very complicated. I confess that I find these elaborate exercises in mosaic work somewhat lacking in verisimilitude.

Let us try for a moment to represent the scene to ourselves as it is told in S. Mark's Gospel, not from our own point of view, as we look back on the origins of Christianity from the vantage-ground of history, but from the point of view of the audience. I venture to think that there was some reason why these Parables were misunderstood by many of those that first heard them. I think that what they found most strange and difficult was not the parabolic form in which Jesus was speaking to them. The difficulty lay in the doctrine itself, the doctrine of the growth of the Kingdom of God.

All through the first century AD the religious part of the Jewish nation expected that the Kingdom of God was suddenly about to appear.[1] The belief is attested by the many Jewish Apocalypses which then were written, some of which survive to our own day. They are now subjects of study for learned men, but when they first were circulated they expressed the hopes and aspirations of the multitudes. At the same time there sprang up a series of leaders who announced themselves as heralds of the new age, men like that Theudas of whom we read in the Acts. Our Lord must have seemed like one of these. He had preached for some time that the Kingdom of God was at hand, and now He had taken a decisive step. He had come to a definite breach with those in authority, and now those who had been attracted by His personality and believed Him to be a teacher sent by the God of Israel, might expect a sign of the approaching catastrophe, or at the very least an assurance that the end was speedily coming. What they heard was very different. They heard that the Kingdom of God was something which could be compared to

[1] Cf. Luke xix 11.

the growth of a plant, that it was like a man sowing his seed, which then grew from stage to stage naturally and silently, until at last the harvest was ripe.

We Christians of the twentieth century have no difficulty in understanding that our Lord's Kingdom was not of this world. We see perfectly well that the development of the Christian character and of the Christian temper among the disciples was the one thing needful to secure the permanence of the Christian Society. That this work could only be inaugurated by the long and intimate intercourse of our Lord Himself with His immediate disciples we now know, seeing that at the time of the Passion they were hardly ready for the terrible strain on their faith. But all this was not obvious in Galilee. Jesus alone was not carried away by the decisive step He Himself had taken; He alone knew that a period of gradual growth was necessary, before His disciples, even those who were most attached and devoted to Him, would be strong enough to count the cost intelligently and follow Him to the end.

Thus we come back to Mark iv 11–13. I cannot see that these verses, when considered in the historical situation, are either inconsistent with themselves or betray the use of two distinct sources by the Evangelist. 'To you the secret of the Kingdom of God has been given: but to the outsiders it must all come in a Parable, that, as Isaiah said, they may see, and yet not see,'—these words mark the separation that had just been made. A few days earlier they would have been inappropriate; but if Jesus be now outside the old Synagogue, the people of the Synagogue are equally outside the new Church. Those whom Jesus had called to Him (Mk iii 13) were inside, the rest were outside. The good Tidings of the Kingdom had been announced to all Capernaum and the country round; those who had not responded had heard indeed, but not understood. To His disciples He will give further explanations, as much as may be needed, but if those outside misunderstand His teaching, He has other work than to go out of His way to answer their cavils. We never read that Jesus refused to explain His words to anyone who came and asked Him, even in the case of 'outsiders';[1] but for the future He had other work to do than rousing the indifferent or restating His Message to those who were hostile.

What follows in Mark iv 13 is equally appropriate to the situation. Jesus asks His own disciples, not without a touch of impatience, 'Know ye not this Parable? How, then, will ye

[1] See, for instance, Lk x 29, 37.

know any Parables?' The Parables of growth ought to have been plain at least to some of His intimate friends. But as yet the nature of the new Kingdom was not clear to any of them. They differed from 'those without' in their willingness to be taught, but they were not yet 'Scribes instructed in the Kingdom of Heaven.' A few months later we find the disciples of Jesus of Nazareth so established in their allegiance that the shock of the Crucifixion of their Master leaves a nucleus of Christians undispersed. We can hardly believe that this could have been the case had our Lord not devoted the greater part of the interval to the special training of His immediate followers. During the greater part of the year before the last Passover our Lord lives a wandering life, in exile from Galilee or in concealment, and His chief work is no longer that of the Revivalist, but of the *Pastor pastorum*.

We are now in a position to go on and consider what answer the Gospel according to S. Mark gives to the first of the questions which I formulated above, the question, *How does the story of Jesus Christ fit into general history?* However obscure the outward life of Jesus of Nazareth may have been, however little the rulers of His country may have concerned themselves with

Him, yet His life must have stood in some relation to the political events of His age. Besides, the whole Gospel narrative is full of the crowd, of the multitudes, believing or unbelieving. Our Lord was no recluse by profession. John the Baptist lived in the deserts away from the haunts of men, yet even he came into collision with the civil power, and ended his life in prison. If, therefore, our Gospels be historical, they should give an intelligible account of our Lord's relations with the civil power; in other words, with the government of Herod Antipas, the Tetrarch of Galilee.

We have just seen that the first period of our Lord's Ministry ended in a definite breach with the Pharisees, that is, with the regular religious and patriotic party among the Jews of Galilee. Their first step, according to Mark, was to concert measures with the 'Herodians,' that is, as I have said above, with persons connected in one way or another with the government administration. Now let us for a few minutes try to forget the religious interest of the Gospel history and fix our eyes only on externals.

It must not be supposed that our Lord and His disciples were in immediate danger because some of the Pharisaic party had approached these 'Herodians.' They had, in fact, done little more than complain to the police, if we may venture to find modern terms for the Gospel phrase. It could not be supposed that Jesus was as yet actively 'dangerous,' and the crowds were more or less on His side. But presently we learn that Herod hears the name of Jesus. There are various reports about the new Teacher at the Court, but Herod is sure that it will be John the Baptist over again (Mk vi 14 ff). Meanwhile, what is Jesus doing? He had crossed the Lake away from Capernaum, but had soon to leave the country (Mk v 17). On His return He had visited His own home, but that also ended in failure (Mk vi 3 ff). The next we hear of Jesus is that He takes apart His more intimate disciples, the Apostles, that He and they may have a short rest (Mk vi 30 ff). Crowds from various quarters follow, and the holiday is interrupted: for our present purpose the important point to notice is, that after these folk have been provided with a meal and sent away, the disciples' boat starts for Bethsaida. It is true that they do not get there, for at the end of the voyage they find themselves, owing to a contrary wind, back in the plain of Gennesaret on the West side of the Lake (Mk vi 45, 48, 53). But Bethsaida, a town and district at the North end of the Lake, had been the intended port. Its importance for us is political. It is outside Galilee, in the Tetrarchy of Philip; the aim of the voyage had evidently been to quit Galilee proper, the Tetrarchy of Antipas.

The return of Jesus and His disciples to Gennesaret produces the familiar scenes. Immediately there are crowds of sick folk and their friends, followed by a controversy with Pharisees and Scribes, some of whom had come from Jerusalem. It was just this that the voyage had been originally undertaken to avoid, and so in the next scene Jesus has gone right away from Galilee towards the Tyrian districts by the Mediterranean coast. Here He is safe and in quiet among a non-Jewish heathen population. From the Tyrian country He goes to the Decapolis, *i.e.* to the predominantly non-Jewish region East and South-East of the Sea of Galilee, making a circuit to the North instead of retracing His steps through Galilee itself.[1]

This journey from Gennesaret to the Tyrian country, and from the Tyrian country by way of

[1] If we follow the text of Mark, Jesus went round by way of Sidon. He would therefore cross the Litani and the Hasbani by the existing route, and proceed by way of Cæsarea Philippi to the country East of the Sea of Galilee. Wellhausen (*Ev. Marci*, p. 60) conjectures that διὰ Σιδῶνος in Mk vii 31 is a mistake of the Evangelist for Bethsaida, the two names being easily confused in Aramaic. But the object of the long journey was obviously to pass well to the North of the Galilean portion of the Tetrarchy of Antipas, and this very likely involved crossing the Litani river.

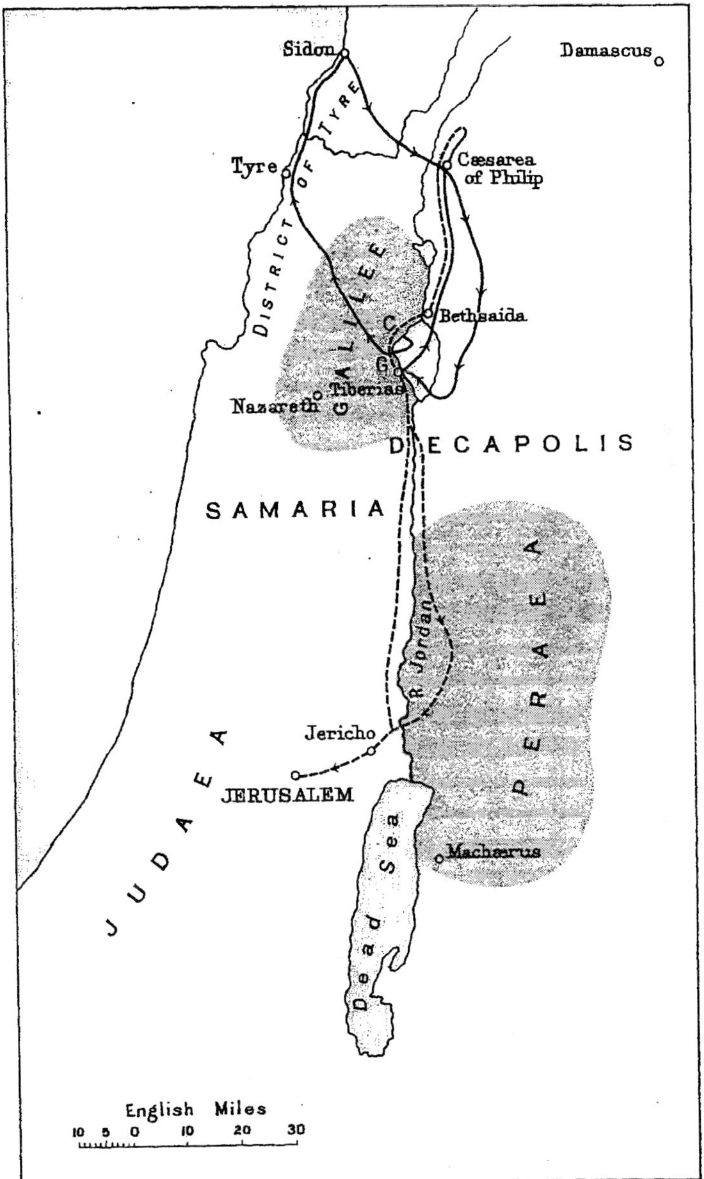

C. = Probable Site of Capernaum.
G. = Plain of Gennesaret
The Tetrarchy of Herod Antipas, Coloured Pink.

the Decapolis to the S.E. shore of the Galilean Lake, does not take long to tell, but it seems to have occupied many months of the short period of our Lord's public Ministry. The grass was still green when the Five Thousand were fed,[1] but now we have arrived almost at the time of S. Peter's confession and the start for Jerusalem to keep the last Passover. The journey must have taken about eight months, say from June to January inclusive, and all this time Jesus had been an exile from Galilee, outside the dominions of Herod Antipas.

Need for rest and quiet is hardly enough to explain this long retirement. Why does Jesus, to use the words of a famous opponent of Christianity, the heathen Celsus, 'run off with his disciples hither and thither'?[2] The itinerary which the Gospel of Mark gives us, meagre as it is, makes the answer quite clear. The parts that are avoided are the dominions of Antipas. The wanderings begin immediately after the fame of Jesus comes to Antipas's ears (Mk vi 14 ff, 31). Jesus was no longer favoured by the Clergy, He was an object of suspicion at the Court, and, like David and Elijah in the old days, He was forced to leave

[1] Mk vi 39.

[2] Μετὰ τῶν μαθητῶν τῇδε κἀκεῖσε ἀποδιδράσκεις (Origen, *Philocalia*, p. 107 = *Contra Celsum*, I, 380).

the country. We are still, let me repeat, concerning ourselves with the mere externals of the Gospel history, and we need not now pause to consider what effect these long journeys in the company of Jesus, through lands mostly heathen or uncultivated, may have had upon the faithful few who remained with Him. Let us turn rather to the effect our Lord's absence must have had upon others. The effect must have been to alienate the lukewarm adherents and to encourage the actually hostile. He was evidently not 'dangerous'—so His opponents said, no doubt.

With the aid of this key to the general history, the key, namely, that it was not safe for Jesus to remain in Galilee, because His enemies had aroused the suspicions of Herod, let us go on with the itinerary. After the feeding of the Four Thousand, S. Mark tells us that He went by boat with His disciples to 'the parts of Dalmanutha' (Mk viii 10). The parts of Dalmanutha are not yet properly identified; there seems to be some error in the transmitted form of the proper name, which is at least as old as the Gospel of Matthew, where the place is called Magedan. Dr. Cheyne suggests a suburb of Tiberias called Magdalnunaya: possibly it is a corruption of Amathus, mentioned by Josephus.[1]

[1] See *Ency. Bibl.* 1635.

Anyhow, we shall not be far wrong in looking for some place on the West side of the Lake, *i.e.* in Galilee. Wherever it was, there were Pharisees there, who come out at once demanding a sign from heaven. The sign, as you will remember, is not given, and our Lord and His companions embark at once for Bethsaida (Mk viii 13, 22). It is all done so hastily that they forget to provision the boat; I cannot doubt that it was, in fact, a hurried flight. And from whom should it be a flight, but from Herodian officials? That is why Jesus warns the disciples, as they sail away, to beware of the influence of Herod as well as of the Pharisees. Why otherwise should Herod have been brought in? Is it not probable that the Pharisees had told Jesus to go at once, because Herod would fain kill him? It seems to me that the story given in Lk xiii 31–33, where our Lord says that it does not befit a prophet to perish outside Jerusalem, belongs to the occasion of the interrupted landing at the place called 'Dalmanutha.'

From Bethsaida they go to the non-Jewish district of Cæsarea Philippi in the Tetrarchy of Philip (Mk viii 27 ff).

And now the time comes for Jesus to start on His final journey to Jerusalem to keep the Passover. He does indeed go through Galilee, but His movements are kept secret, even when He passes for the last time through Capernaum (Mk ix 30, 31, 33). The little company follow the road by the lake and ultimately reach the frontier of Judæa (Mk x 1).[1] Jesus is once more

[1] The route followed by our Lord between Capernaum and Jericho cannot be fully made out. The one thing really certain is that He remained as much concealed as possible during the first part of the journey through Galilee (Mk ix 30), and that He did not resume teaching in public until He 'came to the borders of Judæa' (Mk x 1), *i.e.* as the sequel shews, not very far from Jericho in the Jordan Valley. But there is something odd about the geographical situation implied in Mk x 1 and the parallel verse Matt xix 1. According to the true text of Mark, which is also that of Matthew, Jesus comes 'to the borders of Judæa beyond Jordan' (*εἰς τὰ ὅρια τῆς Ἰουδαίας πέραν τοῦ Ἰορδάνου*—so D 1&c 13&c 28 565 latt syrr). This is generally interpreted to mean, 'He came into Judæa by crossing the Jordan,' *i.e.* that He followed a usual pilgrim route to Jerusalem, in which a passage through Samaria was avoided by crossing over into Peræa, and then crossing back again. This route, indeed, is definitely assumed by the later Greek MSS, which prefix *διὰ τοῦ* to *πέραν*. But *διὰ τοῦ* is not found in any ancient version, and cannot be genuine. The Vatican MS and its usual allies prefix *καί* to *πέραν*. This cannot imply that what follows in the next few paragraphs happens in Peræa, for, in that case, what would be meant by 'coming to the borders of Judæa'? As a matter of fact, the Jordan divided Judæa from Peræa. The odd thing, therefore, about the statement in Mark is that it seems to put our Lord on the Judæan side of the Jordan, while the narrator views the scene, so to speak, from the Peræan side.

It must be remembered that the sentence we are considering occurs in a portion of Mark which has the highest claims to be considered actual history, to be based ultimately on the reminiscences of S. Peter. It is therefore to the point if we here take into account general historical probabilities. We are told that our Lord kept His progress through Galilee as secret as possible, and it is practically certain that the immediate reason for this secrecy was to avoid collision with the Herodian officials. Now, if this were the real situation, to take a journey through Peræa, which

safe outside the territory of Antipas, and—I quote the very words of Mark—'multitudes come together unto Him again; and, as He was wont,

was a portion of Herod's Tetrarchy, seems like incurring a needless risk: the obvious thing to do was to go by the Samaritan route. At the same time, if many friends and adherents were going the usual way by Peræa, it might very well be arranged that the meeting should take place, not at Jerusalem, but at the point where the pilgrim-route from Peræa crossed the Jordan to enter Judæa.

This is the scheme which underlies the story of the journey as given by S. Luke, and I cannot help wondering whether after all it may not be the true account. That S. Luke has inserted a quantity of extraneous matter into his story which belongs to other times and places can hardly be doubted: this is certainly the case with the sayings about Beelzebul (Lk xi 15 ff), and it is hardly likely that Jesus would be taking a meal with Pharisees (xi 37, xiv 1), or that myriads of the people would be gathered together (xii 1), in the midst of the Samaritan country. But it is quite possible that the Samaritan journey itself was found by S. Luke in a previously existing source; at least the story of the Samaritan village that would not receive our Lord because His face was set to go to Jerusalem sounds historical enough (ix 51–56). And it is noteworthy that in this story Peter does not appear, only James and John. I venture to suggest that the historical reason for this was that Peter and most of the other disciples went round by Peræa, that when they arrived at the passage of the river they found Jesus waiting for them in 'the borders of Judæa beyond Jordan,' *i.e.* on the W. side, and finally that one reason why nothing is said about the events of the previous journey is that our Lord and S. Peter had travelled to the spot from Capernaum by different routes and not together.

The net result of this conjecture—for it is little more—is to harmonise the accounts in Mark and Luke. It is therefore well to point out that we are not doing violence to Mark in order to fit it into the scheme of Luke; on the contrary, the considerations which suggest that our Lord's route from Capernaum to Jericho never actually crossed the Jordan are derived from the curious wording of Mk x 1 and from general historical probabilities.

He taught them again.' From this point the narrative becomes once more full of incident, until in due course Jesus enters Jerusalem, not in secret but amid the acclamations of Galilean followers.

When Jesus has reached the neutral ground of Judæa and begun again to teach in public, what is the subject which is discussed? The subject is Divorce. Some persons—in adapting the story Matthew calls them Pharisees—were asking Him whether a man may put away his wife. It was a test question, and we see from what Jesus said afterwards in private to the disciples that it was well understood by Him to be a test question. From his own point of view Herod had been perfectly right. Our Lord's Ministry was in a sense John the Baptist's over again. It began when John was thrown by Herod into prison, and the first watchword of the new Prophet had been a call to repentance, like John's. From Herod's point of view, no doubt, the movement represented another recrudescence of popular religious bigotry, which was easily offended at the fashionable Roman habits of the Herodian family. John the Baptist had lost his life in protesting against the pagan morals of Antipas and Herodias; Jesus in the eyes of many was first and foremost the successor of the Baptist. For months He had been in hiding; now he was again upon the scene, and the question about Divorce could not fail to draw from Him a decisive pronouncement.

I do not think the answer was what His questioners desired. Here as elsewhere our Lord had as little taste for the leaven of the Pharisees as for the leaven of Herod. If they had expected Him to rail at Antipas now that He was safe in Judæa, they were disappointed. To Him the general relations of man and wife mattered more than the amours of this or that half-heathen princelet, and—what must have surprised and shocked His interlocutors—mattered more than the very words of this or that text out of the Pentateuch. His answer offered no palliation for Antipas and Herodias, but His emphatic insistence on the sanctity of marriage is based on the natural constitution of man as opposed to the regulations in the Mosaic Law.

Had this been all the story we should hardly have been justified in assuming any reference at this point to the Herods, but what follows makes it, I venture to think, clear. The disciples, we are told, ask Jesus in private the meaning of what He had said, and He replied: "The woman that leaves her husband and becomes the wife of another commits adultery, and the man that leaves his wife and takes another commits adultery" (Mk x 11, 12). There are certain variations of order and wording in the transmitted text of these words, but all MSS and versions agree in the main point, which is, that the woman that deserts her husband to marry someone else is blamed as well as the man who divorces his wife.[1]

This condemnation of the woman is not found in Matthew and Luke, and it is pretty generally assumed to be a secondary addition, 'based on Roman Law,' says Dr. Schmiedel in *Encyclopædia Biblica*, col. 1851. I venture to think such a view mistaken, and that so far from being a secondary addition it is one of the really primitive features of the Gospel of Mark, a feature which was dropped out or altered when its historical meaning had been forgotten. It was no doubt monstrous to imagine that a Jewess should desert her husband to marry another man, but it was

[1] The offending woman is blamed first, according to the Old Syriac version and the valuable Greek minuscule known as Codex 1, and this is probably the true order. There are also variations in the terms used for the *desertion* of the husband by the wife and for her subsequent *marriage*, no doubt caused by the fact that a woman could neither 'divorce' nor 'marry': she might 'be divorced' or 'be married.'

not quite unheard of. We know the woman and her history. Herodias had left her husband—the man whom Mark calls 'Philip,' but Josephus only knew as 'Herod'—in order to live with Antipas. Antipas also was guilty: he had put away the daughter of the Arabian king Aretas to marry Herodias his half-brother's wife, she herself being his half-niece.

We need scarcely pause to inquire whether Herodias merely deserted her first husband, or whether, like her great-aunt Salome,[1] she availed herself of the methods of Roman procedure and divorced him. Our Lord's previous words shew that He did not regard an immoral act as being any the less immoral for being carried out according to law: in either case I venture to think the saying as reported in Mark clearly implies a reference to Herodias, a reference which is singularly appropriate in the time and place.

Thus the Gospel according to Mark does give an intelligible answer to our question, as to how the story of Jesus Christ fits into the general history of Palestine. The details furnished by the Gospel explain the silence of profane historians. John the Baptist had openly with-

[1] Josephus, *Ant.* xv 7_{10}.

stood Herod, and had perished in consequence. Jesus came, indeed, as the successor of John; but as soon as His activity reached the ears of Herod and aroused his suspicions, Jesus gave up teaching in public and left the country. By doing this, He was working for the future, but He lost His hold on the present. He lost His hold on the Galilean crowds; but we have seen in the earlier part of this Lecture that He had already given up the task of rousing the people, and had begun to confine Himself to the more thorough instruction of His own followers, before the hostility of Herod was fairly awakened.

What the doctrine of Jesus Christ was we have yet to consider. At present we have been dealing almost entirely with the external framework in which His life is set. But I venture to think that what I have put before you goes far to vindicate the claim of the Gospel according to S. Mark to be a historical document, a document really in touch with the facts of history. In S. Mark we are, I believe, appreciably nearer to the actual scenes of our Lord's life, to the course of events, than in any other document which tells us of Him, and therefore if we want to begin at the beginning and reconstruct the Portrait of Christ for ourselves we must start from the

Gospel of Mark. The other Gospels, even the Gospels according to Matthew and Luke, give us an interpretation of Jesus Christ's life. An interpretation may be helpful, illuminating, even inspired, but it remains an interpretation. The thing that actually occurred was the life which Jesus Christ lived, and our chief authority for the facts of that life is the Gospel according to Mark.

We must be prepared resolutely to hold fast by the result we have attained. Ideas may develop, interpretations may become more noble and more profound, but the facts of ancient history do not develop. They remain the same. We must resist the temptation to try and fit into the historical framework supplied by Mark all the tales and the sayings of Christ that we find in the other Gospels. We must beware of regarding as additions to the sacred Biography things that are in reality interpretations of it. Not that there is nothing which may legitimately be done by the harmonist; I have ventured to put before you an instance just now, by combining Lk xiii 31 ff with Mk viii 11 ff. But such interpretations must always be made with the utmost caution. If the narrative of Mark has a historical background, and in its main outlines and arrangement fits without violence into the framework of secular circumstances and events, we are not at liberty seriously to disturb the proportions of this narrative and to change its general character, in order to interpolate into it stories derived from a wholly different view of the Ministry.

IV.

THE COMPOSITION AND LITERARY CHARACTER OF THE GOSPELS OF LUKE AND MATTHEW.

Date and Authorship of 'Luke' and 'Acts.'

THE Third Gospel is not a book complete in itself. It is only the first portion of a larger historical work, which was apparently designed to be executed in three volumes. The third volume is not extant; in fact, there is very little reason to suppose that it was ever actually written, but the absence of an adequate peroration at the end of the Acts of the Apostles (which forms the second volume of the series), shews us that a further instalment must have been contemplated. The date of 'Luke' and 'Acts' can be determined within narrow limits, if the arguments used below are sound. On the one hand, both the Gospel and the Acts contain details drawn directly from the *Jewish Antiquities* of Josephus, a work published in 93 or 94 AD; on the other hand, the literary evidence indicates that the author of the Gospel and of the Acts is none other than that companion of S. Paul, whose travelling diaries are largely quoted in the latter portion of the work. The Gospel and the Acts may therefore be assigned to the decade 95–105: we shall not be far wrong if we say in round numbers about 100 AD.

The evidence which convicts the Third Evangelist of having used the *Antiquities*, not always with complete accuracy, is very well brought together by Prof. P. W. Schmiedel in *Encyclopædia Biblica*, articles 'Theudas' and 'Lysanias.' In Josephus, *Ant.* xx 5, we read:

> "While Fadus was procurator of Judaea, a certain charlatan, Theudas by name, persuaded a very great number of people to take their effects with them and follow him to the river Jordan; for he told them that he was a prophet, and said he would at the word of command divide the river and give them an easy passage through it; and by these words he deluded many. Fadus, however, did not permit them to gain aught by their folly, but sent a squadron of cavalry against them, which, falling upon them unexpectedly, slew many of them and took many alive. Taking Theudas also alive, they cut off his head and carried it to Jerusalem."

This would be between 44 and 46 AD.

Josephus then goes on to say that the procurator Alexander of Judæa (about 46–48 AD) put to death some of the sons of Judas the Galilean, a personage who had incited the Jews not to pay their taxes in the time of Quirinius, about AD 6 (*Ant.* xx 5_2).

Now in Acts v 34 ff a speech is put into the mouth of Gamaliel in which these two men, Theudas and Judas the Galilean, are mentioned one after the other as agitators who had come to grief after making a great stir for a short time.

"For before these days rose up Theudas, giving himself out to be somebody; to whom a number of men, about 400, joined themselves: who was slain; and all, as many as obeyed him, were dispersed and came to nought. After this man rose up Judas of Galilee in the days of the enrolment, and drew away some of the people after him: he also perished; and all, as many as obeyed him, were scattered abroad."

Here, if anywhere in the Acts, the details of the speech must be due to the author, for all the Christians had been put outside. There are strong reasons for believing that the passage in *Ant.* xx $5_{1,2}$ supplied the material for Gamaliel's speech. The verbal resemblance between the two passages is considerable; so much so, that Eusebius quotes *Ant.* xx 5_1 in his Ecclesiastical History as a confirmation of the narrative in Acts.

The account in Josephus is consistent, and his information about these agitators, for aught we know to the contrary, is accurate. The passage in Acts, on the other hand, occurs in a speech where it is probable that the narrator is freely setting down such details as seemed appropriate;

it is chronologically faulty, for Gamaliel was speaking before 34 AD, before the rebellion of Theudas took place, and yet this rebellion is mentioned as if it preceded the times of the Census of Quirinius and the birth of Jesus. When therefore we find a passage where Theudas and Judas are spoken of, one after the other and in reverse chronological order, occurring in a standard history, it is natural to conjecture that this passage was in the mind of the author of the book of Acts. That the author of the book of Acts should have been careless in his choice of suitable historical instances to put into the mouth of Gamaliel is not very surprising, and surely quite excusable: the important point is not his inaccuracy, but his acquaintance with the *Antiquities* of Josephus. If he had read the *Antiquities*, and I cannot help drawing this inference, we must date the composition of the book of Acts later than 94 AD.

It should be remarked that if we admit the literary connexion between the Acts and the *Antiquities* we cannot arrive at an earlier date for Acts by postulating a common source for Luke and Josephus. The problem is not to explain how the author of Acts should have heard of Judas of Galilee and of Theudas, but why he should mention them together in the wrong order.

Almost equally cogent is the evidence about Lysanias of Abilene. The story of the public ministry of John the Baptist starts off in the Third Gospel with a very elaborately given date: "in the 15th year of the reign of Tiberius Caesar, Pontius Pilate being governor of Judaea, and Herod being tetrarch of Galilee, and his brother Philip tetrarch of the region of Ituraea and Trachonitis, and *Lysanias tetrarch of Abilene*, in the high-priesthood of Annas and Caiaphas, the word of God came to John" (Lk iii 1, 2). The 15th year of Tiberius is 29 AD, unless the Evangelist is reckoning by the system of Nerva, which would give 28 AD.

But Lysanias was not at that time Tetrarch of Abila: he had been, according to Strabo (xvi 2_{10}, p. 753), lord of the hill country of the Ituraeans, and he was executed by Mark Antony in BC 36. Nevertheless the territory that he had ruled over continued to bear his name. Josephus (*BJ* ii 11_5, §215) speaks of 'the so-called Kingdom of Lysanias,' and in *Ant.* xx 7, §138) he says that in 53 AD Agrippa II received the tetrarchy of Philip and Batanaea together with Trachonitis and Abila, adding that this last had formerly been the tetrarchy of Lysanias (*Λυσανίου δ' αὕτη ἐγεγόνει τετραρχία*).[1] Can we doubt that the Third

[1] *Cf. Ant.* xix §5, 275, Ἀβίλαν τὴν Λυσανίου.

Evangelist was writing with this passage of Josephus in his mind? Josephus tells us that after 53 AD Philip's Tetrarchy and Trachonitis, together with Abila that had been the Tetrarchy of Lysanias, belonged to Agrippa II: the natural inference might well be that before 53, and therefore in the time of Tiberius, Philip's Tetrarchy belonged to Philip and Lysanias's Tetrarchy—to Lysanias.[1] We need to explain why Lk iii 1 mentions Abilene at all, and further why the writer when mentioning it should fall into a gross chronological error: the way that Josephus mentions Abila and Lysanias explains both difficulties on the hypothesis that the Evangelist derived his information from a somewhat careless perusal of the Twentieth Book of the *Antiquities*.

We now come to the evidence which tends to shew that the whole of Luke and Acts is the work of one author, including the travelling diaries in which the writer speaks in the first person plural (Ac xvi 10–17, xx 5–15, xxi 1–18, xxvii 1–xxviii 16). That these diaries are the genuine records of a fellow-traveller of S. Paul cannot well be doubted. If they were not so,

[1] Most of these regions had previously been made over to Agrippa I in AD 34 (*Ant.* xviii 6_{101}, §237), but in telling us this Josephus makes no mention of Abila in naming the 'tetrarchy of Lysanias.'

they would be an incredible miracle of deceptive art, and one adapted not so much to attract the early Christians as to take in modern historical and archæological scholars: among a large number of other details may be mentioned the correct geographical information in Ac xx, xxi, and the designation of the Maltese noble as a πρῶτος, *i.e. Primus* of the island, a title confirmed by an inscription.

Accepting then the 'We-sections' of Acts as genuine excerpts from the travelling diary of a companion of S. Paul, the question arises whether the author of the diary is identical with the author of the Acts. Now in Sir John Hawkins's *Horae Synopticae*, pp. 148 ff. (2nd ed., pp. 182–189), the reader will find a number of carefully drawn up tables of Greek words and phrases characteristic of the 'We-sections,' of the rest of Acts, and of the Third Gospel. It would be absurd to attempt to reproduce Sir John Hawkins's work here, because the strength of the argument consists in the number of instances of agreement and the absence of serious instances of disagreement. What is really remarkable is that so much agreement with the rest of the Lucan writings can be noted in the 'We-sections,' which amount in all to only 97 verses, nearly half of which is occupied with the account of a shipwreck.

As a mere illustration, not as a substantive proof, let us take the only voyage described in the Third Gospel, that of Lk viii 22–25. This is a little narrative of 94 words, the substance of which (with most of the wording) is taken direct from Mk iv 35–41. The only other source from whence the wording of 'Luke' is here derived is the literary instinct of the evangelist. The parallel in Matt viii 18, 23–27, also founded on Mark, will serve to indicate what points might seem to invite alteration. What, therefore, is peculiar to the Third Gospel will give us the individual style of the compiler of that Gospel. Several points illustrate the question before us. At the start (*v.* 22) *καὶ ἀνήχθησαν* is inserted, *ἀνάγεσθαι* in the sense of launching forth into deep water being frequently used in the 'We-sections' and twice again in the other parts of Acts, but not in the rest of the N.T. In *v.* 23 we find the word *πλεῖν* 'to sail, travel by water,' which is not used in Matthew and Mark, but comes four times in the 'We-sections.' Again, in *v.* 23 the English versions find it necessary to supply the words 'with water,' where it says that 'they' (*i.e.* the boat) 'were filling.' The mention of *κύματα* 'waves' is curiously avoided. This is paralleled by Ac xxvii 41, where according to the true text (א* AB arm) we read that the stern of S. Paul's ship was dashed to pieces 'by the violence,' *i.e.* by the violence of the waves, as later MSS put it and as the English Bible understands it. But the writer, perhaps from familiarity with nautical Greek, does not bring in the waves by name.

Thus in this short narrative we find three parallels of language between the peculiarities of the story in Luke and the style of the writer of the 'We-sections.' The only link between either of the other two accounts and the 'We-sections' is the fact that S. Mark finds occasion to mention the stern (πρύμνα), a part of the ship which is mentioned in Acts xxvii 41, but obviously this is a mere coincidence.

While we are considering this passage it may be worth while to point out that the other deviations of Lk viii 22–25 from Mark which do not happen to find a parallel in the short compass of the 'We-sections' are nevertheless thoroughly characteristic of the Lucan writings. Here, as elsewhere in Luke, the Sea of Galilee is carefully called a *Lake* (λίμνη) and not a *Sea* (θάλασσα); and the word for 'being in jeopardy' (κινδυνεύειν) occurs twice in Ac xix, otherwise only once in S. Paul and never elsewhere in the N.T. The agitated cry of the disciples 'Master, master, we perish' is also characteristically Lucan. The regular title *Διδάσκαλε*, *i.e.* 'Teacher,' corresponding to the Hebrew title *Rabbi*, is used in all the Gospels for the title by which our Lord is addressed. But in Luke the *disciples* do not call Him *Διδάσκαλε* or *Rabbi*; they call Him either *Κύριε* ('Lord'), or as here *'Επιστάτα* ('Master'). In Luke *Διδάσκαλε* is the title given to Jesus by strangers or by half-declared adversaries.[1] The change of Mark's *Διδάσκαλε* in Luke viii 24 into *'Επιστάτα* is therefore thoroughly in keeping. The doubling of the vocative is also a Lucan characteristic. No writer of the Old or New Testament so often gives sayings with this doubling. Besides 'Jerusalem, Jerusalem' (which Lk xiii 34 shares with Matt xxiii 37), we have 'Martha, Martha' (Lk x 41), 'Simon, Simon' (Lk xxii 31), and 'Saul, Saul,' in all three places where S. Paul's conversion is narrated in Acts (ix 4, xxii 7, xxvi 14). I do not suggest that the compiler of the Third Gospel invented the doubling in all these places; in Lk xiii 34 it must certainly have stood in the source which he was transcribing. But these many examples shew that he appreciated the force of a double vocative, so that we need not be surprised to find a doubled vocative in Lk viii 24, in a

[1] In Lk xxi 7 the use of Διδάσκαλε is an indication that the whole of the chapter is in this Evangelist's view spoken to the people generally.

sentence which shews other marks of having been remodelled in language by the evangelist.

These remarks may serve to illustrate the literary unity of the Lucan writings. To come back to the main issue, I think that we may venture to endorse the verdict of Sir John Hawkins, based as it is on a very full induction, that "there is an immense balance of internal and linguistic evidence in favour of the view that the original writer of these sections [that is, the 'We-sections'] was the same person as the main author of the Acts and of the Third Gospel, and, consequently, that the date of these books lies within the lifetime of a companion of S. Paul" (*Hawkins*, p. 154; 2nd ed., p. 188). Nevertheless, in view of the great historical importance of this conclusion, it may be well to consider what other view consistently with the evidence it is possible to take. It may be said that we have only proved that the 'We-sections' are taken from a real diary, the work of a companion of S. Paul on his travels; and also that the Third Evangelist edited and partly rewrote this diary for his book of Acts, just as he edited and partly rewrote Mark's narrative when he incorporated it in his own Gospel. The sections taken from Mark are full of 'Lucan' characteristics as they appear in the present Gospel of Luke, but these 'Lucan' characteristics are due to the Third Evangelist, not to Mark the original author of these sections. May it not be that the 'Lucan' characteristics of the 'We-sections' are due not to the original diarist, but to the editor, *i.e.* the Third Evangelist himself?

A complete and satisfactory answer to this objection can hardly be given, certainly not from linguistic evidence alone. In dealing with the work of the Third Evangelist we are dealing with the work of a very expert writer. How easily the Gospel according to Luke reads! How strongly marked all through is the linguistic evidence which shews the hand of the Evangelist! And yet we know that it is built up upon Mark, and that much of the wording of many whole paragraphs has simply been transferred from Mark. Now in studying the Acts we are in just the same position as we should be if Luke was the only Gospel that had survived. How can we distinguish between the work of the diarist and that of the editor of the Acts?

Our answer must be that we cannot safely distinguish. Even if Sir John Hawkins be in the main right, as I think he is, we cannot hope to disentangle the work of Luke the diarist from the work of Luke the editor of the Acts. If the Evangelist did not scruple to rewrite sayings that were given in his sources as the very words of Jesus, whenever the occasion seemed to demand it, can we suppose that he treated his own travelling notes with greater reverence? We cannot doubt that the travelling diary has been 'written up' to suit the dignity of a historical work. The story of Eutychus, with its almost pointless allusion to the many lamps in the upper room (Ac xx 8), a touch quite in harmony with a really contemporary account, may very well have been taken over from the diary unchanged. But that is no reason for believing that the diarist took full notes of S. Paul's speech at Miletus, or that (if he did so) he reproduced them unaltered.[1] And though I can well believe that during the shipwreck S. Paul had faith enough to act in the sensible and courageous way related by the diarist, thanking God that he had been spared to eat another meal and heartening up his companions in misfortune to do the same, yet the words of his speech do not sound like a real report (Ac xxvii 33[b], 34). 'Not a hair of your head shall perish' (*v.* 34) seems to have been a favourite phrase with our Evangelist: he had already interpolated it into the eschatological Discourse of our Lord

[1] In Ac xx 25 *κηρύσσων τὴν βασιλείαν* is in the style of Lk ix 2 and of Ac xxviii 31 rather than in that of S. Paul, while *διὰ τοῦ αἵματος τοῦ ἰδίου* in *v.* 28 recalls Ac i 25 (*εἰς τὸν τόπον τὸν ἴδιον*). Similar examples could be culled from almost every verse.

(Lk xxi 18) and now he puts it into S. Paul's mouth.

Why, then, should we regard the substance of the traveller's diary as having been really a diary made by the editor of Acts? The main reason appears to me to rest ultimately upon a question of literary good faith. To put the matter quite plainly—and a familiar phrase will explain my meaning best—I think the device of saying 'we' when you mean 'they' is rather *cheap*, and I do not think the editor of the Third Gospel and the Book of Acts was given to using a cheap literary device. It is so easy to use and so effective, that I cannot imagine why, if this writer thought it worth his while to employ it at all, he should have used it only in certain chapters of the Acts. On the hypothesis that the 'We-sections' are not his own diary but someone else's, the editor of Acts must have almost entirely rewritten these sections, so full are they of 'Lucan' phraseology. Under these circumstances it becomes disingenuous to leave the impression that the writer of the book was really there, when he was not there. And all, we may well ask, to what purpose? To us, of course, it makes a considerable difference, because it affects our judgement as to the date of the work. But the public for which the work was originally designed knew the date of the work and something about the author. I do not see what reason there was for trying to induce the excellent Theophilus to believe that the writer of the Acts had been shipwrecked with S. Paul by means of a literary trick. It was probably a matter of common knowledge whether he had been at one time a companion of Paul, or not. The case is quite different with the speeches in the Acts. These no doubt, even the speech of Gamaliel, represent what the author thought the various personages would have said, and in some cases they may even have been expanded from notes taken at the time.[1] The author does not say he was there, any more than he professes to have overheard the conversations of our Lord with His disciples. The case is different again from Epistles circulated in the name of Peter or Paul, but not really his. In such a case the false ascription, if believed in, does add to the authority of the letter. But in the case we are considering the amount of extra authority gained for the whole work among contemporaries by posing as a companion of S. Paul on some of his later journeys must have been small. Readers who had accepted the Gospel of Luke without extracts from the author's diary would not need such extracts to authenticate the Acts of the Apostles.

[1] See Ac xx 25, 38.

Of course, if the extracts really were taken from a diary by the author he might very well be proud to incorporate them in the way we actually find them incorporated.

For these reasons I still continue to hold the old-fashioned belief that the 'We-sections' in the Acts are really taken from a travelling diary made by the Editor of the whole book. As I have already explained, this view does not imply that the diary has been incorporated entire into the Acts, or that it has not been occasionally rewritten and added to in order to fit it for incorporation into a literary work. What is asserted is that 'we,' where it occurs in the narrative of Acts, really does mean that as a historical fact the Editor of the whole book was present.

But we have seen that there is considerable reason to believe that the Acts and the Gospel of Luke were compiled by someone who had read Josephus's *Antiquities*, book xx: that is to say, that they can hardly be earlier than 100 AD. Are the two opinions compatible?

I venture to think the two opinions are compatible. The travellers' diaries, of which the 'We-sections' in Acts consist, shew that their author accompanied S. Paul from Troas to

Philippi about AD 50; there is nothing to shew that he was more than a young man of twenty. Thus he would have been born about AD 30. Consequently he would not be more than 70 years old when he published the two books dedicated to Theophilus which we possess. Is this really improbable? Does it not rather explain the very different degrees of accuracy which we find in the works of the accomplished writer whom I shall still not hesitate to call S. Luke? When he uses his own old diaries, made on the spot and at the time, he is full of information which surprises us now by its minute correctness. He gives the right title to the *Praetors* of Philippi and the *Politarchs* of Thessalonica. Yes; but he was actually there or in the immediate neighbourhood, and keeping a diary. When on the other hand he comes to describe the political situation in Palestine about the time he himself was born, we find him falling into error, error none the less real for being excusable. We do not know under what conditions he had access to the works of Josephus; he may have only had the opportunity for a rapid perusal, with but little time to make notes or extracts for his future use. For the ordinary events of secular history a Christian writer at the end of the 1st century would be dependent on the ordinary channels of information. For the events connected with the rise of his own sect he might have special sources to draw upon. He may have conversed during the course of his life with those who had themselves seen the Lord. At the same time, the fact that S. Luke uses the Gospel according to S. Mark as his main source for the Gospel history seems to me to make it unlikely that he had much personal intercourse with those who had been the Companions of the Ministry, men who could themselves have supplied the skeleton of a narrative from their own reminiscences. A comparison with the First Gospel makes it highly probable that S. Luke also used the so-called *Logia* Document in addition to the Gospel of Mark. But the important point which I have attempted to demonstrate in the preceding paragraphs is that the Third Gospel was compiled in his old age by a former companion of S. Paul, not earlier than the reign of Nerva.

The Composition of the Gospel according to Matthew.

The Gospel according to Matthew, unlike the Third Gospel, cannot be dated with precision, nor are we in a position to name the compiler.

Something however can be gathered about the sources which he had at his disposal and the circle of ideas in which he moved. Like S. Luke, he was a competent writer, he treats the wording of his predecessor with entire freedom, rearranging and combining them into a well-fused whole. This makes the reconstruction of his lost hypothetical sources an extremely hazardous, if not impossible, task. As I said in the Introductory Lecture, there can hardly be a greater error in Synoptic criticism than to treat the Evangelists as if they had worked like the harmonist Tatian, who made up a single narrative by piecing together the words of the several Gospels almost without alteration.

The happy circumstance that Mark, Matthew and Luke have all survived enables us to discover that Matthew and Luke are based on Mark, but if Mark were not actually extant I very much doubt whether modern criticism would have been able to reconstruct it from the other Synoptists. This consideration should render us very cautious in making statements about the contents or arrangement of the other sources on which we may imagine Matthew (or Luke) to have been based. It is indeed highly probable that, besides Mark, another document was used in common by Matthew and Luke, of which the main contents were a collection of Sayings of the Lord. This document is usually supposed to have been what Papias calls the *Logia* composed by S. Matthew, but when we attempt to go into details it is found that the opinions of investigators differ widely on almost every point, and a different interpretation of the passage in Eusebius will be given below. Instead, therefore, of attempting to reconstruct the lost materials out of which the Gospels according to Matthew and Luke may have been built, let us examine the demonstrable procedure of the First and Third Evangelists with regard to the Old Testament and S. Mark's Gospel.

In the case of S. Luke the first part of the answer is simple. S. Luke uses the 'Septuagint,' the ordinary Bible which the Church inherited from the Greek-speaking Jews. Notably this is the case in the story of the Nativity (Lk i, ii), where the LXX, and not any Hebrew or Aramaic document, has perceptibly coloured the style and language of the whole narrative.[1]

The quotations peculiar to the Gospel according to Matthew have wholly different characteristics.

[1] Compare the use of ἀδυνατεῖν in Lk i 37 and Gen xviii 14. But this is only one instance out of many. Others will be found in my own article on the *Magnificat* in the *Journal of Theological Studies* for Jan. 1906, or in Prof. Harnack's in the *Sitzungsberichte* of the Berlin Academy for 1900, pp. 538–556.

A few of them are indeed taken from the LXX, but the greater number are based on the Hebrew, some of these exhibiting curious inaccuracies arising out of a misconception of the Hebrew text. The Hebrew basis is particularly clear in the passage 'Out of Egypt have I called my son' (Matt ii 15). This is a quotation of Hosea xi 1 that agrees literally with what we find in the present Hebrew text; but it differs both from the LXX, which has 'Out of Egypt I have called back his children,' and from the Targum, which has 'Out of Egypt I have called them sons.'[1] The quotation in Matt xxvii 9, 10, alleged to be made from 'Jeremiah the prophet' but really based on Zech xi 13, owes its presence in the Gospel to a confusion between the Hebrew words for 'potter' and for 'treasury.' This confusion exists in the Massoretic text, but the LXX has another reading and the Targum turns the 'potter' into a Temple official. Thus the Evangelist appears to have derived his curious interpretation from the Hebrew, and not from the Greek Bible or from the main stream of

[1] I quote the Targum, because it might be supposed to contain a popular Jewish interpretation of the verse. Wellhausen (*Matt.*, p. 11) explains a similar literal following of the Hebrew in Matt iv 15 by assuming that the Evangelist used 'Theodotion.' It is therefore important to notice that this explanation does not fit Matt ii 15, for in Hosea xi 1 Theodotion has [ἐξ Αἰγύπτου] ἐκάλεσα αὐτὸν υἱόν μου.

popular Jewish exegesis. At the same time, seeing that in this passage (Matt xxvii 9, 10) he assigns words taken from Zechariah to Jeremiah, and that in xiii 35 he appears (according to the text approved by Dr. Hort) to assign Ps lxxviii 2 to Isaiah, it is improbable that he was quoting direct from a Hebrew copy of the Prophets. Equally clear is it that the words 'In His *Name* shall the *nations* hope' (Matt xii 21) are taken from the LXX of Isaiah xlii 4[b], for the Hebrew text has 'the *isles* shall wait for His *Law*.' And similarly 'Out of the mouth of babes and sucklings Thou hast perfected *praise*' (*κατηρτίσω αἶνον*, Matt xxi 16[b]) agrees with the Greek of Ps viii 2, while the Hebrewtext has 'Thou hast ordained strength.'

These last passages shew that the Evangelist was after all not unfamiliar with the Greek Bible. This is not surprising: the surprising part is the influence of the Hebrew text in a Greek Gospel. Now, as we have seen, the evidence does not point to the direct use of a Hebrew MS of the Old Testament: we must look rather to a collection of *Testimonia* as the immediate source of our Evangelist's quotations. The collection must have been made from the Hebrew, but the names of the several Prophets or Psalmists do not seem to have been attached to the quotations, nor were the words always cited with scrupulous accuracy. To collect and apply the Oracles of the Old Testament in the light of the New Dispensation was the first literary task of the Christian Church. Several such collections survive, and one of them, the *Testimonia* edited by Cyprian, is the source from which a whole series of Latin writers quote Scripture.

We may go on to conjecture that the original collection of Messianic proof-texts was made by Matthew the Publican in Hebrew, and that it is the use of this document by our Evangelist which gives his work the right to be called the Gospel according to Matthew. This collection of texts, in a word, may have been the famous *Λόγια*, of which Papias speaks (Euseb. *HE* iii 39), which each one interpreted as he could. The chief objection to this view is that such a quotation as that in Matt ii 15 ('Out of Egypt have I called my son') seems to assume the story of the Flight into Egypt, and it is difficult to believe that this story had a place in the work of the Apostle Matthew. I do not think we are in a position to solve the difficulty. The *Logia* of S. Matthew is hopelessly lost, and we do not know what it really contained. What is really demonstrable, and of great importance for us in estimating the value of the stories peculiar to the canonical Gospel of Matthew and in investigating their origin, is that the quotations by which some of them are illustrated are derived from the Hebrew Bible and not from the Greek. This consideration does not of itself make the stories historical or even probable, but it does tend to prove that they originated in Palestine. In no other part of the Empire can we assume a knowledge of the Old Testament Scripture in the original language.

Thus the answer to the first question we asked, as to the knowledge and methods of the First and Third Evangelists, is that S. Luke uses the Greek Bible, but the First Evangelist draws his proof-texts direct from the Hebrew (or rather from a collection of *Testimonia* derived from the Hebrew), although he too occasionally uses the ordinary Greek translation.

We must now consider the way in which Matthew and Luke have used the Gospel of Mark. This is practically the question which was considered in the second of these Lectures, and all that will be needed now is a statement of results.

Matthew, we find, shortens the narrative of Mark, retaining the main features, but cutting down details and (like S. Luke) suppressing the mention of the various human emotions of our Lord, *e.g.* anger, annoyance, amazement.

Matthew freely transposes the earlier parts of

the story, which thereby becomes a series of disconnected anecdotes. The confusion is still further increased by the interpolation of long discourses into the framework taken from Mark: however interesting and authentic these discourses are in themselves, they completely break up the unity of the historical narrative. But very little of the material supplied by Mark is altogether omitted.

Besides the long discourses, Matthew introduces into the Marcan narrative certain stories not known to us from other sources, such as Peter walking on the water, Judas and the pieces of silver, the Earthquake at the Crucifixion, the Guard at the Tomb. There are grave difficulties in making out a claim for considering any of these stories as serious history. At the same time it should be remarked that their tone and language suggest, like nearly all the other peculiarities of this Gospel, a Palestinian origin. For example, the story of the earthquake speaks of Jerusalem as 'the Holy City' (Matt xxvii 51^b–53), and we have already seen that the quotation from the Prophets by which the story of Judas and the pieces of silver is illustrated is derived from the Hebrew and not from the Greek Bible.

In view of the Palestinian origin of the elements peculiar to Matthew, it is worth while once more to emphasise the remarkable fact that the Passion narrative in the First Gospel is based upon Mark. Both in the selection of incidents and their relative order Matthew follows unquestioningly the corresponding narrative in Mark.

The procedure of S. Luke offers a notable contrast to all this. He freely omits large portions of Mark, and in the Passion he deserts Mark to follow another story of the last scenes. But the sections of Mark which are incorporated in Luke are given in the same relative order; and although as in Matthew much in the narrative is curtailed, yet there is not the same tendency to interpolate fresh incidents in the Marcan stories. There are fresh incidents in Luke, but they are kept separate.

It appears to me that the inference drawn from these facts by Dean Armitage Robinson is legitimate. He considers that if we wish to reconstruct the order and arrangement of the lost document used by Matthew and Luke, that document which I will *not* call 'the Logia,'[1] we must take the outline of it from Luke rather than from Matthew. We must subtract from Luke the first two chapters and those sections of the Third Gospel which are simply derived from Mark: what is left will give

[1] Wellhausen calls it Q.

us an approximate outline of the document in question.[1] In making use of the Second Gospel S. Luke inserted it in his own narrative καθεξῆς, in order; there is great probability that he did the same when making use of that lost document from which he has taken so much of what is to us of the highest value.

But fascinating as are these schemes of reconstruction, we should never forget how precarious is the foundation upon which they rest. We can no more reconstruct this lost Gospel in detail than we could reconstruct from Matthew and Luke alone the Gospel according to S. Mark. We cannot get behind the three Synoptic Gospels in the sense of being able to dispense with either of them. Each of the three contains authentic matter not represented in the other two; each of them represents a different view of our Lord's Life and Teaching. We must frankly recognise that the Gospel according to S. Mark is nearer both in time and in atmosphere to the actual course of events, but the other two Synoptic Gospels enable us to fill in many details without which the resultant Picture would be sadly incomplete. S. Mark supplies us with the crown, but many of

[1] J. A. Robinson, *The Study of the Gospels* (1902), especially pp. 87, 95, 111.

the most precious jewels must be added from the other Gospels.

One very common misconception may be here conveniently noticed. Some writers speak of 'the Triple Synopsis' and 'the Double Synopsis,' meaning by the former phrase the incidents or sayings found in all three Synoptic Gospels, and by the latter those found in Matthew and Luke. Such phrases are somewhat misleading, as they inevitably suggest that the portions comprised under the Triple or the Double Synopsis are better attested than those which are found in one document only. But to those who hold that Matthew and Luke actually used our Mark, and another document besides, it is evident that the *consensus* of all three Synoptics resolves itself into the single witness of Mark, and the *consensus* of Matthew and Luke is in many cases only to be regarded as the single witness of the lost document discussed in the foregoing paragraphs. Thus the story of the Gadarene swine rests really on no more evidence than the story of the blind man at Bethsaida, *i.e.* upon the witness of the Second Gospel. And similarly the Parable of the Seed growing secretly, related only by S. Mark, is really no worse attested than the Parable of the Vineyard, which is given in all three Gospels. The only real double attestation is to be found in those few passages, mostly short striking sayings, which appear to have found a place in the common source of Matthew and Luke as well as in Mark.

These passages we shall consider in detail in the next Lecture, when we begin to study the teaching of Jesus as recorded in the Synoptic Gospels. But before we leave our survey of the lost common source of Matthew and Luke, which (following Wellhausen and others) I shall call Q for convenience, let us consider one important question connected with it, viz. whether it contained a story of the Passion. Practically this is equivalent to asking whether Q was a 'Gospel,' like one of our Gospels, or whether it was a mere collection of discourses.

The Judgement-Parable of the Sheep and the Goats (Matt xxv 31–46) would make so dramatic a conclusion to a collection of the Lord's Discourses that we might at first sight be tempted to regard it as the actual peroration of Q. And this view, we must admit, seems to be borne out by the remarkable fact that not a single phrase in the last three chapters of Matthew can be supposed to come from Q. Even in the account of the Last Supper and the Words from the Cross Matthew has nothing to add to what Mark tells us.

The account of the Passion in Luke is very different. The disputes in the Temple courts with the Pharisees and Sadducees of Jerusalem are given by Luke from the corresponding sections of Mark, and the same is true for the eschatological Discourse (Lk xx, xxi). There are many verbal changes, much indeed is re-written, but no other source but Mark appears to have been used. The opening paragraphs of Lk xxii are also derived from Mark. But when the Evangelist comes to the Last Supper itself he has other material. From this point the Gospel of Mark is no longer the basis of his narrative. It only supplies a few touches here and there, like the mention of Simon the Cyrenian in Luke xxiii 26. The rest, whatever its historical value and whatever may have been the source from which Luke took it, is certainly not derived from Mark. We have seen that Luke does not, as a rule, disturb the relative order of the sources which he employs, and so the question arises whether this narrative of the Passion may not have been derived from the same source as most of Luke's non-Marcan material, *i.e.* from Q itself.

The safest criterion that a passage comes from Q is that it should be found both in Matthew and in Luke. We cannot expect to find many such passages in this part of the Gospel, for we have seen that in the Passion Matthew is based on Mark, not at all on Q. Nevertheless some of the peculiar matter in Lk xxii is actually given in earlier chapters of Matthew. The section Lk xxii 24–30 contains a saying of Jesus on the occasion of a strife for precedence among the apostles. It begins with a parallel to Mk x 42 ff, a saying occasioned by the request of the sons of Zebedee for precedence. But it goes on to give the promise that the apostles should sit on twelve thrones judging Israel, which is parallel to Matt xix 28, a non-Marcan verse, interpolated after the usual manner of Matthew into the main framework of the Marcan narrative. This at once suggests that we have here a fragment of Q, and consequently that Q contained a story of the Passion as well as of the discourses. We know that Q was not confined to discourses alone, for the same arguments which prove that it contained a discourse corresponding to the 'Sermon on the Mount' prove also that it contained the story of the Centurion's boy (Matt viii 5–13, Lk vii 1–10). There is nothing therefore surprising that it should have given an account of the last scenes.

Whatever view we may take — and I am most anxious not to put before you a piece of literary reconstruction of this kind without reminding you how doubtful this reconstruction of lost documents must remain—there is, I venture to think, a considerable element of valuable history in S. Luke's account of our Lord's Passion, from whatever source he may have drawn his information.

The Christian tradition tells us of Peter's Denial, of the Trial of our Lord by the 'chief priests,' and of rough horseplay practised on Him when a prisoner. But Mark and Luke do not agree as to the time or order of these events. Our Lord was arrested in the middle of the night when the apostles were heavy with sleep; He was crucified in 'the third hour' next day according to Mk xv 25, *i.e.* between 9 and 10 AM, but perhaps it may really have been a little later. Now I may be uncritical and credulous, but I confess that I am impressed with the account given by Luke, regarded as a narrative of events. Here as elsewhere, of course, the wording of the Third Gospel reflects the style and personality of the Evangelist: we must not assume that he treats the unknown source Q otherwise than he treats the extant Gospel of Mark. But the main course of the action is more intelligible in this section as Luke gives it, at least from the point of view of the chief priests. We can hardly suppose that the Jewish grandees kept vigil all night on account of the Galilean Agitator; according to S. Luke they did not do so. Our Lord is arrested in the dead of night, and as we should expect He is simply detained in custody until the great folk get up in the morning (Lk xxii 66). A prisoner, and deserted by His followers, He is naturally exposed to the vulgar insults of the Temple police who had arrested Him (*vv.* 63–65); in point of fact, they have nothing else to do. Meanwhile Peter slinks into a corner of the great court; we are even told that he shewed his face in the light of the fire (*v.* 56). He denies His Master, as we know, during the hours that slowly pass by. All the action takes place in the court: in one corner is the Prisoner, in another is Peter and the group of servants. I can very well believe that the one group was visible to the other, and that the Lord really did turn and look upon Peter (*v.* 61). At last the day breaks and the elders of the people gather together, chief priests and scribes; they give their Prisoner a hasty trial (*vv.* 66–71) and as soon as He is condemned they bring Him at once before Pilate (xxiii 1 ff).

According to Mark, who is of course followed by Matthew, the chief priests try Jesus in the dead of night, and the rough horseplay and buffeting appears to be done by some members of the Council themselves while they are waiting till it is time to go to Pilate, not by the Temple guards waiting till it is time for the Council to assemble. I venture to think that S. Luke's account is the more probable.

Among the incidents peculiar to Luke is the interview with Herod Antipas (xxiii 4–16), commonly treated by critical historians as fictitious. It has recently been the subject of an independent study by Dr. Verrall, whose work, like Lachmann's before him, has not received from professional theologians the attention which is its due. But until the arguments brought forward in 'Christ before Herod' have been successfully met, the inclusion of the story how Herod treated the Good Physician with cynical generosity must be held to illustrate the excellence of S. Luke's historical information rather than his credulity or inventiveness.[1]

[1] 'Christ before Herod' first appeared in the *Journal of Theological Studies*, x 321–353 (Apr. 1909): it has been reprinted by Dr. Verrall in his *Bacchants of Euripides and Other Essays*, pp. 335–390. He understands Lk xxiii 11 to mean: 'But Herod, with the armed forces of Galilee at his back, thought Jesus of no importance and jested at the notion, but he presented Him with a robe of honour and sent Him back to Pilate.' Properly speaking, there was no 'trial' before Herod: Pilate takes the opportunity of Herod being at hand to ascertain whether the government of Galilee regarded Jesus as a dangerous agitator (*vv.* 5, 6). For σὺν τοῖς στρατεύμασιν, compare σὺν χειρὶ ἀγγέλου in Acts vii 35: it almost means 'supported by' or 'relying upon.' See also 1 Cor v 4.

We may note in passing that the accusation which the chief priests bring against our Lord to Pilate not only is calculated to impress the Roman Governor, but also contains the genuinely Jewish phrase χριστὸν βασιλέα. That the Jews told Pilate that the accused prisoner forbad the people to give tribute to Cæsar might have been surmised by the Evangelist; he would not have been likely to have hit upon a phrase exactly corresponding to *Malka Meshiḥa* or, as we commonly render it, 'King Messiah.' The occurrence of the technical Jewish phrase suggests to us that in this passage S. Luke is using a valuable source.

Investigations of this kind, which attempt to weigh the merits of conflicting or parallel accounts, have always a somewhat coldblooded and judicial spirit in them, a spirit which cannot but be out of harmony with that in which we can study the Passion of our Lord to our soul's profit. Yet these historical questions must be faced, if our estimate of the Gospel is to be lifted out of the region of mere inherited sentiment. And perhaps, if we have learnt to regard the peculiar matter in Lk xxii and xxiii with more respect as a historical document, we may be able to hear with renewed attention some of the words of Jesus, which S. Luke assigns to the night of the Last Supper.

These words (Lk xxii 24–38) are of very great

interest, and I venture to think that the concluding section is not only a genuine saying of the Lord, but also appropriate in the historical situation. The earlier part may possibly not belong to the last evening; for Mark also has the saying about the kings of the Gentiles having dominion over their subjects while the chief of the disciples of Jesus was to be the servant of his brethren, and in Mark it is placed on the journey to Jerusalem, not after the Last Supper (Mk x 42 ff). Yet, after all, the desire of the sons of Zebedee to sit on the right hand and on the left of their Lord may very well have found expression when they were actually seated at supper with Jesus, perhaps occupying the very places that they coveted in the heavenly kingdom.[1] Our Lord's allusion to His own approaching death, when He would give His life as a ransom for many (Mk x 45), also suggests the last tragic night rather than the approach to Jerusalem. Be this as it may, I find it difficult to believe that the words which follow are not a true, and a misunderstood, reminiscence of the night of our Lord's arrest. They are among the saddest words in the Gospels, and the mournful irony with which

[1] If there be any historical truth in what we read of this meal in the Fourth Gospel, the struggle for precedence may have been the immediate cause why Jesus Himself began to wash the feet of the disciples.

they are pervaded seems to me wholly alien from the kind of utterance which a Christian Evangelist would invent for his Master. 'When I sent you forth without purse and wallet and shoes, lacked ye anything?' And they said: 'Nothing.' But He goes on to tell them that now they must take their purses and wallets, and that he who had no sword must get one, even if he has to pawn his cloak to buy it, for soon Jesus and His followers will be counted among lawless folk.[1] The disciples do not understand: they take it all literally, and someone says, 'See, here are two swords!'

It seems to me easier to believe that these words were remembered and recorded, than to think that they could have been invented by any early Christian of whom we have ever heard. It is impossible to believe that the command to buy a sword was meant literally and seriously: it is all a piece of ironical foreboding. The early Christian missionaries did not, so far as we know, go out on their travels armed; it is only because these words are so familiar that they do not give us a shock.

[1] The allusion to Isaiah liii 12 does not agree with the LXX, for Lk xxii 37 has μετὰ ἀνόμων while the LXX has ἐν τοῖς ἀνόμοις. In the words which follow, 'The things concerning me have an end' is a better translation than 'hath fulfilment'; our Lord had already used τέλος ἔχει (Mk iii 26).

Yet there they stand in the Gospel according to S. Luke, and we are entitled to draw from them the conclusions that they suggest. They are sad enough indeed; but if they are historical, as I believe them to be, they afford us a very welcome glimpse into the mind of our Lord. They shew us that there was in Him a vein of what I have no other name for but playfulness, a tender and melancholy playfulness indeed, but all the more remarkable that it comes to outward expression in moments of danger and despondency. We feel that we are listening to the words of the same Master, who excused the woman for the waste of her precious ointment that might have been so profitably spent in works of charity. This kind of playfulness is totally alien from ignorant fanaticism, and indeed it is totally alien from the general spirit of early Christianity. That it appears at all in the Gospels is in itself a proof that the Evangelists and the sources from which they drew sometimes remembered better than they understood.

V.

THE TEACHING OF JESUS CHRIST.

WE come now to the Sayings of our Lord as handed down for us in the Christian tradition. And before we consider any part of these Sayings in detail I think it will be well to call to mind some general considerations about the circumstances of their utterance and their preservation. The considerations I mean are all perfectly obvious and plain, but their very plainness and obviousness make them run some risk of being slurred over.

Jesus Himself wrote nothing, and the only words which He is said to have taught His disciples are the words of the Lord's Prayer. Even this short form of words has been handed down with notable variations. He ordered the apostles to say to those to whom they preached 'the Kingdom of God is at hand' (Matt x 7, Lk x 9), but this is rather a doctrine than a formula. It does not appear that it was part of His method to give His disciples watchwords or anything in the nature of a set phrase. On the contrary, the Gospels tell us that He expressly commanded His followers that they were not to defend themselves by set apologies, but to say what the Spirit impelled them to say, as the occasion suggested. There is no trace of any systematisation of the teaching; the private expositions of the Parable of the Sower, of the new doctrine concerning Pollution (Mk vii 17) and concerning Divorce (Mk x 10), are all as informal as expositions can be. I do not mean indefinite: the teaching is always clear and definite, but it is essentially occasional. It arises out of what passes at the moment.

The effect of all this can be very broadly stated. It tended to heighten the personal impression of our Lord upon His disciples. It is the Lord Jesus and not His Sayings which was the subject of the earliest preachers of Christianity. Doubtless part of the personal impression included a vivid sense of our Lord's guiding principles of life, His daily and hourly intercourse with His Father in Heaven, and the sureness and authority which this heavenly intercourse gave Him in discerning right and wrong. They saw and felt His independence of earthly standards, His impatience with the self-satisfied, His compassion for those in need. This was what was necessary.

It was necessary that the disciples should reverence and love their Master; far more necessary than that they should remember His phrases. But the conditions were not specially favourable for accurate reminiscence. People talk vaguely of the marvellous achievements of Oriental memories, but I think you will find on investigation that these feats are all connected with systematic instruction. The wisdom of this or that famous Rabbi, of this or that renowned sage, has been handed down to posterity by the recollections of his pupils; but in all such cases there was a conscious committing to memory of instruction or doctrine. The same is true of the preservation of the Qoran. Mohammed's discourses were to a considerable extent preserved through the memories of the faithful, but they consist of sentences of a marked rhetorical character and end with a rhyme.[1]

How different is all this from the recorded Sayings of our Lord! As I said just now, they are occasional, they arise out of some event, some circumstance of His life. The Sayings for the most part form the point of an anecdote, or are themselves couched in the form of a story, like

[1] In mentioning the Mohammedan tradition we may profitably remind ourselves of the existence of a vast mass of 'Traditions' of the Prophet which is in no sense genuine historical reminiscence.

several of the Parables. There is no indication in the Gospels that any of our Lord's hearers were taking notes at the time, whether mental or written. Indeed, we are told in one place that it was only after He had risen from the dead that His disciples remembered He had said such and such things.

Moreover, the aim of the early Christians was practical; they aimed at making saints, not historians. The memory of Jesus survived among His servants, His Presence was still felt in their midst; and we must be prepared beforehand to find that a clear distinction was not always drawn between what He would have said and what He really did say. 'The labourer is worthy of his hire' (or, 'of his food'), said Jesus, according to Matthew and Luke; with S. Paul this has become the formal statement that the Lord ordained that they which preach the Gospel should live of the Gospel (1 Cor ix 14)—an example which clearly shews how sayings detached from a historical context harden into rules from which most of the distinctive phraseology of the speaker disappears. Another instance of the same kind is to be found in the Sayings about Divorce, which we considered in a former lecture. In Mk x 2–12 we have the whole story in its historical setting, and the Saying of the Lord at the end takes its colour from the events of the age and the circumstances of the place where the Saying was uttered. In Lk xvi 18 we have much the same principle of conduct laid down, but the historical setting is gone: it belongs to Christian Ethics rather than to our Lord's Biography.

We need, therefore, a kind of starting-point for the consideration of our Lord's doctrine, some external test that will give us a general assurance that the Saying we have before us is really from Him, and is not the half-conscious product of one school of His followers. Where shall we find such a test?

It appeared to me that the starting-point we require may be found in those Sayings which have a real double attestation. The main documents out of which the Synoptic Gospels are compiled are (1) the Gospel of Mark, and (2) the lost common origin of the non-Marcan portions of Matthew and Luke, *i.e.* the source called Q. Where Q and Mark appear to report the same saying, we have the nearest approach that we can hope to get to the common tradition of the earliest Christian society about our Lord's words. What we glean in this way will indicate the general impression His teaching made upon His disciples.

The list of Sayings that here follow is arranged according to the order of Mark. The Saying is usually repeated with comparatively trifling verbal variations, and in the same context, by Matthew and Luke, or by one of them ; but these repetitions practically contribute nothing for our purpose, and I have not given them here. The Saying that I give after the verse of Mark is taken from a different context, usually from Luke, as we have seen reason to believe that the Third Evangelist keeps his sources more apart than Matthew does. Matthew, on the other hand, seems often to combine Sayings taken from Q with those taken from Mark, so that his form of these Sayings is generally not so instructive for the purposes of this comparison.

1. Mk iii 4 (*copied in* Lk vi 9).

And He saith unto them, 'Is it lawful on the sabbath day to do good, or to do harm? to save a life, or to kill?' But they held their peace.

Lk xiv 5, 6 (*compare* Matt xii 11).

And He said unto them, 'Which of you shall have [an ass or] an ox fallen into a well, and will not straightway draw him up on a sabbath day?' And they could not answer again unto these things.

[Most Greek MSS have *υἱὸς ἢ βοῦς*, *i.e.* 'a son

or an ox.' It is quite impossible that this can have been the original form of the *Saying*, but its very harshness is in favour of its genuineness in the text of *Luke*. Probably it goes back to a mistake in translation. In Aramaic 'son' is *bar* (בר, sometimes written ביר, *e.g. Pesikta*, 75[a]), and 'the well' is *bêrâ* בירא. If the original Aramaic ran something like מנו מנכון דבבירא תורה נפל, it is easy to imagine how the mistake may have arisen. In the parallel Matt xii 11, 12, only one animal is named—a *sheep*—and it is supposed to fall into a *pit*.]

2. Mk iii 22–26.

> And the scribes which came down from Jerusalem said, 'He hath Beelzebul,' and, 'By the prince of the devils casteth He out the devils.' And He called them unto Him, and said unto them in parables, 'How can Satan cast out Satan? And if a kingdom be divided against itself, that kingdom cannot stand; and if a house be divided against itself, that house will not be able to stand; and if Satan hath risen up against himself, and is divided, he cannot stand, but hath an end.'

Lk xi 15–18 (*compare the non-Marcan portions of* Matt xii 24–26).

> But some of them said, 'By Beelzebul the prince of the devils casteth He out devils.' And others, tempting, sought

of Him a sign from heaven. But He, knowing their thoughts, said unto them, 'Every kingdom divided against itself is brought to desolation, and a house against a house falleth; and if Satan also is divided against himself, how shall his kingdom stand? Because ye say that I cast out devils by Beelzebul.'

[It is evident that Mk iii 22–26 and Lk xi 15–18 report the same Saying of Jesus, notwithstanding the many differences and the very small amount of actual coincidence in language. It is further evident, if we tabulate the many similarities of language between Lk xi 14–23 and Matt xii 22–30, that S. Luke has not entirely rewritten the passage himself, but has preserved much of the wording of his immediate source. That being the case, it is difficult to believe that any common document underlies Mark and Luke at this point, other than the common memory of the first circle of disciples. The reason why these Beelzebul sayings are so well remembered and reported is, I believe, to be explained partly by their striking and picturesque imagery, but still more by the fact that they were spoken at the moment of the great breach with the Jewish clergy of Capernaum.]

3. Mk iii 27

'But no one can enter into the house of the strong man and spoil his goods, except he first bind the strong man; and then he will spoil his house.'

Lk xi 21–23 (*compare the non-Marcan portions of* Matt xii 28–30).

'When the strong man fully armed guardeth his own court, his goods are in peace; but when a stronger than he shall come upon him, and overcome him, he taketh from him his whole armour wherein he trusted, and divideth his spoils. He that is not with me is against me; and he that gathereth not with me scattereth.'

[Here again the verbal resemblance between Mark and Luke is very small, though there are some marked coincidences between Luke and Matthew. In all this section I believe Matthew to present a text conflated by the Evangelist out of Mark and the 'non-Marcan document' (Q), which Luke has here preserved free from contamination with Mark.]

4. Mk iii 28–30.

'Amen, I say unto you, All things shall be forgiven unto the sons of men, the sins and the blasphemies wherewith soever they shall blaspheme: but whosoever shall blaspheme against the Holy Spirit hath never forgiveness, but is guilty of an eternal sin': because they said, 'He hath an unclean spirit.'

Lk xii 10.

'And every one who shall speak a word against the Son of Man, it shall be forgiven him: but unto him that blasphemeth against the Holy Spirit it shall not be forgiven.'

[Matt xii 31, 32 seems to be partly remodelled by the Evangelist from the parallel in Mark, which indeed forms the basis of the narrative in Matt xii.]

5. Mk iii 31–34 (*retold from Mark in* Lk viii 19–21).

> '. . . Whosoever shall do the will of God, the same is my brother, and sister, and mother.'

Lk xi 27, 28.

> '. . . Blessed is the womb that bare thee . . . !' But He said, 'Yea rather, blessed are they that hear the word of God, and keep it.'

[Lk viii 19–21 contains the story of our Lord's mother and brethren standing outside because of the crowd. In that place it is doubtless taken from Mark, like the rest of Lk viii. Lk xi 27, 28, on the other hand, comes between the sayings about Beelzebul (parallel to Mk iii 22 ff) and the saying about the Lamp and the Stand (parallel to Mk iv 21): it is therefore difficult to avoid the inference that it is another reminiscence of the same story as Mk iii 31–34.]

6. Mk iv 3–9 (*The Parable of the Sower*).

[We may conjecture that the Parable of the Sower stood in Q, but the text of Matt xiii 2 ff and Lk viii 5 ff seems wholly derived from Mark.]

7. Mk iv 21 (*rewritten from Mark in* Lk viii 16).

And He said unto them, 'Is the lamp brought to be put under the bushel, or under the bed? Is it not to be put on the stand?'

Lk xi 33 (*compare* Matt v 15).

'No man, when he hath lighted a lamp, putteth it in a cellar, but on the stand, that they which enter in may see the light.'[1]

8. Mk iv 22 (*copied from Mark in* Lk viii 17).

'For there is nothing hid, save that it should be manifested; neither was anything made secret, but that it should come to light.'

Lk xii 2 (*compare* Matt x 26).

'But there is nothing covered up that shall not be revealed, and hid that shall not be known.'

9. Mk iv 23.

'If any man hath ears to hear, let him hear.'

Lk xiv 35.

'He that hath ears to hear, let him hear.'

[This Saying is also reported at the end of the Parable of the Sower in Mk iv 9, and parallels.

[1] Most Greek and Latin documents add 'neither under the bushel' after 'cellar,' but the clause should be omitted from Lk xi 33, on the sufficient authority of the Sinai Palimpsest, supported as it is by several groups of important Greek MSS.

The very varied attestation of this Saying is good evidence that our Lord really used this phrase, most likely on several occasions. It clearly shews that He expected His more intelligent hearers to understand something of the real meaning of His Parables.]

10. Mk iv 24[b].

'. . . With what measure ye mete it shall be measured to you.'

Lk vi 38.

'For with what measure ye mete it shall be measured to you again.'

11. Mk iv 25 (*rewritten from Mark in* Lk viii 18).

'For he that hath, to him shall be given; and he that hath not, from him shall be taken away even that which he hath.'

Lk xix 26 (*compare* Matt xxv 29).

'I say unto you, that unto every one that hath shall be given; but from him that hath not, even that which he hath shall be taken away from him.'

[A saying like this may very well be genuine in both contexts; it is inserted in this List because whether it was uttered once or twice, it has certainly been twice remembered.]

12. Mk iv 30–32.

And He said, 'How shall we liken the Kingdom of God? or in what parable shall we set it forth? As to a grain of mustard seed, which, when it is sown upon the earth, being a thing less than all the seeds upon the earth, yet when it is sown, groweth up, and becometh greater than all the herbs, and putteth out great branches, so that the birds of the heaven can lodge under the shadow thereof.'

Lk xiii 18, 19 (*compare the non-Marcan portions of* Matt xiii 31, 32).

He said therefore, 'Unto what is the Kingdom of God like? and whereunto shall I liken it? It is like unto a grain of mustard seed, which a man took, and cast into his own garden; and it grew and became a tree, and the birds of the heaven lodged in the branches thereof.'

[Here again the language of the two parallel passages could hardly be more different, considering the essential similarity of thought and imagery.]

13. Mk vi 4.

And Jesus said unto them, 'A prophet is not without honour, save in his own country, and among his own kin, and in his own house.'

Lk iv 24.

And He said, 'Amen, I say unto you, No prophet is acceptable in his own country.'

[Both extracts come from the account of Jesus at Nazareth, but S. Luke places the story at the beginning of the Ministry, and the rest of the context is very different. The Saying reappears in Joh iv 44, when Jesus is journeying from Jerusalem and Samaria to Galilee.]

14. Mk vi 10, 11 (*condensed in* Lk ix 4, 5).

And He said unto them, 'Wheresoever ye enter into a house, there abide till ye depart thence. And whatsoever place shall not receive you, and they hear you not, as ye go forth thence, shake off the dust that is under your feet for a testimony unto them.'

Lk x 5[a], 7, 10, 11 (*compare* Matt x 11–15).

'And into whatsoever house ye shall enter . . . in that same house remain, eating and drinking such things as they give: for the labourer is worthy of his hire. Go not from house to house. . . . But into whatsoever city ye shall enter, and they receive you not, go out into the streets thereof and say, "Even the dust from your city, that cleaveth to our feet, we do wipe off against you: howbeit know this, that the Kingdom of God is come nigh."'

["There is no doubt—and Matthew has rightly recognised the fact—that Mk vi 7 ff and Lk x 1 ff are variants, which must be compared together" (Wellhausen, *Ev. Lucæ*, p. 49).]

15. Mk viii 12[b].

'Why doth this generation seek a sign? Amen, I say unto you, there shall no sign be given unto this generation.'

Lk xi 29 (*compare* Matt xii 39, *also* xvi 4[b]).

'This generation is an evil generation : it seeketh after a sign ; and there shall no sign be given to it but the sign of Jonah.'

[Note that 'the sign of Jonah,' which occurs also in Matt xii 39, xvi 4[b], is differently expanded in Matt xii 40 and Lk xi 30.]

16. Mk viii 15.

And He charged them, saying, 'Take heed, beware of the leaven of the Pharisees and the leaven of Herod.'

Lk xii 1[b].

'Beware ye of the leaven of the Pharisees, which is hypocrisy.

[The context is quite different.]

17. Mk viii 34 (*rewritten in* Lk ix 23).

And He called unto Him the multitude with His disciples, and said unto them, 'If any man would come after me, let him deny himself and take up his cross, and follow me.'

Lk xiv 25–27.

Now there went with Him great multitudes : and He turned, and said unto them, 'If any man cometh unto me, and hateth not his own father, and mother, and wife, and children, and brethren, and sisters, yea, and his own life also, he cannot be my disciple. Whosoever doth not bear his own cross, and come after me, cannot be my disciple.'

[Lk ix 23 is certainly based directly upon Mk viii 34, but S. Luke has given a peculiar turn to it by adding 'daily' (καθ' ἡμέραν) to 'take up his cross.'][1]

18. Mk ix 37^b.

> 'Whosoever receiveth me, receiveth not me but Him that sent me.'

Lk x 16 (*compare* Matt x 40).

> 'He that rejecteth me rejecteth Him that sent me.'

[The special interest of this passage is the formula 'Him that sent me,' so characteristic of the Fourth Gospel. Similar phrases occur in Matt xv 24, Lk iv 18, 43, so that in all our sources—in Mark, in Q, and in the peculiar elements of Matthew and Luke, as well as in John—our Lord is made to describe Himself as being conscious of a definite Mission from the Most High.]

19a. Mk ix 42.

> 'And whosoever shall cause one of these little ones that believe on me to stumble, it were better for him if a great millstone were hanged about his neck, and he were cast into the sea.'

Lk xvii 2.

> '. . . It were well for him if a millstone were hanged about his neck, and he were thrown into the sea, rather than that he should cause one of these little ones to stumble.'

[Here the context is quite different.]

---

[1] Most Greek MSS (not the best) and most 'Western' texts omit 'daily.' On ἔρχεσθαι in Lk ix 23, see *Enc. Bibl.* 1775, note [4].

19b. Mk ix 43–48 (*condensed in* Matt xviii 8, 9).

'And if thy hand cause thee to stumble, cut it off: it is good for thee to enter into life maimed, rather than having thy two hands to go into the unquenchable fire.[1] And if thy foot cause thee to stumble, cut it off: it is good for thee to enter into life halt, rather than having thy two feet to be cast into hell. And if thine eye cause thee to stumble, cast it out: it is good for thee to enter into the Kingdom of God with one eye, rather than having two eyes to be cast into hell where "their worm dieth not and the fire is not quenched."'

Matt v 29, 30 (*no parallel in* Lk).[2]

'And if thy right eye causeth thee to stumble, pluck it out and cast it from thee: for it is profitable for thee that one of thy members should perish, and not thy whole body be cast into hell. And if thy right hand causeth thee to stumble, cut it off, and cast it from thee: for it is profitable for thee that one of thy members should perish, and not thy whole body go into hell.'

20. Mk ix 50.

'Salt is good: but if the salt have lost its saltness, wherewith will ye season it? Have salt in yourselves, and be at peace one with another.'

Lk xiv 34 (*compare* Matt v 13).

'Salt therefore is good: but if even the salt have lost its savour, wherewith shall it be seasoned?'

---

[1] Omit here εἰς τὴν γέενναν with the Sinai Palimpsest, &c.

[2] It seems to me probable that Luke the Physician preferred to leave out the metaphor of amputation. Compare the curtailment of Mk v 26 in Lk viii 43.

21. Mk x 11, 12.

And He saith unto them, 'Whosoever shall put away his wife, and marry another, committeth adultery against her: and if she herself shall put away her husband, and marry another, she committeth adultery.'

Lk xvi 18 (*another form in* Matt v 31, 32).

'Every one that putteth away his wife, and marrieth another, committeth adultery: and he that marrieth one that is put away from a husband committeth adultery.'

[For the historical setting, see Lecture III.]

22. Mk x 42–45.

And Jesus called them to Him, and saith unto them, 'Ye know that they which are accounted to rule over the Gentiles lord it over them; and their great ones exercise authority over them. But it is not so among you: but whosoever would become great among you, shall be your minister: and whosoever would be first among you, shall be servant of all. For even the Son of Man came not to be ministered unto, but to minister, and to give His life a ransom for many.'

Lk xxii 25–27.

And He said unto them, 'The kings of the Gentiles have lordship over them; and they that have authority over them are called Benefactors. But ye shall not be so: but he that is the greater among you let him become as the younger; and he that is chief, as he that doth serve. For whether is greater, he that sitteth at meat, or he that serveth? . . . but I am in the midst of you as He that serveth.'

[The context again is quite different.]

23. Mk xi 22, 23.

And Jesus answering saith unto them, 'Have faith in God. Amen, I say unto you, Whosoever shall say unto this mountain, "Be thou taken up and cast into the sea"; and shall not doubt in his heart, but shall believe that what he saith cometh to pass; he shall have it.'

Lk xvii 6.

And the Lord said, 'If ye have faith as a grain of mustard seed, ye would say unto this sycamine tree, "Be thou rooted up, and be thou planted in the sea"; and it would have obeyed you.'

[Wellhausen (*Ev. Marci*, p. 97) remarks that 'into the sea' seems to suit Galilee rather than Jerusalem. But need this use of Galilean imagery imply more than that the words were uttered by a Galilean Prophet to Galilean fishermen? It is a saying that might very well have been spoken more than once.]

24. Mk xi 24.

'Therefore I say unto you, All things whatsoever ye pray and ask for, believe that ye have received them, and ye shall have them.'

Lk xi 9 (*compare* Matt vii 7).

'And I say unto you, Ask, and it shall be given you; seek, and ye shall find; knock, and it shall be opened unto you.'

25. Mk xi 25.

'And whensoever ye stand praying, forgive, if ye have aught against any one; that your Father also which is in heaven may forgive you your trespasses.'

Matt vi 14, 15.

'For if ye forgive men their trespasses, your heavenly Father will also forgive you; but if ye forgive not men their trespasses, neither will your Father forgive your trespasses.'

[It is hardly likely that these verses from the Sermon on the Mount were derived from Mark.]

[26.] Mk xii 32–34[a].

The scribe said unto Him, 'Of a truth, Master, thou hast well said that He is One; and there is none other but He: and to love Him with all the heart, and with all the understanding, and with all the strength, and to love his neighbour as himself, is much more than all whole burnt offerings and sacrifices.' And when Jesus saw that he answered discreetly, He said unto him, 'Thou art not far from the Kingdom of God.'

Lk x 25–28.

> And He said unto him, 'What is written in the law? how readest thou?' And he answering said, 'Thou shalt love the Lord thy God with all thy heart, and with all thy soul, and with all thy strength, and with all thy mind; and thy neighbour as thyself.' And He said unto him, 'Thou hast answered right: this do, and thou shalt live.'

[I have inserted Mk xii 32 ff and Lk x 25 ff in the list, because at the first glance they are real doublets; *i.e.* different accounts of the same event drawn from different sources. They agree in the very remarkable circumstance that the duty of love to God and one's neighbour is emphasised by the learned interlocutor of our Lord. In Mark this is comprehensible, for what the scribe says is merely a generously appreciative echo of our Lord's great answer. But in Luke the case is different. There we are surprised, first, to find that the Jewish Doctor actually anticipates our Lord's doctrine without having been prompted, and then that he is unwilling to apply his own principles.

Wellhausen (*Ev. Lucæ*, p. 52) further points out that the Parable of the Good Samaritan (which immediately follows) is strictly speaking an answer to the question, 'Whose neighbour am I?' not to 'Who is my neighbour?' I should have been inclined rather to say that it is an answer to the question, 'What is my duty towards my neighbour?' But in either case the inconsequence remains. Wellhausen considers that the answer of the scribe and the Parable are really separate stories, which have been joined together by the Evangelist. The Parable has a Samaritan hero, consequently the Evangelist has placed the whole compilation in the Samaritan section of his Gospel; but the lawyer who answers so well at first is only the scribe of Mark xii 30 ff transferred to an earlier place, like the sermon at Nazareth in Lk iv. On this theory, which on the whole seems best to explain the facts, the answer of the lawyer is only Mk xii 28–34 itself, rewritten by Luke to suit the Parable which follows. It is not therefore a doublet of Mark at all.]

27. Mk xii 38, 39 (*copied in* Lk xx 45, 46).

> And in His teaching He said, 'Beware of the scribes, which desire to walk in long robes, and salutations in the marketplaces, and chief seats in the synagogues, and chief places at feasts.'

Lk xi 43.

> 'Woe unto you Pharisees! for ye love the chief seats in the synagogues, and the salutations in the marketplaces.'

[Mk xii 40 goes on to accuse the Scribes that they 'for a pretence make long prayers,' προφάσει μακρὰ προσευχόμενοι. In Matt xxiii 5 the Scribes and Pharisees are said to 'make broad their phylacteries.' The Jewish Phylacteries were called *Tephillîn*, a word which means 'prayers': apparently, therefore, Mark has misunderstood a saying which referred originally to the ostentatious size of the *Tephillîn* worn by the professedly religious.]

28. Mk xiii 11 (*rewritten in* Lk xxi 14, 15).

'And when they lead you, and deliver you up, be not anxious beforehand what ye shall speak: but whatsoever shall be given you in that hour, that speak ye: for it is not ye that speak, but the Holy Spirit.'

Lk xii 11, 12.

'And when they bring you before the synagogues, and the rulers, and the authorities, be not anxious how or what ye shall answer, or what ye shall say: for the Holy Spirit shall teach you in that very hour what ye ought to say.'

29. Mk xiii 15, 16.

'. . . And let him that is on the housetop not go down, nor enter in to take anything out of his house: and let him that is in the field not return back to take his cloke.'

Lk xvii 31.

'In that day, he which shall be on the housetop, and his goods in the house, let him not go down to take them away: and let him that is in the field likewise not return back.'

[The whole of the section Lk xvii 20–37 is really a doublet of Mk xiii 3–37, and both should be compared with the final chapter of the *Didache*. Except the last five verses of Matt xiii, the section Lk xvii 20–37 seems to me to contain the most authentic reminiscences of what our Lord may have said on this subject at various times.]

30. Mk xiii 21.

'And then if any man shall say unto you, "Lo, here is the Christ"; or, "Lo, there"; believe it not.'

Lk xvii 23.

'And they shall say to you, "Lo, there!" "Lo, here!" go not away, nor follow after them.'

31. Mk xiii 34, 35.

'As a man, sojourning in another country, having left his house, and given authority to his servants, to each one his work, commanded also the porter to watch. Watch therefore: for ye know not when the lord of the house cometh, whether at even, or at midnight, or at cockcrowing, or in the morning.'

Lk xii 37, 38.

'Blessed are those servants whom the lord when he cometh shall find watching: amen, I say unto you, that he shall gird himself, and make them sit down to meat, and shall come and serve them. And if he shall come in the second watch, and if in the third, and find them so, blessed are those servants.'

I have read out to you this list of Sayings, familiar as they are, because of their historical importance. No one would deny that they are important taken singly, but I wish to draw your attention now to their importance as a collection. When we study the life and work of the great personages of history and thought there are two distinct things that we should desire to know about them. We desire to know their deeper teaching, to see and recognise the first formulation of some great idea, which comes new and strange from the brain of a man in advance of his time, an idea perhaps not destined to be fully understood and appreciated for many a long day. But we need also to understand the impression made by the man on his contemporaries; we want to know what he stood for to them, as well as what he stands for to us. And this last kind of knowledge is the most necessary for us to have when we are studying those who are great because of the influence they have had upon the general course of events, not only because of what they wrote or said.

Now I am not going to claim that the list of Sayings which I have read to you are the deepest or the most original of the recorded Sayings of our Lord. It may very well be that some of the most profound of the Sayings of His that have survived at all are recorded only by a single Evangelist. But if we are asking what was the teaching of Jesus Christ which impressed His followers generally, or what was the main impression made by His teaching, then I think we are justified in pointing to this list that I have drawn up. It may not be the most profound or subtle view that we can obtain of our Lord's doctrines, but we have reason to consider it, so far as it goes, a true view. At least it will be useful to us as a corrective: any other Portrait of the Lord which we may draw must not be inconsistent with the Portrait attested by the mouth of our two witnesses.

Not that it is by any means easy to put together the Sayings in our list and weave them into a body of systematic doctrine. I shall not attempt to do so; I shall only offer a few scattered remarks on some features of the teaching which more or less prominently emerge.

To begin with, we may pass by several of the Sayings which really have rather a biographical than a religious interest, such as the saying about the Prophet in his own country (13), and the directions for the early missionary journeys of the apostles (14). Let us go on to the attacks upon the Scribes and Pharisees (27). The Scribes were the trained theologians of Israel, the Pharisees were the religious world of Israel. They therefore represented that element in the Jewish people with which a religious Teacher might have been expected to be in harmony. We do actually read that our Lord's contemporaries found it strange that He should consort with the irreligious, and it is quite obvious that His answer to their complaint is at least partly ironical. He did not believe that the Scribes and Pharisees were whole and in no need of a Physician, and I do not think that He consorted with those whom the Pharisees regarded as sinners solely because He saw that they were in the greatest need of repentance.

The opposition of Jesus to the Scribes does really stand in some need of elucidation. We Christians only hear of these folk as the opponents of our Lord. We hear Him cry 'Woe unto you, Scribes and Pharisees, hypocrites!' We do not know any Scribes and Pharisees, but perhaps we do know some hypocrites, and we are content to think of Scribes and Pharisees as another term for hypocrites. But it is a very serious indictment to draw up against the Jewish people. My friend Mr. Claude Montefiore has recently protested, not without reason, against the picture of the Rabbinical religion which is commonly drawn by

Christians out of materials supplied by the Christian Gospels. He complains that learned theologians, some of whom are orthodox in nothing else, agree in representing the Rabbinical religion as mechanical and unspiritual, although as a matter of fact and history it has been the sustaining force which has knit together and kept alive the Jewish nation unto this day. It has been held by many Jews that Jesus was really too emphatic in denouncing the Scribes, that He called them a generation of vipers merely because they rejected His doctrine.

Let us be fair to the Jews. Let us admit first of all that the Christians may have only too easily remembered their Master's words against some Scribes, and afterwards set them down in such a way that they seem like an accusation against all the Scribes. That this is not mere fancy may be seen by comparing Matthew with Mark. Mark tells us how Jesus told the people to beware of the Scribes who desired the chief seats in the Synagogues while (as His phrase goes) they 'devoured widows' houses'; at the same time he tells us of the enthusiastic praise given by one of the Scribes to our Lord's summary of the Law as a joining together of the commands to love God and one's neighbour (26). But though this Scribe was commended by Jesus,

Matthew tells us nothing about him that is good. According to Matthew, he was 'tempting' Jesus, and he says nothing to Jesus in reply. Yet if we are to judge the Jews out of what we read in the Gospels, we ought not to forget what Mark tells us about this Scribe.

But in the next place we may ask ourselves how far the Rabbinical religion is the immediate descendant of the main current of the Judaism of the 1st century AD. Between the Judaism of the time of Christ and the Judaism of the early Middle Ages intervened two catastrophes, or rather one catastrophe in two great shocks, such as hardly ever befel any nation that has survived. The two great Jewish rebellions in the times of Vespasian (AD 70) and of Hadrian (AD 135) ended in utter collapse, and most of the leading features of the older Judaism perished in them for ever. In AD 70 perished the Jewish State, the Temple, the annual pilgrimages to the Feasts, the Priestly aristocracy, all the worldly political hopes of the Jews. Everything which the Gospels connect with the Sadducees or with the Herods disappeared for ever. The Revolt of Bar-Cochba against Hadrian was equal to the Great Revolt in fierceness; it also contained a Pharisaic element. Bar-Cochba was supported by Rabbi Aqiba, himself in some ways to be regarded as the founder of modern Judaism. Aqiba died a martyr, and with him died the last effort of militant Pharisaism.

What was left to the Jews? We may answer with S. Paul 'much every way,' for they were left with the Oracles of God; but they were left with little else. In these awful catastrophes had perished a great part of what Jesus had most opposed. Thousands of Jews had been killed outright: we cannot doubt that many of the survivors lost their nationality and became merged into the Gentiles. Very likely many became Christians: it is difficult, for instance, to explain certain features in the rise of Christianity in Edessa, except on the supposition that the original congregation was largely composed of converted Jews. The Remnant who were left, who still remained Jews, were attached to their religion from motives which were in many ways akin to the motives that made men Christians. They had learnt that the Kingdom of God was not of this world; there was now no inducement to serve the God of Israel left for those who did not still love Him and trust His promises. Can we wonder that Judaism tended to become a more spiritual religion, narrow indeed in its outer aspect, but animated within by humility and grace, even by mysticism?

But in so far as the Rabbinical religion is all this, it has been metamorphosed from the prevailing Judaism of the 1st century. I do not think we need deny the real spirituality of the Rabbinical religion because we believe what the Gospels say about the Scribes, or that we need disbelieve what the Gospels say about the Scribes in the 1st century because we recognise the real spirituality of the Rabbinical religion. We have a right to believe that the spiritual descendants of the Scribes whom Jesus denounced perished in the two Revolts during the century after the Crucifixion, while the spiritual ancestor both of the Jews who became Christians and the Jews who developed and maintained the Rabbinical religion is represented by the Scribe who was 'not far from the Kingdom of God.'

Even on the one point where the Synoptic Gospels have been said to have given a wholly false representation of the teaching of the Rabbis, viz. the doctrine of 'Corban,' it seems to me dangerous to disbelieve the Gospel evidence. It is said that the Rabbis never failed in inculcating a man's duty to his father and mother, that parents came before vows. But I can quite understand that while the Temple was still standing the duty of a religious vow might seem to some a more direct service to God, and therefore more binding, than a man's ordinary duty to his parents. At least it is our plain business to remember, before we blame the unnatural casuistry of the Rabbis, that on a different occasion our Lord also declared that whoso had left father or mother for His sake would receive a hundredfold reward.[1] The real moral of the dispute about Corban for the Christian theologian is that it shews the very great stress which our Lord laid under ordinary circumstances upon the ordinary natural duties of life as compared with ecclesiastical and ritual fervours; and therefore it brings into prominence the exceptional character of the exceptional demands which He made towards the end of His Ministry on those who wished to follow Him then. That He had the right and the power to make these demands He did not doubt; but however often the occasions may recur, they remain exceptional.

The real cause of quarrel between our Lord and the Scribes seems to me to be that it was a quarrel between erudition and intuition, between

[1] Similarly, the Saying of Jesus in Mk iii 31 ff about his mother and brethren (5) is historically connected with the attempt of His relatives to arrest Him as a madman. Hence the difference of tone between this passage and Mk vii 9 ff.

traditionalism and originality. With us the word 'originality' tends to be used for mere cleverness, but in its true sense it is the very word for the great characteristic of our Lord's teaching, especially as compared with the principles of the Scribes. It was, in fact, so original as to be superficially inconsistent. The tradition of the Elders (said He) is inconsistent with the Word of God, the Law revealed to Moses: well then, the tradition of the Elders must go. But in the matter of Divorce (21) it is the Law of Moses itself that was given for the hardness of men's hearts; well then, the Law of Moses must go. In the matter of the Sabbath (1) it is the very Law of God, which, according to the Jewish view, God Himself has kept from the beginning, that comes into conflict with duties of kindness and beneficence; well then, even the Law of God is to be broken, as David did. What does all this mean, but that the supreme sanction lay not in any Code or set of Rules, however promulgated, but in an enlightened conscience, a mind really in harmony with the mind of the Father in Heaven? We have learnt the lesson so well that we do not see the difficulty. Our difficulty is to know what enlightenment is, but that was not the difficulty of the Scribes. They did not doubt that it was worse for a man to be paralysed than to be sound; they doubted whether it was worse for a man to be paralysed or for the Sabbath to be broken.

Closely connected with all this is the way of looking at events which Jesus called blasphemy against the Holy Spirit (2–4). The opponents of our Lord, who said that He cast out devils by Beelzebul the prince of the devils, did not deny that the devils were really cast out and the sufferers benefited. It is very likely that if we were to be transported back to Palestine we should use very different medical terms both for the diseases and the mode of cure, but that is not the question. What the Scribes said was in effect: 'We admit that you have cured the man, but we do not recognise the treatment; it must have been unlawful.' They do not say, as doctors sometimes say of quacks, that such and such a treatment is sure to have evil effects afterwards. That again is another question altogether, which is not raised in the Gospels. What is called in the Gospels blasphemy against the Holy Spirit is the refusal to acknowledge a manifest benefit to have been the work of 'the finger of God.'[1]

[1] In this matter Jesus is truly consistent with Himself, for He refused to condemn the man who 'cast out devils' in His name, although not one of His followers.

But the rejection of Tradition and of external Authority is a very serious course to take. Even if we believe that our Lord was right and the Scribes wrong in the particular disputes that took place between them, that does not give us a rule for other times and other questions. Moreover, to substitute unintelligently the rule of Jesus for the rule of Moses is to act clean contrary to the principle which Jesus taught. There was no dispute between our Lord and the Scribes as to the canonicity of the Pentateuch, or whether God had really given commandments to Moses. The question was whether a rule, which was admitted to have all the sanction that a code of rules can have, could retain its binding force in changed and inappropriate circumstances. How is the Christian to get and to retain that sure and intuitive judgement of right and wrong that his Master had?

It seems to me that the answer which Jesus gave is contained in the two groups of Sayings about Humility (22) and about Watchfulness (31). It is difficult to know where to begin, for there are so many familiar Sayings of our Lord on these subjects which all mean much the same thing in the end. It is characteristic of His whole teaching that there can be no doubt about right and wrong for those who have eyes to see and ears to hear. Those whose eyes are clear—Jesus said 'simple'—can see clearly, but most folk have one eye fixed on the Will of God and the other on their own private advantage, with the natural result that they see double and their whole outlook is confused. And therefore He strove again and again to set the ambition of His disciples away from their private advantage and to turn it towards the service of their brethren. Only he whose ambition it was to serve the others was great among His followers (22); only he who was at peace with those around him could pray aright to the common Father of him and them (20, 25); and even in prayer only he who was so far forgetful of his private wishes as to believe that he had virtually received what he had asked for could hope to be heard by God (23, 24).

And I venture to urge that in something of this kind lies the permanent ethical value of the many Sayings about the duty of Watchfulness. 'Watch therefore, for ye know not when the lord of the house cometh'; 'Blessed are those servants whom the lord when he cometh shall find watching,'—what do these and similar Sayings really mean, when stripped of their eschatological dress?

The hope of the Second Coming of the Son of Man has faded with us into an unsubstantial dream. We are not expecting a new heaven and a new earth—at least, not in our time. And consequently all the thoughts and the imagery which imply the near approach of a tremendous catastrophe have in them something strange and unreal to us. Yet it is imperative that we should realise the point of view of our Lord's contemporaries, if we are to understand His teaching about the approaching End. It is no use to allegorize altogether the idea of the Second Advent, still less to regard 'The Kingdom of God is within you' as the only genuine teaching of Jesus, and all the rest as carnal misunderstanding on the part of the disciples. The true way is to accept the Coming of Messiah upon the clouds of heaven to gather together His elect from every quarter as the natural picture, the natural way of expressing faith and hope in the triumph of good over evil, all that people mean nowadays by the vague word Progress. The age in which our Lord lived did not believe in Progress; it was too bad an age, at least for the class of people among whom Christianity grew up. The only progress they had seen was progress to the bad. To associate ideas of natural growth with the coming of God's kingdom was a strange notion, which the disciples were hardly able to grasp when they heard their Master speak of it. If they thought of growth at all in this connexion, it was in the awful imagery of the Apocalypse, where there is growth and harvest and vintage indeed, but it is gathered into the great winepress of the wrath of God.[1]

And, on the whole, men were justified in looking forward at that time to Catastrophe rather than Progress. The Jewish State and the Jewish Nation, as history had known them, did come to a violent end; and the survivors—Christianity and Rabbinical Judaism,—however good a title they may make out for themselves to be legitimate heirs of the old order, are not the old order itself, but a new state of things. A time of Catastrophe means a time when more than usual it is necessary to make the right choice. Most paths lead to swift destruction, most lines of action end in immediate ruin.

What, then, did our Lord command His faithful followers? If we confine ourselves to the Sayings which have come down to us doubly reported, those parts of His Teaching which appear in S. Mark and elsewhere as well, we find that He told them to watch like servants waiting

[1] Apoc xiv 19.

through the night for their lord to return (31), but they were not to be mere passive spectators. There was the double danger before them, first of hailing as a new revelation that which was not a revelation at all, but the will-o'-the-wisp of a false prophet (30); and then the equally fatal course of not being ready to act when the decisive moment came (29).

Our Lord was proved right by the event, when He bade His disciples look forward to a time of trial and crisis, followed by a total change of the conditions of their life. The actual event was very different in detail from what had been expected, but the mortal shock was real enough. The Christendom of the second and succeeding centuries was a very different thing in almost every particular from the Kingdom of God that had been looked for by the disciples in Galilee and in Jerusalem. But it was, as a matter of fact, the line upon which the movement which our Lord started was destined to go; and that the Christian movement survived at all, or survived with a real memory of what it had started from, is a proof that the disciples had learnt their lesson. They endured to the end and were saved themselves. Much of what they most valued was in their old home, the doomed House of Israel; but they had learnt that they must not go back and attempt to salvage their property. So when the Jewish State came to an end, Christianity was left.

A common accusation often brought nowadays against the early Christians is that their ethics and their morality are inappropriate for a stable society that hopes to attain a higher standard of comfort for its members by gradual amelioration. It is a sufficient answer to say that had the early Christians devoted themselves to the well-to-do philanthropy of the nineteenth century they never would have survived at all. But I venture to think that our answer need not stop there. We have learnt to see that the crisis which marks the conclusion of the old order is a continual process, that it is always in operation, and that what is unfit for the new order is being continually cast out. No generation, and least of all our own, can pass away without far-reaching changes in the modes by which alone men can express their aspirations after the Eternal that changes not. The old formulas, the old symbols, must always be reconceived or die. It is for us still to take heed to ourselves, lest our hearts be overcharged with the politics of the moment and the dregs of old disputes that once were fresh, and the new era come upon us suddenly as a snare. This is what Jesus Christ tells us when He says, as

S. Luke paraphrases a still older form of His words: 'Keep watch at every season, making supplication that ye may prevail to escape all these things that shall come to pass and to stand before the Son of Man.'

VI.

THE GOSPEL IN MATTHEW AND IN LUKE.

ἔλεγον οὖν αὐτῷ Σὺ τίς εἶ; εἶπεν αὐτοῖς ὁ Ἰησοῦς Τὴν ἀρχὴν ὅτι καὶ λαλῶ ὑμῖν.

IF the Style is the Man, then we are in a position to know something of the compiler of the Gospel according to Matthew. We have already learned a good deal in the course of these Lectures about the composition of this work. We have seen that it is based upon Mark, but in the earlier portion the material taken from Mark has been freely transposed and curtailed in order to make room for a collection of the Sayings of our Lord, which are introduced at appropriate places in the re-arranged narrative. In addition to these Sayings, a story of the Birth of Jesus Christ is prefixed to the Gospel, with a genealogy which goes from Abraham through David to Joseph.

All through the Gospel, in the parts taken from Mark, in the Nativity story and the other additions to the narrative, and not least in the

Sayings ascribed to our Lord Himself, we find the same peculiarities of language, a peculiar style marked by the recurrence of certain formulas and favourite expressions. To such an extent is this the case that there is hardly a paragraph in the Gospel that does not contain one or more. The *Kingdom of Heaven*, used by Matthew where other Evangelists speak of the 'Kingdom of God,' is the best known of them, but there are many others equally characteristic. Such, for instance, is the way in which after the longer discourses of our Lord, the Evangelist takes up the narrative with, 'And it came to pass when Jesus had finished these sayings. . . .';[1] or again, the way in which a new paragraph begins with 'then.'[2] The Parables themselves are stereotyped, they begin 'The kingdom of heaven is like to this or that,'[3] and they tend to end up with 'There shall be the wailing and the gnashing of teeth.'[4] You will find a list of the Words and Phrases characteristic of S. Matthew's

[1] Matt vii 28, xi 1, xiii 53, xix 1, xxvi 1, contain this formula with slight variations.

[2] In the narrative 'then' occurs in Matthew 60 times, in Mark *never*, in Luke *twice*; in discourses 'then' occurs in Matthew 30 times, in Mark *six* times, in Luke *thirteen* times.

[3] Matt xiii 31, 33, 44, 45, 47, xx 1, xiii 24, xviii 23, xxii 2, xxv 1; this formula never is used in the other Gospels.

[4] This formula occurs at the end of a Saying of Jesus in Matt viii 12, xiii 42, 50, xxii 13, xxiv 51, xxv 30; elsewhere only Lk xiii 28, where it stands at the beginning of a Saying.

Gospel on pp. 4–7 of Sir John Hawkins's *Horae Synopticae*, a list which repays very careful study. But indeed one hardly needs to read such a list to be convinced of the general facts.

Yet I wish I could think of some other word than 'formality' by which to name the chief characteristic of the First Evangelist's literary style. Formality suggests frigidity, generally with a certain measure of incapacity, and these are not among his defects. On the contrary, Matthew has great literary skill, as well as dignity. Everything that he says is put with admirable clearness and lucidity; what he writes down he has first understood himself. If there is an exception to be noted he notes it. A wife is not to be divorced, said Jesus, according to Mark and Luke; Matthew adds the exception *saving for the cause of fornication.* 'Blessed are the poor and the hungry,' said Jesus (Lk vi 20, 21); Matthew explains that the 'poor' are the poor *in spirit*, and the 'hungry' are those who hunger *after righteousness.* At the end of the scene in which Jesus spoke to His disciples in the boat about the leaven of the Pharisees, Matthew adds 'Then'—notice the typical Matthæan cast of the sentence,—'then understood they how that He bade them not beware of the leaven of bread, but of the teaching of the Pharisees and the

Sadducees' (Matt xvi 12). Some twenty verses later, after the Transfiguration, Matthew reports (from Mark) the sayings of Jesus about Elijah coming to restore all things, but he adds, 'Then understood the disciples that He spake unto them of John the Baptist' (Matt xvii 13). Similarly, he points the moral of the Parable of the Vineyard, already sufficiently obvious, by making our Lord say, after the telling quotation about the Stone that the builders rejected, 'Therefore say I unto you, the Kingdom of God shall be taken away from you, and given to a nation bringing forth the fruits thereof' (Matt xxi 43).

This last illustration of the First Evangelist's method is highly characteristic. It is magnificent, but it is not history; at least it is not history, if by history we mean the nearest possible approach to giving a cinematograph view of a past scene, accompanied by a record on the gramophone. Such a record would indeed be precious, but even if we had it we should want something more. We should still want a Commentary, something which would give us the moral of what we were seeing and hearing.

I do not think that Matthew—it is convenient to call the Compiler of the Gospel according to Matthew by the traditional name—aimed at being a Chronicler. This statement would not be true of all the Evangelists. Mark and Luke are, in a way, Chroniclers; that is, a very great part of their intention is to tell the story of the events more or less as they came to pass. With Matthew the case is different. He is not especially concerned to paint the most lifelike picture possible of Jesus of Nazareth as He walked the earth in what was, even when Matthew wrote, a past age. His aim rather is to shew forth the real significance of one who had come in the fulness of time, fulfilling the ancient words of prophecy, proving Himself thereby to be the legitimate King and Lawgiver of the new Nation which is the true Israel of God.

'The Kingdom of God shall be taken away from you and given to a nation bringing forth the fruits thereof'—this is the motto, the special doctrine, of the Gospel according to Matthew. The disciples are a new legitimate Israel, come to take the place of the old Israel, and bound together by a New Law which takes the place of the Old. The keynote of the work is not the opposition of Law and Grace, as in S. Paul, but the opposition of the Old Law and the New Law.

It is very difficult to dwell upon the leading characteristics of Matthew without seeming to fall back into the phrases of Baur and his followers, to whom the main event in the development of the early Church was the struggle between 'Paulinism' and the primitive Jewish Christianity of the original apostles. I am not trying to revive the antiquated heresies of the Tübingen School. We need not doubt that S. Paul really wrote, and wrote with truth, that James and Cephas and John gave him the right hand of fellowship; and I venture to think, with (I suppose) the great majority of modern students of early Christian literature, that it is absurd and fantastic to explain expressions in the Parables given by Matthew, such as the 'enemy' of xiii 25 who sowed Tares among the Wheat, as covert allusions to the Apostle of the Gentiles. Nevertheless there remains a certain element of truth in the contention of the Tübingen theologians. There is, it was inevitable that there should be, a real difference between the outward aspect of Christianity in the Gentile communities founded by S. Paul, in which the Christians were dissenters from the heathen view of life, and the Jewish or semi-Jewish communities in Palestine, in which the Christians were a sect or school among the Jews. To be a Christian at all in a heathen city meant an inevitable change of life in every social and domestic custom. The religion of a man's neighbours was the service of Demons, a thing altogether irrational or wicked from the Christian's point of view. There were scandals, of course, in the little Christian societies, but on the whole the pressure of the outside world tended to keep things straight within the fold. But in the Jewish communities the moral position of the Christianised Jews was different. Here it could not be asserted as a self-evident proposition that the Christian's manner of life was better than the Jew's. The Christian and the Jew worshipped the same God, they appealed to the same sacred Scriptures, the same Saints of old supplied acknowledged examples of godly conduct. It might well seem that except the righteousness of the Christian exceeded the righteousness of the Jews around them, they could not enter into the kingdom of heaven. On every point debatable questions of conduct would arise, and the Christians felt the need of Rules which might guide their actions with reference to the rules observed by their more conservative neighbours.

In no book of our New Testament is this conception of a New Law for Christians so prominent as in the Gospel according to S. Matthew. No book of the New Testament is so full of thoughts and expressions which have a real parallel in Rabbinical literature. The Evangelist is, so to speak, a Christian Rabbi, though no doubt he would have disclaimed the title.[1] If the Gospel of Mark is most closely in touch with History, the Gospel of Matthew is most closely in touch with the Talmud. Like the other Gospels it is in form a narrative of the earthly life of Jesus Christ, but it sets forth that life with reference to the questions that most nearly concerned a Church composed of Palestinian Christians. No doubt the Evangelist feels himself and his brethren separated from the mass of his unbelieving fellow-countrymen. The Christians form an Ecclesia, a Society, of their own (xviii 17), distinct from ordinary Jews (xxviii 15). The separation had been made absolute when 'all the people' had answered Pilate by saying 'His blood be on us, and on our children!' (xxvii 25). But even so, the unbelieving Jew is nearer than the Gentile and the tax-gatherer (xviii 17): he that is outcast to the Jew is outcast also to the Evangelist.

I imagine it to be one of the most delicate of the problems which confront the investigator of the Gospel History to determine how far the Sayings of Jesus reported only in the Gospel according to Matthew are, in the narrower sense, historical: how far, that is, they are a literal translation into Greek of words which Jesus once spoke,

[1] Matt xxiii 8.

and how far they represent the practice and the hopes and fears of those of His countrymen who believed on Him a generation after the Crucifixion. Happily the problem is less important than at first sight appears, at least to those who believe with our Evangelist, that in a very real sense the risen Lord was with His disciples all the days, and that the Church in Palestine as well as in Corinth and in Rome was really carrying out the work that Jesus had originated. But when we seek to pick out the particular sayings which happen to have come down to us unmodified in word and expression, we are attempting a task which is in most instances impossible to carry out. It is not only a question whether this or that sentence or illustration comes really from a later time:[1] the Evangelist all through is thinking of his own age and the condition and needs of his fellow-Christians. It is this which everywhere influences the representation that he gives of the events of the past generation. "The Kingdom of God here and now, according to Matthew's representation," says Wellhausen (*Einl.* p. 105), "is an institution founded by Jesus, and conversely the thought of the Kingdom is inseparable from its Founder. On this assumption Jesus has the design to found it on earth, and so appears from

[1] *E.g.* the mention of Zacharias, son of Barachias, in Matt xxiii 35.

the beginning as Messiah. From the beginning He specially teaches His own disciples, to shew them in detail how the Society of His followers must be constituted and what kind of experiences will befall it. He does not scatter His teaching about on every soil heedless of its success or failure, but sows the Kingdom of God with the 'Word of the Kingdom,' and this Kingdom of God when called the Field is the same as in the Parable of the Vineyard. We cannot help recognising that the Ecclesia, the Church, is meant, although the name is generally avoided on historical grounds. Especially is this clear when Jesus speaks of Scribes and Stewards of the Kingdom of God, of the Labourers, some of whom have long worked in it, and some only for a short while, and of its worthy and unworthy members; or again, when He says that John the Baptist, though he be the greatest of Jews, yet is less than the least member of the Kingdom of Heaven. The identification of the Kingdom and the Ecclesia is entirely comprehensible, seeing that the Christian Society was undeniably the work of Jesus, and it was considered to be the porch of Heaven itself. But this Kingdom, as it is set forth in Matthew, is altogether 'Christian'; it cannot have been thus set forth, or rather presupposed, by Jesus Himself. For in this Gospel

He really presupposes the Kingdom without considering any explanation about it necessary. He addresses His disciples as though they were already members of His Society and organised as such; He transfers Himself into a future state of things as if it were then actually present."[1]

Professor Wellhausen's characteristic judgement of the general standpoint of the Gospel according

[1] I have ventured to paraphrase the German so much in order to make this isolated quotation clear that I give the original here also. Wellhausen's actual words are: "Das gegenwärtige Reich, wie es namentlich bei Matthäus erscheint, ist die Stiftung Jesu und hat ihn zum notwendigen Korrelat. Unter dieser Voraussetzung hat er die Absicht, es auf Erden zu gründen und tritt eben damit von Anfang an als Messias auf. Er lehrt von Anfang an speziell seine Jünger, um ihnen aus einander zu setzen, wie seine Gemeinde beschaffen sein soll und was ihr widerfahren wird. Er streut nicht unbekümmert um den Erfolg auf beliebigen Boden seine Lehren aus, sondern er sät durch das Wort vom Reich das Reich Gottes an, welches mit dem Saatfelde oder der Pflanzung in dem selben Sinne verglichen wird wie mit dem Weinberge. Dass er darunter die ἐκκλησία versteht, deren Namen er aus historischen Gründen in der Regel vermeidet, lässt sich nicht verkennen; es erhellt besonders deutlich, wenn er von Schriftgelehrten und Verwaltern, von älteren und jüngeren Schichten, von würdigen und unwürdigen Mitgliedern des Reiches Gottes spricht, oder wenn er sagt, der Täufer obwol der grösste Jude sei doch kleiner als das geringste Mitglied des Reiches Gottes. Die Gleichsetzung der βασιλεία und der ἐκκλησία begreift sich vollkommen, da die Gemeinde unleugbar die Wirkung Jesu war und für die Vorstufe des Himmels galt. Aber sie ist durchaus christlich und kann nicht von Jesu selber vollzogen oder gar vorausgesetzt sein. Denn er setzt sie in der Tat voraus, ohne eine Erklärung darüber für notwendig zu halten. Er redet zu seinen Jüngern, als wären sie schon seine Gemeinde und als solche organisirt; er versetzt sich in eine zukunftige Situation, als wäre sie gegenwärtig."

to Matthew appears to me worthy of very careful attention and to contain a great deal that is undeniably true. We miss altogether in this Gospel the historical perspective which meets us in Mark. In Mark the story moves from situation to situation, from the beginning to the crisis; in Matthew, as in the Epistle to the Hebrews, the Master is depicted as 'Jesus Christ, the same yesterday and to-day and for ever.' The Church, the organised body of believers in Jesus, is, as Wellhausen says, presupposed all through, and this anticipation of the events has doubtless coloured the turn of many a phrase. But I venture to think that Wellhausen has pushed a legitimate argument further than it is wise to go, and that we shall make a mistake if we refuse to accept a great deal of the teaching of this Gospel as a true representation of what Jesus taught. I find it difficult to believe that the Parables and Sayings which speak of the Kingdom of God as a thing to be realised here on earth would have retained so fresh and unecclesiastical an atmosphere, if they were both in spirit and in substance the work of an age later than our Lord. Nowhere in early Christian literature, except in the three Synoptic Gospels, do we find that picturesque outlook on men and nature that finds its expression in the Parables of Jesus. The

Acts of the Apostles is full of speeches of Peter and Paul and other Christians of the early times. These speeches are either the work of the speakers themselves, or of the compiler of the Acts, who is himself one of the Evangelists. But there is never a Parable among them, and not many Sayings like the Sayings in the Gospels.

As an instance of what I mean, let us take the Parable of the Tares and its Explanation (Matt xiii 24–30, 36–43). Both Parable and Explanation are found in Matthew only, and the Concordance will shew you that they exhibit in a very marked degree the linguistic peculiarities of the First Evangelist. No doubt, therefore, the wording, both of the Parable and of the Explanation, is the Evangelist's wording. But how very different they are in their inner structure! They both mean the same thing; you cannot doubt that the explanation is, in a general way, correct. Indeed it is too correct: the Field is the world, the Enemy is the devil, this figure in the scene means this, and that means that, until the whole picture of the Harvest of men has melted away, and the just are represented as shining like the sun, instead of lying stored like wheat in a barn. I can well believe that the Explanation is altogether the handiwork of the Evangelist or of his contemporaries, but the original picture of the good and the bad, growing together unhindered until the harvest is ripe, seems to me to come from another and a more creative mind. And I know of no one else to whom to ascribe this picture save our Lord, who taught His disciples to imitate their Father in Heaven whose sun shines alike on bad and good, and whose rain falls on the just and the unjust.

I think also that we may easily go too far in pressing the logical consequences of the belief that the world was speedily coming to an end. It is true that the Ministry was a short period when we look at it from the point of view of general history, and that doubtless the disciples expected that the Kingdom of God was immediately to appear. But if a particular twelve or thirteen months be a very short space of time when viewed from a distance, it is sufficiently long for those who are actually passing through it to raise questions which can only be settled by an appeal to eternal principles. We know from the Gospel of Mark that besides the main events of the Ministry there was plenty of time for disputes about precedence to develop among our Lord's nearest followers.[1] We saw in the first of these Lectures how many days there were which are unchronicled by the Evangelists. Yet

[1] Mk ix 34, x 35.

in each of them our Lord and the disciples must have eaten and slept—or gone without food and sleep,—in each of them there must have been a round of more or less ordinary occupations, quite sufficient in themselves to call forth the Sayings that we find recorded.

The actual fact of the dislocation of Mark's order by Matthew justifies us in paying very little attention to the order in which we find the Sayings of Jesus grouped in Matthew's Gospel; the way in which Matthew often, but not always, modifies the language of Mark warns us that we must expect Matthew to have similarly modified the language of his other, and to us lost, sources. But the very fact that Matthew after all retains so much of what is primitive in Mark, should teach us that Matthew has probably retained much of what is primitive in his other sources. However short our Lord and His disciples may have imagined the time would be before the End —and Jesus expressly declared that He did not know the day or the hour—there was yet plenty of time to go wrong in, plenty of time for a discrimination between the faithful and the unfaithful, the false prophet and the true. And therefore I think that we shall do better to regard these Sayings of Jesus in the Gospel of Matthew, in which a Christian community seems more or less to be presupposed, rather as adaptations of what the disciples had remembered of their Master's teaching than as new inventions made for the purpose. It is easy to apply the Sayings in the Gospels to the varying needs of the moment: you may, in fact, hear it done in any pulpit every Sunday in Church and Chapel. But it is not so easy to make new Sayings and new Parables like those in the Gospels of Matthew and Luke; at least, that kind of speech does not make itself heard in the extant remains of what the first four generations of Christians wrote.

For these reasons, while we cannot suppose that the order in which the various Sayings of Jesus are given in Matthew at all represents the chronological order in which they were spoken, yet there is not the same reason to regard them as unauthentic in substance. They are arranged, and here and there altered in expression, to meet the needs of the Christian community in Palestine towards the end of the first century; but I venture to think that the greater part of the substance of the Teaching, and all that is most fresh and picturesque in its expression, come from historical reminiscence of the Master's words.

There are two points upon which I ought to touch before we leave the Gospel of Matthew. These are the appeal to prophecy and the representation of Jesus Christ as the Son of David. Both points illustrate in a very marked degree the legal, we may almost say constitutional, ideas of the First Evangelist. It is very easy for us at the present time to do less than justice to the 'Argument from Prophecy,' as our fathers called it. When we read in the Gospel of Matthew 'Now all this was done that it might be fulfilled which was spoken by the Lord through the Prophet, saying . . .' (Matt i 22 f, xxi 4 f), we simply do not agree with the Evangelist. And we do not agree for two reasons. In the first place, we have come to look at the Old Testament in a different light. We do not believe that the sayings of the Prophets and Psalmists were so many dark riddles to themselves and their contemporaries, without real significance except in regard to certain future events which were to happen centuries after. If the Prophet said 'Tell the daughter of Zion, behold, thy King cometh unto thee riding upon an ass,' this must have had its primary and sufficient meaning in the time of the Prophet: we cannot believe that it needed Christ's Entry into Jerusalem to justify its existence. In the second place, even if there be among us any who still hold that this verse from Zechariah was really a prediction of our Lord's Entry, I still do not think they would be satisfied with the Evangelist's form of words. They would assert, I am sure, that the Prophet said these words because our Lord was going to enter Jerusalem thus. I do not think they would agree with Matthew that our Lord healed those that were sick, 'that what was said through Isaiah the Prophet might be fulfilled' (Matt viii 16, 17). They would say that our Lord healed the sick, because it was His will and kindness to do so, and that therefore Isaiah had been inspired to prophesy such things of Him.

The difference between our standpoint and that of the Evangelist is that between him and us lies the whole edifice of Christology. We know what Jesus of Nazareth has been to the world; the Evangelist lived in an age which was only beginning to find out. The argument from Prophecy is ultimately an attempt to shew that the Life and Mission of Jesus was no Divine freak or caprice, but a part of a well-ordered whole. To the pious Jew the utterances of the Prophets had very much the same place in their idea of the world as what we call the Laws of Nature have for us: they were things which had been formulated by men, yet they were not constituted by man, but by God. How what we call the Old Testament had acquired this sacred character is another matter, but that it had acquired the character is undisputed.

The power of the argument from Prophecy, both the motive force which prompted its use and its effect upon those who were influenced by it, was that it attempted to legitimatise the Gospel History, to shew that it was the legitimate outcome of the religion of holy men of old.

It cannot be said that the early Christians in general, or the First Evangelist in particular, were very successful in their use of the Old Testament. They rarely rise above surprising us by their verbal ingenuity. All the more remarkable is it therefore to notice that the only references to the Old Testament in the Gospels which have any real validity for us to-day are those which are ascribed to our Lord Himself. We know from Mark that 'Love God and love your neighbour' was what He regarded as the sum of the meaning of the Old Testament, and Matthew repeats the story, with the characteristic addition that on these commandments hangs the whole Law and the Prophets also.[1] But besides this, Matthew twice (ix 13, xii 7) makes our Lord quote from Hosea 'I desire mercy, and not sacrifice.' This verse (Hosea vi 6) is one of those flashes of spiritual insight which light up here and there the tortuous and despondent utterances of the most obscure of all the Hebrew Prophets. To bring it out from

[1] Matt xxii 40: a Rabbinical phrase, cf. *Berachoth*, 63*a*.

its obscurity shews not only a knowledge of the letter of the Old Testament, but also a real appreciation of the genius of Hebrew religion. The Evangelist in his own person alleges Hosea's word 'Out of Egypt have I called my Son,' as being fulfilled by the Flight into Egypt. Now we cannot prove by critical analysis that the Evangelist found the quotation 'I desire mercy and not sacrifice' in his source as being quoted by Jesus; but is it not hard to believe that these two quotations represent the same person's study of Hosea? All we can say for certain is that the one quotation shews insight and intelligence, and that the other does not. The fact remains, that the quotations from the Old Testament, which are given as quotations made by Jesus, shew a very different degree of literary tact from those made by His followers. Are we to say with the Jews in the Fourth Gospel 'How knoweth this man letters, having never learned?'[1]

[1] Other instances of really appropriate quotation from the OT are to be found in Mk vii 6, 7 = Matt xv 6 ff (Isaiah xxix 13); Matt xxi 16 (Ps viii 2); and Lk xxii 37 (Isaiah liii 12, see above, Lecture IV. p. 141). In Matt xxi 16 the quotation from the Psalm is given according to the text of the LXX, but it seems to me that a tradition that Jesus had quoted, perhaps often quoted, a particular text might survive independently of the version in which he had quoted it, and independently of other traditions of His Sayings. The *words* of the OT were familiar to very many Jews, even if in a merely mechanical way. But to remember that the Master used to quote such and such a text is one thing; it was quite another to pick out

To return to our Evangelist. Another line by which he tried to mark out the place of his Lord in the universal scheme of things was to regard him as the Heir of David. The Gospel according to Matthew may well be called *The Book of Jesus Christ, the son of David.* According to Mark, blind Bartimæus had indeed called out to the Galilean Prophet by this title, but no special stress is laid on the wayside beggar's words. Matthew not only gives this tale (xx 30, 31): in his Gospel our Lord is recognised as Son of David by the two blind men (ix 27), by the multitudes (xii 23), by the Canaanitish woman (xv 22), and by the children in the Temple itself (xxi 9, 15). Jesus is the King of the twelve tribes of Israel (xix 28), who is ultimately to reign over all the nations (xxv 34). In a word, the special aim of Matthew is to represent our Lord as the legitimate Heir of the royal house of David. That the Messiah should be merely a Son of David was not enough. There were doubtless many sons of David alive at the time; but the Evangelist wanted the legitimate Heir of the Divine promises made to David. That is why in this Gospel the Genealogy of Joseph is taken through the line of the Kings of

for oneself appropriate utterances from what Tyconius calls 'the unsurveyed forest of prophecy.' It is only in this way that we can explain the quotation of Ps lxxxii 6 in Joh x 34: possibly there is an allusion to the same verse in Lk vi 35 (*ἔσεσθε υἱοὶ Ὑψίστου*).

Judah, and why the usurper Herod is alarmed when he hears that the legitimate ruler has been born within his dominions.[1]

In reality the Kingdom of Jesus Christ was not of this world, and Jesus Himself never claimed obedience as the Heir of David's line. His only reference to any connexion between David and the Messiah is the paradox with which He prefaces His attack in the Temple courts on the Scribes and their ways. When He quoted Psalm cx, and asked how the Messiah could be David's son when David called him Lord, Matthew tells us that none of the Scribes could answer. No wonder: there is no answer, except that the current method of arguing from single texts taken at random from the Old Testament can only prove what is believed already. The real answer is—'Beware of the Scribes.'[2]

But even in the matter of the representation of our Lord as the Heir of David, we may easily do less than justice to the point of view of the Evangelist. The Heir of David—what was the worth of the inheritance when the Gospel according to Matthew was being com-

[1] A full discussion by the present writer of the text and interpretation of the Genealogy, and of the story of the Nativity according to Matthew, will be found in *Evangelion da-Mepharreshe*, vol. ii, pp. 258-266.

[2] Mk xii 38, Lk xx 46: contrast Matt xxiii 2, 3.

piled? Palestine was trodden under the heel of the Roman power, Jerusalem was left desolate, the Temple in ruins, the Jewish nation enslaved and broken. The tabernacle of David was fallen, and the only worth of the inheritance was spiritual and ideal. We cannot doubt that to the Evangelist the Royal descent of our Lord from David, and through David from Abraham, symbolised the belief that the still infant Church, immature, weak and insignificant as it then was, was yet the true Israel of God, foreseen from of old and destined in due time to triumph over the heathen world. And it is due to the Evangelist to remember that the triumph to which he looked forward was a triumph of incorporation. The disciples were to make disciples of all the nations. More than that: the final test was not whether men had called Jesus 'Lord,' but whether they had been kind without looking for reward. As I said in the Introductory Lecture to this series, the important thing for our study of early Christianity is not whether the Parable of the Sheep and the Goats in Matt xxv is a literal translation of words once spoken by Jesus, or to discover the real time and place where they were first uttered. The important thing is to recognise that this is the kind of teaching which the Evangelist thought worthy to put in his Lord's mouth, and which the Church accepted as worthy. At the same time, the more we study the special aims and tendencies of the Synoptic Evangelists, the greater the gap appears between the theories which they themselves elaborate and the circle of ideas in which the Sayings of Jesus move. Again and again we find ourselves in the presence of something which may or may not be authentic historical reminiscence, but is in any case totally unlike the other remains of early Christian literature. We cannot tell whether the tale be well remembered, or how many steps there may have been in its transmission, but the difference of spirit is unmistakeable, and we take knowledge of the Evangelists that they have been with Jesus.

The Gospel according to S. Luke brings us into a different atmosphere, and one more difficult to characterise than that of the First Gospel. This is mainly due to the fact that the Third Evangelist is more of a compiler and less of a theorist than Matthew. In a word, he is more of a historian. I do not mean that all his historical statements will better stand rigid investigation, but I certainly believe that he intended to write history; and further, that he wrote history as we write it, by putting together such materials as came to his hand. I have already given you in the Fourth Lecture some reasons for believing that the chief materials out of which this Gospel is constructed are Mark's Gospel and the lost Document which we have called Q; and further that, speaking generally, the Evangelist (whom I still believe to be Luke the Physician, sometime a companion of the Apostle Paul, and now writing in his old age) has set down the events and sayings that he relates very much in the same order as they were given in the sources he used, while making many stylistic changes and minor alterations. Where S. Luke follows his sources exactly, he preserves for us very valuable fragments of history: I have already given you an instance when we were examining the story of our Lord's arrest in Gethsemane, at the end of the Fourth Lecture. On the other hand, some of the expedients by which this Evangelist attempts to weld his materials together can hardly be accepted by the scientific historian. This is conspicuously the case with regard to his representation of our Lord's last journey to Jerusalem. Even if we agree with Luke as to the route followed, it is obvious that the greater part of the sayings and anecdotes which are assigned to this journey do not really belong to it,[1] but to an earlier period in the Ministry. Apparently the Evangelist, finding that the record of the journey from Capernaum to near Jericho was almost a blank, inserted at this point all the stories of our Lord's teaching for which no appropriate place offered elsewhere. No doubt many paragraphs come directly out of the lost source Q, notably Lk xi 15–36.

But, as I have had occasion to remark several times in the course of these Lectures, the lost sources of the Evangelists cannot be recovered in such a way that we can really examine their structure and their spirit. It is more profitable to examine the special aims of the Evangelists themselves, the special aspects of the Christian movement which the Evangelists thought well to emphasise. And although it is not so easy to make this characterisation in the case of Luke as in that of Matthew, it is almost more necessary to attempt to do so, because we are dealing with the only writer who carries on the tale beyond the Resurrection. The trustworthiness of the Gospel of Luke is the measure of the trustworthiness of the Book of Acts; the special point of view from which the Gospel History is looked at in this Gospel will shew

[1] On the course of this journey, see the Note at the end of Lecture III (pp. 96, 97).

us the special point of view from which the Acts must have been written.

To put the question in a less pretentious but more manageable form: what features are there in the Gospel of Luke, which are either wholly absent from, or less conspicuous in, the other Gospels? There are, of course, many Sayings and Parables given in Luke which are not found elsewhere. The Parables of the Good Samaritan, of the Prodigal Son, of the Pharisee and the Publican, are conspicuous instances. And, as I have just said with regard to the Parables found only in Matthew, we shall do well to remember that nothing in the least like them in form or style is to be found in Christian literature outside the Synoptic Gospels. But the presence of these Parables in Luke does not answer our question: their teaching, after all, is much the same as what is given in the other Gospels.

It appears to me that the two tendencies which are really characteristic of the writings of S. Luke are a tendency towards voluntary poverty and a tendency towards asceticism. Neither of these ideals, as I understand the matter, belonged by nature and choice to the earliest form of the Christian movement. Our Lord ate and drank with those who invited Him, so that His opponents called Him gluttonous and a winebibber. His disciples provoked comment because they did not fast, and Jesus Himself taught the doctrine, so amazing to a Jew, that nothing a man takes into him can defile him.[1] The sacrifices which, when occasion arose, He demanded from His followers were for the sake of the Cause,[2] not directly for their personal benefit in time to come. For the Cause, for the sake of the Gospel, our Lord was not afraid to call upon the disciples to give up everything, but that was because the circumstances required the sacrifice, not because the goods of this life were in themselves bad.

This is the same attitude of mind that we find in the letters of S. Paul. S. Paul, like his Master, wished his disciples to be free from anxiety about worldly matters. Marriage and property were not unlawful, but they were roots which attached a man to this world; and S. Paul felt sure that the time was short and that the fashion of this world was passing away.[3] We never do justice to the theory and practice of the first two generations of Christians, if we forget even for an instant that there brooded over them the shadow of the anticipated End of all things.

After the Fall of Jerusalem and the extinction of the Jewish State the Christian Churches began

[1] Mk vii 15 ff.
[2] Mk viii 35.
[3] See especially 1 Cor vii 27–32.

gradually to find out that the end was not yet, but the view of life which was reasonable in Judæa for half a century after the Crucifixion continued to assert itself as the ethical ideal in the Christian communities. There was indeed much to encourage asceticism in their ranks. For the first three hundred years the Christian Church had a precarious existence, sometimes actively persecuted by the State, sometimes left alone, but never formally permitted to live. In such circumstances earthly ties, whether of property, or of wife and children, are more or less of an encumbrance; they tend to make a man less eager, less wholehearted. And so there sprang up the notion that these things are inconsistent with the highest Christian life; that the ideal Christian should be penniless and unmarried.

This point of view makes itself felt all through the writings of S. Luke. "Blessed are ye poor; for yours is the Kingdom of God!" "Woe unto you that are rich, for ye have received your consolation! Woe unto you, ye that are full now, for ye shall hunger!"[1] "Sell that ye have, and give alms; make for yourselves purses which wax not old."[2] Abraham says to the rich man in the parable, "Remember that thou in thy lifetime receivedst thy good things, and Lazarus in like

[1] Lk vi 20, 24, 25. [2] Lk xii 33.

manner evil things; but now here he is comforted, and thou are tormented."[1] These Sayings go further, are more uncompromising, than what we find in the other Gospels. And as to the other point, I think it is impossible to read through this Gospel and the Acts without feeling that all the writer's sympathy is for the unmarried and the widows, from Anna the daughter of Phanuel, who had been a widow for eighty-four years, to the four virgin daughters of Philip the evangelist. The tendency of Luke is perhaps most clearly seen in the wording of our Lord's reply to the Sadducees, whereby it is made to appear that those who are worthy to attain the resurrection from the dead do not marry like ordinary men and women. According to Mark our Lord says, 'When they shall rise from the dead, they neither marry, nor are given in marriage'; but in the Gospel of Luke the words of the answer are: 'The sons of this world marry, and are given in marriage: but they that are accounted worthy to attain to that world, and the resurrection from the dead, neither marry, nor are given in marriage.' The wording has been made, as I cannot but think, intentionally ambiguous. It was with good reason that the heretic Marcion, who rejected marriage altogether for Christians, chose out the Gospel of

[1] Lk xvi 25.

Luke as the only one which could be made to fit with his own teaching.

The tinge of ascèticism and, if I may use the word, of communism which pervades the Gospel of Luke is just one of those things which are easier felt than demonstrated. It is not strong enough to disturb the balance of the story, but its presence is, I think, indubitable to every attentive reader. I have mentioned it with some emphasis for two reasons: in the first place, because it was a real constituent element in early Christianity; and, secondly, because it is a little over-emphasised in this Gospel, if we may judge by comparing it with the others. We may therefore go on to assume that the stress laid upon this side of Christian life in the Acts in the very earliest period of the Church's existence is also a little over-emphasised, and that if it had been Matthew who had written the history of the Church in Jerusalem we should have heard more of their community of customs and morals, and less of their community of property. All through the Acts, in its presentation both of Christian practices and of Christian beliefs, the tale is being told by the same voice that speaks to us in the Third Gospel.

In conclusion, there is one point connected with early Christian asceticism that ought not to escape notice. We must never forget that Christian asceticism has generally tended towards the equalisation of the sexes. The historical opposite to the ascetic ideal was not that in which woman was looked upon as the equal complement of man, but one in which woman was looked upon as the divinely ordained household drudge or the plaything of man. The old idea of the family, at least in the times we are considering, meant the relegation of the woman to the background. And so the Gospel which most strikes the ascetic note is also that which tells us most of the part played by women in the Gospel history. It is an old observation that the Nativity Story is told by Luke from the woman's point of view. But elsewhere also women play a prominent and independent part in the narrative. The Widow of Nain; the woman that was a sinner who wiped the feet of Jesus; Joanna the wife of Chuza and Susanna, who ministered unto Jesus of their substance; Martha who served, and Mary who listened; the 'daughter of Abraham' who was loosed from the bond of Satan on the Sabbath; the women who bewailed and lamented Jesus on His way to the Cross,—all these come into the Gospel story through S. Luke alone. Some of these personages are certainly historical, of others we may not be so sure. But their presence corresponds to what is certainly a fact of history, to wit, the appeal made by the earliest Christian preaching to women, and their response.

The point of view of Luke differs from that of Matthew, and both differ from Mark. In the Gospel of Mark, whenever and wherever it was written, we are the nearest to the events and the spirit of the time. In Matthew we see the Gospel History more or less as it was understood by a Christian who had ceased to be a Jew, but who still retained much of the lore of the Synagogue. In Luke we have the Gospel History as told by one who had enough ordinary Greek culture to know that there was something in the new doctrine which was of more value to men and women than what they would get from the world around them. We have seen in the last Lecture what the two main sources from which these Gospels are built up told us of the teaching of Jesus Christ. We have considered to-day some of the special features emphasised by Matthew and by Luke; we have seen in what directions the evangelical legend tended to grow under their hand. Yet, after all, the Portrait they draw remains essentially the same. Verse after verse, Saying after saying, might be quoted to you from the three Synoptic Gospels, and, unless you happened to have special knowledge or had given special attention to such matters, you would be unable to say to which Gospel they really belonged. Morally, ethically, spiritually, they are all in the same plane. We cannot doubt that the common impression which they present of the way in which our Lord spoke, the style of His utterance, the manner of His discourse to rich and poor, to learned and unlearned, is based on true historical reminiscence.

VII.

THE FOURTH GOSPEL.

Nam dicere ut est quis potest? audeo dicere, fratres mei, forsitan nec ipse Johannes dixit ut est, sed et ipse ut potuit.

S. AUGUSTINE, *in Joh.* i.

WE come now to consider the Fourth Gospel, the Gospel according to John. And before we begin our investigation we shall, I think, do well to remember the immense influence which this work has had for century after century. No work could hold so great a place before the world so long, without intrinsic merit of an extraordinary sort. However peculiar the aims and methods of the author of this work may be, however out of harmony may be the world of ideas in which he lived with that which surrounds us at the present day, we shall not be likely to arrive at a true solution of the problems which the work offers by belittling it. If the history turn out to be no history, it must be because it was intended to teach something to the author more important than history. If the rhetoric does not always ring true, if the argument sometimes fails really to appeal to us, it is more probable that we have misunderstood than that the writer was really at fault. Our duty is to criticise, and that fearlessly, but yet with reverence and with misgiving of our own infallibility.

It will not be necessary here to investigate in detail the external evidence for the Fourth Gospel. The belief that it was written by the Apostle S. John was fully established in most parts of the Christian world as early as the decade 170–180 AD, and clear indications of its use, especially among some of the Christian 'Gnostics,' can be traced back to a period some fifty years earlier. It is true that these indications are weak just where we might have expected them to be most precise: S. Polycarp, according to tradition a disciple of S. John at Ephesus, does not quote at all from the Fourth Gospel, either in his Epistle or in the prayer which he is said to have prayed at the stake, and the utmost that can be claimed is that certain phrases in a single passage in his Epistle are parallel to some leading phrases in 1 and 2 John.[1] This passage in S. Polycarp is certainly

[1] Polycarp, *ad Phil.* vii: 'For whosoever doth not confess Jesus Christ to have come (ἐληλυθέναι) in the flesh is antichrist, and whosoever doth not confess the witness of the cross is of the devil, and whosoever perverteth the oracles of the Lord to his own desires and says there is neither resurrection nor judgement, he is the first-born of Satan.' Compare 1 Joh iv 2, 3; 2 Joh 7.

important as shewing that Johannine watchwords, like 'antichrist' and 'confessing Jesus Christ to have come in the flesh,' were actually used by orthodox circles in Asia Minor. But it is remarkable that S. Polycarp should exhibit no further trace of the influence of the Johannine theology.

The external testimony to the traditional authorship of the Fourth Gospel is, in a word, indecisive. It is not unfavourable to the genuineness of the tradition, but it is quite insufficient to prove it. We may therefore go on to examine the internal evidence. And here the first question which must be asked is whether this Gospel is really a historical work. We have seen that S. Mark's Gospel has a very good claim to be so regarded: how does the Fourth Gospel compare with S. Mark?

The comparison of the Synoptic narrative with that of 'John' is an old and very simple study. The details are all familiar, and the problems do not depend upon the niceties of Hellenistic Greek or the various readings of MSS. It is a matter of historical discrepancy in two perfectly clear and definite accounts. The fact is, that the narrative in 'Mark' and the narrative in 'John' cannot be made to agree, except on the supposition that one or the other is, as regards the objective facts, inaccurate and misleading. I shall hope later on to attempt an explanation: what we are now concerned with is the question whether the Fourth Gospel can be trusted as a narrative of events.

The discrepancy between the Fourth Gospel and the Synoptic narrative, *i.e.* S. Mark's Gospel, comes to a head in the story of the Raising of Lazarus. It is not a question of the improbability or impossibility of the miracle, but of the time and place and the effect upon outsiders. According to 'John,' Jesus had been in Jerusalem in the winter preceding the Crucifixion (x 22), and after that visit had gone away to where John the Baptist had been baptizing (x 40). There He heard that Lazarus of Bethany, brother of Martha and Mary, was ill (xi 1 ff); and when at last Jesus comes to Bethany, Lazarus has been dead four days (xi 17, 39). Jesus goes to the tomb, accompanied by Martha and Mary and a 'multitude' of the Jews (xi 19, 42). He calls Lazarus from the tomb; and when he comes forth bound in his grave-clothes, Jesus says, 'Loose him, and let him go' (xi 44). This stupendous miracle produces, according to 'John,' exactly the sensation that we should expect. Many of the Jews that witnessed the scene believed on Jesus, though some of them went away to the Pharisees and told the news (xi

45, 46). The chief priests and Pharisees hardened their hearts and decided forthwith that Jesus must be killed (xi 47–53); but the common people were much impressed, and when Jesus (who had gone into the country, to 'Ephraim') returned to Bethany, they came to gaze on Him, and also upon Lazarus (xii 9). To such an extent was this the case that the chief priests took counsel to put Lazarus to death also (xii 10). This natural interest on the part of the crowds caused them to welcome Jesus with a triumphal entry (xii 12–16); and stress is laid on the public character of the miracle and the many independent witnesses of it (xii 17, 18).

The story of the Raising of Lazarus was a favourite with the early Christians. The quaint mummy-like figure of Lazarus in the arched door of his tomb is familiar to every student of Christian Art. It was an embodiment of the hope of the Resurrection. But where are we to put the scene into the historical framework preserved by S. Mark? Can any answer be given, except 'there is no room'? If the events occurred as told in the Fourth Gospel, if they were as public as the Fourth Evangelist insists, so fraught with influence upon the action both of friends and foes, they could not have been unknown to a well-informed personage like

'Mark,' nor could he have had any reason for suppressing a narrative at once so public and so edifying. It is true that 'Mark' does not record the Lord's Prayer or many of the most noteworthy sayings of Jesus, but these were not public events like the Raising of Lazarus. Is it possible that anyone who reads the continuous and detailed story of Mark from the Transfiguration to the Entry into Jerusalem can interpolate into it the tale of Lazarus and the notable sensation which we are assured that it produced? Must not the answer be, that Mark is silent about the Raising of Lazarus because he did not know of it? And if he did not know of it, can we believe that, as a matter of fact, it ever occurred? For all its dramatic setting it is, I am persuaded, impossible to regard the story of the Raising of Lazarus as a narrative of historical events.

With this negative conclusion in our minds let us go on to compare other portions of the Fourth Gospel with Mark. The Crucifixion and Resurrection do not present material differences of the order with which we are dealing. There are many variations and discrepancies, but all the Gospels agree in the main facts, as may be realised by comparing them with the apocryphal *Acts of John*. But in other parts of the Gospel story the differences are acute.

The common Christian tradition, attested by S. Paul as well as by the Synoptists, asserts that our Lord at the final meal before His arrest instituted the rite that became the Eucharist. The origin of the Christian rite of the common Sacramental meal must have been known to every moderately instructed Christian, certainly to every one who would undertake to write an account of our Lord's life on earth, and we cannot suppose the Fourth Evangelist to have been ignorant of it. When, therefore, we find him writing an elaborate account of this last meal, including the announcement of the impending betrayal, in which nevertheless there is no mention of the epoch-making words of Institution, we can only regard his silence as deliberate. He must have deliberately left out this exceedingly important incident; and thereby, so far as the mere narrative of facts is concerned, he creates a false impression of the scene. However this may be, it is not for want of sympathy with high Sacramental doctrine. In Joh vi, after the story of the Feeding of the Five Thousand, we read a long discourse of Jesus on this very subject. Jesus here says, 'I am the bread of life' (*v.* 35), and, 'Except ye eat the flesh of the Son of Man and drink His blood, ye have no life in you' (*v.* 53). It is true that a peculiar turn is given to these very strong expressions by the explanation made afterwards to the disciples that it is the spirit that gives life, and that it is the words of Jesus that are spirit and life (*v.* 63). But the Sacramental expressions are not otherwise qualified. It is evident that 'John' has transferred the Eucharistic teaching from the Last Supper to the earlier Galilean miracle.

This is something more than mere historical inaccuracy. It is a deliberate sacrifice of historical truth; and, as the Evangelist is a serious person in deadly earnest, we must conclude that he cared less for historical truth than for something else. To render justice to his work we must do more than demonstrate his untrustworthiness as a chronicler.

A somewhat similar result is obtained by considering the Fourth Evangelist's teaching about Baptism. The descent of the Holy Spirit upon our Lord at His baptism by John is the commencement of the Ministry according to S. Mark. By this act, according to some early theologians, such as Aphraates, He received from the Baptist the sacerdotal gift. But the Fourth Evangelist will have none of it. The scene at the Jordan is indeed recorded by him, and John testifies to the descent of the Spirit upon Jesus; but the central incident, the actual baptism of

Jesus by John is altogether left out (i 29–34). If the intention of the Evangelist had been to tell us what happened, if his intention had been to make us believe in Jesus because of what happened, such an omission would be nothing short of disingenuous. If we are to regard the Fourth Gospel as a narrative of events, we can only say that the writer has given a false impression of what occurred. It is not that the Evangelist disapproves of baptism: on the contrary, he tells us afterwards that the disciples of Jesus baptized their converts (iv 1, 2), and he gives us the conversation with Nicodemus, in which Jesus declares that except a man be born again he cannot enter into the Kingdom of God (iii 3 ff).[1]

It would be easy to go on to criticise the story of the Ministry as related in the Fourth Gospel, to point out the improbabilities of the narrative as it stands, and the continual discrepancies with the Synoptic story that it presents. But it is unnecessary to do so. These improbabilities and discrepancies lie on the surface, they are universally recognised; and those who defend the

[1] It is not quite certain that the actual mention of 'water' in Joh iii 5 is genuine. It appears to have been omitted by Justin Martyr, as is pointed out in Professor Lake's tract upon the 'Influence of Textual Criticism on the Exegesis of the N.T.' (Oxford, 1904). That the mention of the material element should be omitted in the discourse which deals with the doctrine underlying the rite is quite in the manner of the Fourth Evangelist.

Fourth Gospel do so in spite of these things, because of positive merits and excellences, not because the difficulties are denied. But there is one point which I must notice here, a matter far more grave than a faulty system of chronology or a slip in a geographical name. The most serious count against the Fourth Gospel, from the point of view of objective external history, is the attitude assigned to Jesus in His discussions with the 'Jews.' Taking the narratives as they stand, in the Synoptic Gospels the sympathy of the non-Christian reader naturally goes with Jesus against the Pharisees or the Sadducees. We feel that the adversaries of Jesus are narrow, unkind, unintelligent. To such an extent is this the case that recently protests have been raised by a distinguished and learned Jew, to the effect that the Synoptic Evangelists have misrepresented the teachings of the Rabbinical religion. But in the Fourth Gospel it is altogether different. Here I cannot but think that the natural sympathy of the non-Christian reader must go time after time with the Jews. There is an argumentativeness, a tendency to mystification, about the utterances of the Johannine Christ which, taken as the report of actual words spoken, is positively repellent. To heal on the Sabbath was considered by the Jews to be a breaking of the Sabbath. According to Mark, Jesus defends His action by such sayings as that the Sabbath was made for man, not man for the Sabbath; according to Matthew, He quotes Hosea to say that God desires mercy, and not sacrifice; according to Luke, He says that to loose on the Sabbath a bond by which Satan had bound a daughter of Abraham was even better, and therefore as lawful, as loosing a beast from the stall to take it to drink. Our sympathies are clearly here with Jesus against the unreasonable Jews. But in the Fourth Gospel, in similar circumstances, what words are put into our Lord's mouth? Why, He goes on to exasperate the Jews still further by a disquisition about the Father and the Son, asserting to His adversaries that whosoever did not honour the Son (*i.e.* Himself) did not honour the Father (v 23). On a similar occasion, when accused of 'bearing witness of himself,' He is made to say that He has two witnesses in His favour, viz. Himself and the Father (viii 17, 18). Can we wonder that the Jews replied, 'Where is thy Father?' It is quite inconceivable that the historical Jesus of the Synoptic Gospels could have argued and quibbled with opponents, as He is represented to have done in the Fourth Gospel. The only possible explanation is that the work is not history, but something else cast in an historical form.

From this point of view the question of the authorship of the Fourth Gospel is a matter of secondary importance. It is of the highest importance to ascertain the authorship and date of a chronicle, of a narrative of facts, because there the value of the work depends upon the nature of the traditions or sources to which the writer had access. But for a work of philosophy or philosophical history the qualifications required in the writer are mental, rather than local or temporal. We do not need to ask how near he stands to the events, but whether he sees them in their true proportion.

For we have not done with the Fourth Gospel when we have made up our minds that neither the narrative nor the discourses are to be regarded as history, as matters of past fact. The question remains why the Church adopted this Gospel into the New Testament Canon, when so many rivals were excluded. In the answer to this question lies, I believe, the reason which gives a permanent value to the work. It was not the prestige of an apostolic name that made it canonical, for the 'Gospel of Peter' was rejected. Great antiquity and respectful quotation by learned Church writers did not avail to include the 'Gospel according to the Hebrews,' nor did philosophical thought avail the document commonly called the 'Oxyrhynchus Logia.' What was it that the 'Gospel according to S. John' had, that these had not?

I believe the answer to be that the doctrine of the Person of Christ set forth in this Gospel expressed the general conviction of the Church adequately, while the Gospels which failed to become canonical failed mainly because the doctrine of the Person of Christ which they contained failed to satisfy the requirements of the Church. The Christ of the Fourth Gospel is not the Christ of history, but the Christ of Christian experience. Like S. Paul, the Fourth Evangelist did not care to know 'Christ after the flesh,' because he saw both his Lord and his Lord's adversaries *sub specie aeternitatis*.

It is because the Evangelist views the Gospel history from this subjective standpoint, that he allows himself such freedom in remodelling the external events. In the Dean of Westminster's words: "The old disciple needs no documents. . . . The whole is present in his memory, shaped by years of reflection, illuminated by the experience of a lifetime. He knows the Christ far better now than he knew Him in Galilee or Jerusalem half a century before."[1] The

[1] J. A. Robinson, *The Study of the Gospels*, p. 148.

adversaries of Jesus have become his own doubts and unfaithful oppositions; the questioners of Jesus, such as 'Nicodemus' or 'the Woman of Samaria,' are his own questions, his own ignorances, which receive their solution at the hands of the Lord who has come with His Father to make an abode with him. He knows his Lord to be true, and the knowledge of Him to be Life eternal; and therefore all opposition, however specious, is unjustifiable and blind. The Son of God is a Lamp to him who beholds, a Mirror to him who perceives, a Door to him who knocks, a Way to the wayfarer. The true meaning of life could never have been revealed to man, if Jesus had not been sent as the Word from the Father. Who He was could only be seen after He had gone away; what He had been seen to be was nothing in comparison with the underlying reality. It was no mere man whom the Evangelist was preaching, but God unchangeable, God invincible, God higher than all authority and all power, and elder and mightier than all angels and creatures that are spoken of, and than all ages. If those who heard would abide in this, and in this be builded up, they would possess their soul indestructible.[1]

[1] See *Acta Ioannis*, ed. Bonnet, $198^{11ff\ 17f\ 20f}$, 202^{23ff} (or James, *Apocrypha Anecdota*, 12^{18-21}, $14^{5f\ 10f}$, 24^{5ff}, from whom I have adapted the English translation).

It is all a different order of thought from the Synoptic Gospels or objective history.

The substance of the last few sentences has been picked out of the work which above all other surviving fragments of early Christian literature has the closest similarity with the peculiar elements of the Fourth Gospel. This work is the apocryphal *Acts of John*, or rather, I should say, the doctrinal section of that unequal piece of writing. But near as the 'Gospel of John' and the 'Acts of John' are in many ways, their differences are also fundamental, and it is in great part because of these differences that the 'Acts of John' was condemned and forgotten, while the 'Gospel of John' survived to be the spiritual food of many generations.

For although the Fourth Evangelist is no chronicler of events, although his Christ is the *Logos*, the Word of God, that to know is eternal life, yet he firmly holds all the while that this Christ was manifested in time as a human being, a real man of flesh and blood, who really felt as we feel, and above all really suffered and really died, before He rose again from the dead. As we have seen, the Evangelist is careless of events; but to him the Death of Jesus on the Cross was not a mere event, but a something essential, a thing which really came to pass in the eternal order of things. The apocryphal 'Acts of John' sets forth the doctrine that the Crucifixion was a delusion, the Jews gather round the Cross and mock, but Christ is not really there; the 'Gospel of Peter' tells us that Christ felt no pain, and apparently His Spirit is somehow caught up at the last. By a true instinct this specious teaching was rejected by the Church of the second century. The Passion of Jesus Christ must be real, not a stage-play; and if it was to be real, Jesus Christ must have been a real man.

In no early Christian document is the real humanity of Jesus so emphasised as in the Fourth Gospel. That Jesus was a real man is an obvious inference from the Synoptic narrative, but in the Fourth Gospel it is a dogma. It is the Fourth Gospel which tells us that Jesus was tired and asked for water to drink (Joh iv 6, 7), and that He wept at the tomb of Lazarus (xi 35). If we ask what proof there is that Jesus really suffered on the Cross, the answer is ready that the Fourth Gospel declares Him to have said, 'I thirst' (xix 28). Furthermore, we are told, with the most solemn protestations of accuracy to be found in the whole work, that the corpse of Jesus presented a truly human appearance (xix 34, 35).[1] It was no phantom.

[1] According to 1 Joh v 6–8 the living personality has in it three elements, viz. spirit, water, blood. From the 'water' we are

This is the element which differentiates the Jesus of the Fourth Gospel from the Jesus of Gnostic speculation. It was the Fourth Gospel which pointed out the *via media* along which alone the Church could walk. On the one hand, the Church was not prepared to surrender historical reality to a philosophical speculation. The devotion of the first disciples had been kindled by Jesus of Nazareth. It was the belief that their dead Friend had become alive again, and that He had really appeared to them alive after death, which gave the earliest Christians the will and the power to combine on earth into a Society and afforded them enduring hope for the future. It was essential that the Living Christ, whom they continued to serve and to wait for, should have been a real man who had lived and died. Otherwise He was no Firstfruits of the human race, but another species altogether. On the other hand, Christianity is essentially Monotheistic, and it was so all the more consciously and passionately while the whole world outside was given over to the heathen cults and the

begotten, by the 'blood' we are sustained, and the 'spirit' or breath is the immaterial element that enters at birth and leaves at death. The spirit quitted Jesus when He died (Joh xix 30), leaving behind the water and blood of a human body, the existence of which was demonstrated to the onlookers by the spear-thrust of the soldier.

deified Emperor. Whatever else Jesus Christ might be, the Church refused to make Him a demigod. Here the various forms of speculation which we generally denominate 'Gnostic' were ready with terms and conceptions that should bridge the gulf. More than one school of thought, both Jewish and Greek, were teaching that the Word which proclaimed the truth to man was in the beginning with God and was Itself Divine, that It would come or had come to those fitted to receive it. But the Fourth Evangelist alone makes this Word become an actual human being, one who really lived on earth and died under torture as other men would have died in similar circumstances. Whether this conception is really credible to us or not, it is a matter of history that it forms the central idea of the Fourth Evangelist's theology. I believe that it was by virtue of this central idea that the Fourth Gospel won its way to a position of permanent authority in the Christian Church.

I cannot hope to persuade you all to accept the view of the Fourth Gospel which I have put before you. It leaves very grave difficulties unsolved. But I am confident that, speaking generally, some theory of this kind is really forced upon us. Especially am I sure that we shall never do justice to this Gospel, so long as we try to treat it as a narrative of events that were seen and heard of men. It is not a competitor with the Synoptic Gospels.

But, you will say, what becomes of the truth of the Gospel? If neither the words nor the acts of Christ as recorded in the Fourth Gospel belong to the historical Jesus of Nazareth, what, then, is left that has any claim to be called history? There is justice in this criticism, unless we can shew that something is left. A Gospel must be more than a satisfactory piece of theology about our Lord. We require that it should transmit to us something that is really from Him. Can the Fourth Gospel still do this?

What is left is the ideas, the thoughts on God and man around which the Gospel moves. Let us once for all fully recognise that the style and manner of the words put into our Lord's mouth no more represent His historical style and manner than Hellenistic Greek sounds to the ear like Aramaic. 'They are from first to last a part of the author's self,' says Dr. Sanday.[1] The Sayings in the Fourth Gospel are all couched in the peculiar dialect of the Evangelist, and to make them sound like the words of Jesus preserved in the Synoptic Gospels, the style and manner of which, as we have reason to believe,

[1] *Criticism of the Fourth Gospel*, p. 169.

do to some extent reproduce the style and manner of the historical Jesus, we should need to change and to paraphrase. But the ideas are the ideas which animate the Sayings in the Synoptic Gospels. At least, they are often the same ideas, often similar ideas; so that when here and there we find a wholly new idea we have some reason to treat with respect its claim to represent the teaching of Jesus Christ.

Let me give as an instance of what I mean the words of Christ about healing on the Sabbath (Joh v 17 ff). I have already referred to this story. Let us attempt to look all the facts in the face without shrinking, and I think you will find in the end that the peculiar methods of the Fourth Evangelist have really preserved for us something well worth keeping. But the Evangelist has been very far indeed from giving us a mechanical transcript of a scene in our Lord's career. To begin with, we can hardly suppose that the story of the miracle is to be taken as it stands. Apart from the preliminary difficulty of accounting for the presence of Jesus at this time in Jerusalem, it must be observed that the man who had been thirty and eight years in his infirmity is a singularly unsympathetic figure. The cripple at Lystra had faith to be healed (Acts xiv 9), the man with the withered hand in S. Mark is not characterised at all, but this person is just sketched sufficiently to make us dislike him if we think of him as a real human being: 'Sin no more,' says Jesus to him at last, 'lest a worse thing come to thee.' Then again, as I have already observed, the actual words which the Evangelist ascribes to our Lord when the Jews 'persecute' Him for healing on the Sabbath were calculated rather to exasperate than either to appease or instruct them. 'Amen, amen, I say unto you, the Son can do nothing of himself, but what he seeth the Father doing: for what things soever he doeth, these the Son also doeth in like manner. For the Father loveth the Son, and sheweth him all things that himself doeth: and greater works than these will he shew him, that ye may marvel. . . . Marvel not at this: for the hour cometh, in which all they that are in the tombs shall hear his voice, and shall come forth; they that have done good, unto the resurrection of life; and they that have done ill, unto the resurrection of judgement'—and so forth, for the rest of the chapter.

Now, if we look at the form and manner of these words, it is, I am convinced, impossible for one moment to imagine that they can represent an accurate account of any man's defence of himself after outraging the religious susceptibilities of powerful adversaries. It is not in the least the kind of thing which a phonograph would have reported. But are we therefore to conclude that the whole of this chapter out of the Fourth Gospel has no connexion with history at all? Let me put before you something on the other side.

First of all, the subject of the dispute between our Lord and these 'Jews' is historical. It is primarily concerned with the observance of the Jewish Sabbath. This may seem a small thing, but it is a sign that the subject-matter of the Fourth Gospel is not quite so far removed from history as seems to be the case at the first glance. For I do not think the Evangelist is seriously interested in the Jewish Controversy: indeed, this appears from the way in which the conversation shifts from the question of the Sabbath to the question of the office of the Son of God. The general object of the Evangelist in putting this conversation before his readers is to give them the true doctrine about Jesus as the Son of the Eternal Father, not to put them right about Sabbath observance. But just as his doctrine was that the Eternal Son had become incarnate as a particular human being in Judæa, so he knows that the doctrine about the Son and His office must start from real Jewish disputes; in other words, that the doctrine is to be in touch, so to speak, with historical conditions.

And the actual doctrine itself, the principle from which it starts, as distinct from the mere wording of it—is not this also in harmony with what we know otherwise of Jesus? 'My Father worketh even until now, and I work.' Of course we here feel at once the peculiar style of the Fourth Evangelist. But the line of argument, apart from its expression, not only has parallels in the Synoptic Gospels: it exactly reiterates our Lord's doctrine of right and wrong as opposed to the traditionalism of the Scribes. The essential difference between Jesus and the Scribes, between the religion of Jesus and the religion of His adversaries, was that He claimed to know God and God's Will directly, while they were dependent on the tradition of the elders, something that had been taught and learnt. That is what He means when He says that no one knew or knows the Father except the Son:[1] the others only knew the Father through the Word of God.

It was because Jesus knew the Father directly, and not only through the Old Testament, that He was free to judge the religion of the Old Testament by the light of the Father's works; in

[1] Matt xi 27; Lk x 22.

other words, by the light of Nature. 'My Father worketh even until now'—this very Sabbath on which we are disputing—surely this means that the laws of Nature and of Right and Wrong do not observe the Sabbath. The same Father whom Jesus saw making His sun to shine on the evil and on the good, made His sun shine equally on the Sabbath and on the week-day. If all things were delivered unto Jesus by the Father, then all things told Him of the Father, things secular as well as things conventionally sacred.

But is this the sort of reasoning we should expect to get from the author of the Prologue to the Fourth Gospel, if he were merely allegorizing out of his inner consciousness? Is it not more natural to suppose that such a way of thinking about the Sabbath came to him from without rather than from within, by memory or tradition rather than by imagination? The wording is the wording of the Evangelist, he has made it all his own before he gives it back to the world, but the leading thought is the subject and source of his theology, not a product of it.

When the Evangelist goes a little further we are able to see what was really working in his mind, why he thinks it worth while to revive past disputes about the Jewish Sabbath. 'The dead shall hear the voice of the Son of Man: . . . the hour cometh, in which all that are in the tombs shall hear his voice and shall come forth; they that have done good, unto the resurrection of life, and they that have done ill, unto the resurrection of judgement.' We see now why the man who had been thirty and eight years in his infirmity is made so unsympathetic. He is a type of those lying still in their tombs who are to hear the voice of the Son of Man, some of whom only awake to receive their due judgement of condemnation. 'Sin no more,' it is said to him, 'lest a worse thing come to thee.' The Evangelist knew that a crisis in our Lord's life had arisen out of the healing of a man on the Jewish Sabbath; he knew that our Lord had claimed to know the will of His Father in Heaven, and in virtue of that knowledge to dispense with the precepts of the written Law, when they clashed with what He knew directly to be the will of God. All the rest is the Evangelist's setting of the story; at least, I cannot regard it as anything else.

And how different is the picture of the Last Day here presented from what we find in the Synoptic Gospels, in Mk xiii and the parallels in Matthew and Luke! That is depicted as a judgement on the Living, this in the Fourth

Gospel is a judgement on the Dead. In the Synoptic Gospels the disciples are to watch for the signs of the End: 'When these things begin to come to pass, look up, and lift up your heads; because your redemption draweth nigh.' But here, in the Fourth Gospel, they can no longer watch. They are in the tombs, waiting to be aroused by the voice of the Judge.

Thus we come very near to one of the great objects of the Evangelist, which is the deliberate substitution of other ideals for the expected coming of the Messiah on the clouds of heaven. Let me here quote what has been so admirably said on this subject by Dr. Inge:[1] "The Synoptic Gospels, though they doubtless give us a more accurate picture of the outward circumstances of our Lord's ministry, and of the manner and style of his teaching, are pervaded by the idea of the Messianic Kingdom. To the majority of the first and second generations of Christians, the Church was regarded as merely a stop-gap till the Kingdom of God should come. Christ was to return in a few years upon the clouds of heaven to inaugurate the new theocratic kingdom. In correspondence

[1] From a Paper published in the *Proceedings of the Oxford Society of Historical Theology for 1903–4*, pp. 58–68: see now (1911) Professor Inge's Essay on the Theology of the Fourth Gospel in *Cambridge Biblical Essays*, especially pp. 255–257, 259.

with these ideas, a kind of legend grew up, affecting not only the hopes of the future, but the traditions of our Lord's ministry. The demand for evidence of the Messiahship, becoming every year more urgent, was met by heightening the colours of the picture, and modifying those portions of the narrative which ascribed human limitations to Jesus. This process may be seen at work if we compare S. Matthew with S. Mark. Christianity was in some danger of being so closely identified with apocalyptic Messianic dreams that it would have perished when these hopes proved illusory" (pp. 58, 59). "The [Fourth] evangelist wishes to lay a surer foundation, underpinning the fabric which at present rested on the crumbling foundations of thaumaturgic superstition and Chiliastic or Messianic dreams" (p. 65).

In the passage we have been considering we have the link between the eschatological teaching of the Fourth Gospel and that of the Synoptic Gospels. Elsewhere in the Fourth Gospel the doctrine is brought forward that Eternal Life is a condition to be realised here and now through Christ. Jesus is not merely the future Judge; according to the Fourth Gospel He *is* the Resurrection (xi 25), and Eternal Life is to know God and Jesus Christ, whom God had sent (xvii 3).

No one is fully alive who is not in touch with the Father of all (x 10), and Jesus is the Way to the Father (xiv 6). This is only the theological presentment of what the Synoptic Gospels shew us in the movement of history. If Jesus was right in setting aside the Law of God without any other authority than what He derived from His own insight, then He was the Word of God embodied in a Man instead of in a Book. For those who believed on the Christ, His word was God's word, He and the Father were one (x 30). To others also the Word of God had come in the past, and these also were called in Scripture 'Gods' (x 35), but to Jesus alone was given the full measure of the Spirit, and this Spirit was now abiding among His followers and reminding them of what Jesus had said to them (xiv 26). I do not think the Evangelist cared to distinguish between the development of doctrine and historical reminiscence. What I think he did see was the distinction between the doctrines of Christianity and the historical occasions or events with which they were associated in the minds of the ordinary believers. He saw the danger of associating too closely the acts and doctrines of the Christian community with particular events in the career of Jesus on earth. Moreover, the Church had already existed for two generations: even if the Lord were to appear at once, the majority of Christians would have been among the dead. Christianity, therefore, could not be a mere prelude to the Second Coming; it must be a thing timeless, eternal, a state of mind.

Much of this way of thinking is to be found, more or less, in the Alexandrian Jewish philosopher Philo. Philo saw in the Pentateuch a mirror of Divine Wisdom, an embodiment of the Word of the unknowable God. What seems to be narrative is really a description of the unchangeable principles of the moral and spiritual world. The Four Rivers of Paradise are the Four chief Virtues, Egypt is the sensuous body, Rebekah is Perseverance, and much more to the same effect. To quote Mr. Inge again (p. 66): "Philo shows an utter indifference to chronology and historical fact. . . . Every historical event is only valuable as symbolizing some eternal, unchanging truth. . . . The notions of *personality* and of a *real process in time* are completely absent from Philo. Nothing ever really happens in this philosophy."

Nothing, we may add, ever really happens in the world as conceived in the Stoic philosophy. All change was an illusion, there was no development, and therefore history and the truth of history was a thing indifferent. The one essential distinction between these views and that of the Fourth Gospel was the belief in the Incarnation of the Divine Nature in time and place, leading up to the Passion of Christ. That event alone was real; therefore it could not be allegorized or altered. By its existence it restored the idea of real progression and development into the Cosmos. Elsewhere, even in the rest of the Gospel story, the truest picture seemed to the Evangelist to be that which most clearly taught essential doctrines. This, at least, is the only way in which I can picture to myself the Evangelist's procedure.

The line of thought which I have tried to put before you to-day makes the personality of the Evangelist a matter of less importance than it becomes when we attempt to read the Fourth Gospel in order to collect facts about the events of the Ministry. But I still think that many of the old arguments which tended to prove that he had been a Jew of Jerusalem have never been satisfactorily disposed of. Such simple statements as those of Joh x 22, 23 ('It was the Feast of the Dedication at Jerusalem; it was winter weather, and Jesus was walking in Solomon's Porch') are difficult to explain on any other hypothesis. At least the person who supplied the information in the text quoted must have had a real knowledge of the topography of Jerusalem and of the Jewish Calendar.[1]

There is also some evidence which seems to shew that this Jew of Jerusalem, before he became a Christian, must have belonged to the Sadducean party, to have been indeed himself a Priest. The Evangelist Matthew, who must have known something about Jewish parties, finds occasion to bring in the Sadducees by name some half-dozen times, and they are mentioned several times in the Acts. The Fourth Evangelist, though he has so much to say about Jerusalem, does not mention the name. Very likely he regarded it rather as a nickname than a real appellation. According to S. Luke,[2] 'the Sadducees say there is no resurrection, neither angel, nor spirit': the author of the Fourth Gospel writes, of course, from the Christian standpoint, but some of his remarks illustrate curiously the statement in Acts. He believes in these now, no doubt, in and through the Christian revelation, but not otherwise. The Spirit of God descended and rested upon Jesus, but, speaking generally, 'Spirit was not yet' (Joh vii 39) during the Ministry of our Lord: it is given for the first time to the disciples after the

[1] It must not be forgotten that at the time when the Gospel was published the Temple was in ruins and the Feasts had come to an end.

[2] Acts xxiii 8.

resurrection (Joh xx 22). How different is the view which appears in the Gospel of Luke, where Elisabeth and Zacharias, and others besides, are filled with a Holy Spirit! Then again, according to Matthew an angel of the Lord appears to Joseph in a dream, and to Zacharias in the Temple according to Luke. Angels play a very different part in the Fourth Gospel. Two 'angels' are seen sitting in the empty Tomb on the morning of the Resurrection by Mary Magdalene: this is part of the Christian tradition, which the Evangelist accepted, and it is foreshadowed in the saying of Jesus to Nathanael that he shall see the angels of God ascending and descending on the Son of Man, a marvel which is expressly set forth as something exceptionally great (Joh i 51). It was not until the resurrection of the incarnate Word of God that angels were seen by mortal eye. Therefore, when the Voice came from Heaven (Joh xii 28), it is the ignorant multitude, not the Evangelist in his own person, who suppose that an angel had spoken to Jesus.

And the same kind of doctrine is taught about the Resurrection itself. It is 'in Christ,' and in Christ alone. The Pharisees believed in a resurrection; it was indeed the popular belief among the Jewish people. Martha in the midst of her grief is sure that her brother will rise again in the resurrection at the last day (Joh xi 24). I do not think the Evangelist believed in that doctrine apart from his Christianity. Jesus replies to Martha, '*I* am the Resurrection.' In Him, according to the Fourth Evangelist, is Life; by this formula he can express both his new belief in the Christian resurrection and his old disbelief in the Pharisaic resurrection. 'It shall be recompensed to thee in the resurrection of the just' (Lk xiv 14); '*I* will raise him up in the last day' (Joh vi 40):[1] these familiar phrases shew by contrast the difference of conception between the view of a Christianised Sadducee and his brethren. In the sentence from S. Luke the resurrection is viewed as an event which will occur in the providentially ordered nature of things: it is as natural as the Last Day itself. In the sentence from the Fourth Gospel it is part of the new Christian dispensation.

These considerations tend to explain how the disciple who 'wrote' the Fourth Gospel[2] could describe himself as 'known unto the high priest' (Joh xviii 15). They also throw light upon the very curious testimony of Polycrates, bishop of Ephesus, who wrote a letter to Victor of Rome

[1] In the Greek the pronoun is very emphatic: *ἀναστήσω αὐτὸν ἐγὼ τῇ ἐσχάτῃ ἡμέρᾳ.*

[2] Joh xxi 24.

about 190 AD, he—Polycrates—being then a Christian of at least 65 years' standing, in order to defend the Asian custom of keeping Easter by the day of the month, regardless of whether it fell on Sunday or not. 'Throughout Asia,' he says (Eusebius, *HE* v 24), 'great Luminaries have gone to their rest, which will rise on the day of the Lord's Coming, when He cometh with glory from heaven, and shall search out all the Saints, namely, Philip, one of the Twelve Apostles, who sleeps in Hierapolis, and two of his daughters, who died virgins in old age; and the other daughter, who lived in a Holy Spirit, rests in Ephesus; and John too, who leaned on the Lord's breast, who had been a priest and worn the High Priest's mitre,[1] both Witness[2] and Teacher—he sleeps in Ephesus. And Polycarp, too, in Smyrna, both bishop and martyr.' Polycrates then goes on to name other Saints of the Asian Churches, to whose practice he appeals. Here it is definitely implied that the Fourth Evangelist was a member of one of the chief priestly families.

It should be noted that Polycrates, like all the other early witnesses from Asia, avoids calling the Evangelist 'John the son of Zebedee,' or 'John the Apostle.' But, you will say, is not tradition unanimous in identifying this John of Asia, who

[1] τὸ πέταλον. [2] Or, 'martyr': the Greek μάρτυς is ambiguous.

died a natural death in his old age, with John the son of Zebedee? The answer is, that tradition is not quite unanimous, and that there still remain traces of a different tradition which makes the son of Zebedee die a martyr's death at the hands of the Jews.

In a 7th or 8th century epitome, probably based on the Chronicle of Philip of Side (about 430 AD), it is stated that 'Papias in his second book says that John the Divine and James his brother were slain by Jews.'[1] And this statement occurs again with verbal variations in the oldest MS of the Chronicle of George the Monk, a writer of the 9th century. The statement is historically of importance, not because these late chroniclers had independent knowledge of the facts, but because they base their information on Papias, bishop of Hierapolis about 160 AD, who wrote an 'Exposition of the Oracles of the Lord' in five books.

A poor basis, you will say, upon which to overthrow the universal tradition of the Catholic Church. Let me therefore conclude by pointing out that there is one piece of Catholic tradition, familiar to every one, which points in the same

[1] 'De Boor's Fragment,' as it is generally called from its discoverer, was first published in *Texte und Untersuchungen* v 2, p. 170, in 1888.

direction. On the 25th of December the Church celebrates the birthday of our Lord. The birthdays of Martyrs, for purposes of commemoration, are the days of their martyrdom. It is therefore very right and proper that the commemoration of S. Stephen, the first martyr, should be fixed upon the 26th of December, the day after Christmas Day. The next day, as we all know, is S. John's day—S. John the Apostle, not S. John the Baptist. What is the reason for this? The full answer is, of course, a long story, but it will be enough here to say that we can trace back the beginnings of our Calendar to the beginning of the 6th century in the West, and to the beginning of the 5th century in the East. In a Calendar of Carthage, drawn up shortly after 505 AD, we read:

Dec. 25, commemoration of our Lord Jesus Christ, the Son of God.

Dec. 26, commemoration of S. Stephen, the first Martyr.

Dec. 27, commemoration of S. John Baptist, and of James the Apostle, whom (*quem*) Herod slew.

Here we have the same series of names as in our Calendar, together with a commemoration of James the brother of John, but John the Apostle has been turned into John the Baptist. The same Carthaginian Calendar gives June 24 for the Baptist's commemoration, so that he is commemorated twice in this list, and John the Apostle not at all.

Still older and more weighty is the testimony of the ancient Syriac Calendar of the Church of Edessa. The venerable MS in which this Calendar is preserved is dated 411 AD, and the Calendar itself may be a generation older. It begins with December 26 thus:

> The names of our lords the martyrs and victors, and their days on which they gained their crowns.
>
> In the month Kanun the first [*i.e.* December].
>
> On the 26th, the first martyr, at Jerusalem, Stephen the apostle, the head of the martyrs.
>
> On the 27th, John and James, the apostles, at Jerusalem.

Then follows a commemoration of Paul and of Simon Kephas, 'the head of the apostles of our Lord.' This oldest Martyrology gives a clear answer to our question, why we commemorate John the son of Zebedee the next day to S. Stephen. We really commemorate him with his brother as martyrs. The Church tradition, therefore, when we look into it, attests the statement ascribed to Papias, and thereby strengthens the cause of those who distinguish between John of Ephesus, to whom we owe the Fourth Gospel, and the Apostle John the son of Zebedee. As Dr. Sanday suggests in his recent book on the Fourth Gospel (p. 98), the 'disciple whom Jesus loved' may have been no more than a youth when our Lord lived on earth and was crucified.

Of this at least I am quite certain: the Fourth Gospel is the work of one to whom belief in Jesus Christ was not a new external condition, impressed upon him from without, after his mind had already acquired its individual characteristics. He had long been conscious, we may be sure, of the presence of the Paraclete within him, guiding him into all truth as to the inner meaning of the life and light which came into the world when the Word of God was manifested, not perhaps without some admixture of ancestral disdain for the materialistic superstition of the masses, both of believers and unbelievers. And now in his old age, when the popular expectations had proved false, as he knew they would, and the Antichrist that was to come and set up his impious kingdom a little before the End had not after all made his appearance, he finds himself confronted by new dangers from the other side. Other thinkers, more spiritual (as they would consider) than he, are saying that the Son of God was not a real man at all, for flesh and blood cannot inherit the Kingdom of God. This to the Evangelist was the greatest error: to deny the coming of Jesus Christ in the flesh was the doctrine of Antichrist.

The Fourth Gospel is written to prove the reality of Jesus Christ. But the Evangelist was no historian: ideas, not events, were to him the true realities, and if we go to his work to learn the course of events we shall only be disappointed in our search.

VIII.

THE GOSPEL CANON.

THE actual process by which our Four Gospels arrived at their present rank of pre-eminence is quite obscure. From about 170 AD onwards the Gospel Canon enjoys practically unchallenged supremacy, as we see from Tatian's Harmony, from the document known as the Muratorian Canon, and from S. Irenæus. Somewhat earlier than Tatian must be placed an interpolated edition of the Four Gospels, which seems to have been set forth in Rome, and from which the more important 'Western Interpolations' in Greek and Latin Biblical MSS are ultimately derived. This brings us back to about 150; but the literary history of our Gospels during the first half of the second century is unknown. Justin Martyr doubtless used all the Four in Rome about the middle of the century, and Marcion certainly used Luke about 130–140. Earlier still are the allusions which indicate a use of Matthew by S. Ignatius. But there is nothing to shew that Marcion was acquainted with any other of the Canonical Gospels than Luke, and very little to shew that S. Ignatius used any other Canonical Gospel than Matthew; while the verbal inaccuracy of Justin's quotations suggests that even in his day the 'Memoirs of the Apostles' had hardly yet taken their place beside the Law and the Prophets as part of the written Word of God. At the same time, Trypho, Justin's Jewish opponent, is quite aware that the way to become acquainted with Christian doctrine is to read what is written ἐν τῷ λεγομένῳ εὐαγγελίῳ (*Tryph.* § 10). Thus 'The Gospel' has already become the name of a Book.

We have really to distinguish three stages in the process by which the Gospel Canon was formed. Of the 'many who took in hand' to write of Jesus Christ, the Four Gospels alone remained in favour. The rest either failed altogether to attract, or were discovered to teach heresy. There is first the stage in which 'the Gospel' changed its meaning from the announcement of the Kingdom of God to a narrative, or a set of narratives, about Jesus Christ. Then there is the stage in which our Four Gospels won their way to recognition. Lastly, there is the stage in which these Four attained full and exclusive canonicity. The final stage was thus one of exclusion.

Certain 'Gospels' had been adopted locally, such as the 'Gospel of Peter' at Rhossus, near Antioch, but one by one these unauthorised works were suppressed. On the other hand, the attempt made by Tatian to combine the unrejected Four into a single account failed everywhere, except in the still unconsolidated Syriac-speaking community of Edessa. Whether the Church made the ideally best choice from the point of view of the modern historical investigator is a matter that cannot be scientifically demonstrated, for the simple reason that the rivals of the canonical Four have not survived in full. But the abiding interest which each and all of the Four have excited during eighteen centuries is enough to shew that the Church chose well. And it should not be forgotten that those of the non-canonical Gospels, which we know enough of to pass judgement upon, shew a sensible inferiority. Marcion's Gospel is in every way inferior to Luke, and the Gospel of Peter is inferior to either of the Synoptic accounts of the Passion. It is, in fact, because the canonical Gospels paint such an eternally fascinating Portrait, that we welcome every scrap that may claim to give another view, however inadequate.

In one respect I venture to think the modern historical investigator is more fortunate than from general considerations he might have expected. We are indeed fortunate that the Gospel according to Mark should have been included in the official Canon. Many of the special ideas and tendencies of the First and the Third Evangelists are in close touch with the ideas and tendencies of second-century literature. I have tried to shew in the preceding Lecture that the theology of the Fourth Gospel met the wants of the Church, that it pointed out the way along which the conflicting currents of Christian thought and feeling might run together. In any case, the Fourth Gospel is unique. But it is difficult to understand what attraction was offered to Christians of the second century by the Gospel of Mark, which the Gospels according to Matthew and Luke did not offer, either singly or taken together, in a more eminent degree. Probably its traditional connexion with S. Peter may have had a determining share in recommending it, and the appeal of Irenæus to historical tradition against Gnostic theorizing may help us to understand how such an old-fashioned book as the Gospel of Mark, S. Peter's 'interpreter,' should have survived. It is, we find, very little quoted before it became part of the official fourfold Canon, that is, before the time of Irenæus, and it is certain that it ran a very serious risk of being forgotten altogether. As every one knows, the genuine text ends at Mk xvi 8, in the middle of a sentence describing the terrified departure of the women from the empty tomb. There is no reason to doubt that the Gospel went on to describe some of the appearances of Jesus to the disciples after the Resurrection. The narrative is incomplete as it stands, and it is much more likely that the mutilation was accidental than intentional. Had it been intentional, the break would never have been made where it is, at *ἐφοβοῦντο γὰρ* . . . : even the sentence is left incomplete. But all our MSS ultimately go back to this mutilated text; it is therefore evident that at one time no more than a single mutilated copy was in existence, or at least available. The work had dropped out of circulation, it had lost its public, and we can only guess at the reasons which led to its resuscitation.

The fact, however, remains. By its inclusion in the Canon we are to-day in possession of a document in warp and woof far more primitive than the Churches which adopted it. The fine instinct which reserved a place for the Gospel of Mark among the books of the New Testament shews the Catholic Church to have been wiser than her own writers, wiser than the heretics, wiser, finally, than most Biblical critics from S.

Augustine to Ferdinand Christian Baur. It is only in the last half-century that scholars have come to recognise the pre-eminent historical value of that Gospel which once survived only in a single tattered copy.

It may be convenient here to give a short

Chronological Summary.

From what has been said in the foregoing Lectures, it will be evident that no very definite date can be assigned to any of the Gospels, except S. Luke's. But we may distinguish four periods of 40 years each, reckoning from the Crucifixion.

I. 30–70 AD. Oral Period. No written 'Gospel' appears during this period, nor any formal shaping of the Gospel history as a whole. S. Paul's accounts of the Lord's Supper (1 Cor xi 23 ff) and of the Resurrection (1 Cor xv 3 ff) do not appear to have any *literary* connexion with what we read in our Gospels. To the end of this first Period we may assign the fly-sheet underlying Mk xiii (in Greek), and S. Matthew's Collection of Messianic Prophecies (in Hebrew).

II. 70–110 AD. Period of the writing of the Gospels.

Gospel of Mark, 70–80 AD.

" " Luke (and Acts), 100 AD.

Gospel of Matthew, 90–100 AD., in any case before 110 AD.

„ „ John, 100–110 AD.

III. 110–150 AD. Period of the catholic reception of the Gospels.

IV. 150–190 AD. Period of the canonization of the Gospels. By the end of this period the Idea of the Fourfold Gospel (*Iren.* 192) is fully established.

The Influence of the Gospels on the Church.

The fact that the Church came to accept the Four Gospels is a proof that each of these works satisfied in a general way the Church's requirements. Had it been otherwise, the Gospel in question would never have attained to canonicity. At the same time, it would be absurd to regard the Church's requirements as being in any way occupied with details; these the Church has learnt from what the Evangelists have supplied. The Church's picture of Jesus Christ is not unfairly summarised in the so-called Apostles' and Nicene Creeds; it is the written Gospels that have preserved for us the winning personality of the Son of Man.

The history of Christology is not that of a simple advance from an original unitarian psilanthropy to the ultimate recognition of the Deity of Christ. Naturally it took many generations of Christian thought to evolve a form of words which should satisfactorily define the exceptional Nature of the Founder of the new Religion in terms of current philosophical conceptions. But from the first there existed the sentiment of devotion, the temper of mind which was assured that no title was too high to give, no homage too high to pay, to the Son of God who had been sent from Heaven to overcome death and open the gates of everlasting life to those who believed on Him. For the first thirty years or so practically all Christians were converts: those who doubted how far the Message was true did not become Christians at all. And unless the extant literature gives a totally false impression of the general state of mind among Christians, the interest of the nascent Church was not in the least directed towards the past. In the words of the earliest written Christian document that we possess, the converts had "turned unto God from idols to serve a living and true God, and to wait for His Son from heaven, whom He raised from the dead, even Jesus who delivereth us from the wrath to come."[1] Those that had entered the Church by baptism were to set their minds on the things that are above, where

[1] 1 Thess i 9, 10.

Christ is, seated on the right hand of God. It was true that the Christians in consequence of their belief submitted to new rules of conduct, and that these rules consisted in great part of reminiscences of the words of the Lord Jesus who had taught 'sweet reasonableness' and longsuffering (*ἐπιείκειαν καὶ μακροθυμίαν*), rules such as: "pity, that ye may be pitied; forgive, that ye may be forgiven."[1] But the Gospel was not a formal Code, still less a Biography. No pictures of early Christianity have been conceived more fundamentally false, both to the spirit and the letter of historical fact, than those which represent S. Matthew or S. Peter as delivering catechetical lectures on the 'Life of Christ.'

The actual course of events was very different from what the first generation of believers had anticipated. The End, so confidently awaited, was not yet. One by one the Companions of the Ministry went to their graves, and when the cataclysm of the Jewish War broke up for ever the one community in which there could have been common first-hand knowledge of how our Lord had lived and moved among men, the great majority of Christians were Greek-speaking inhabitants of the Levantine cities, a population far removed in spirit and in culture from the pro-

[1] Clem. Rom. *ad Cor.* xiii.

vincial Judaism of Galilee. What wonder that Christianity began to mix with alien elements and to appear in forms which alarmed the more conservative believers?

A few words may be said here on the influence of S. Paul. To us, and to the whole Church for the last seventeen centuries, S. Paul is preeminently the writer of the Epistles. We, like the Church in general, recognise the wisdom that was given him, while at the same time we find in these Epistles 'some things hard to be understood, which the ignorant and unstable wrest, as they do also the other Scriptures, unto their own destruction.' The Epistles come to us as part of the sacred Canon; consequently they are studied, and careful study shews us that, strange and unfamiliar as is the whole world of thought in which they move, they are the product of a great mind occupied with extraordinary circumstances. Of course, to us the Epistles, or parts of them, are verbally familiar; but I feel sure that, if we had not so often heard them read and commented on, we should find great parts of them most incomprehensible on a casual hearing. To the careful student, as I said, they are documents of very high interest. The Epistle to the Galatians and the Second Epistle to the Corinthians give in the most lively and moving way the indignant self-defence of an intensely earnest and sincere religious innovator, withstanding absolutely alone in the midst of a heathen world the attacks of his co-religionists, themselves a mere sect of the isolated Jews. The adversaries of Paul are convincd that his doctrines are not only mistaken but absolutely anarchical, destructive of the ancient ordinances of religion. Yet in the First Epistle to the Corinthians, and elsewhere also where occasion offers, we see the destructive anarchist labouring, and labouring with fervour and practical good sense, to build up the infant communities which he had founded on the basis of a new morality, equally alive to the real claims of Freedom and of Order.

All this is profoundly interesting, profoundly instructive. But a good deal of what is best in the Pauline Epistles does not lie on the surface. They are in their outward form and in their whole manner of composition occasional pieces, the product of an age of transition. The Churches to which S. Paul wrote, and over whose development he watched with such anxious ardour, were neither in their formal theology nor their outward organisation so many early examples of the Catholic communities of later times. Nor were they simple colonies of converted Jews. Their interest to us historical students lies just in this, that they were something between—the first result of principles, so to speak, in the process of fashioning for themselves an appropriate embodiment. But for that very reason they presented little practical interest to the next generation.

As I said, S. Paul is to us pre-eminently the writer of the Epistles, the founder of 'Paulinism.' But this cannot be said of the portrait of Paul which we find in the Acts. If our only knowledge of the Apostle of the Gentiles were drawn from the Acts, we should not know that he ever wrote any Epistles, and we certainly should have had no idea of his style or manner of writing. This, as you all know, has often been used as an argument to prove the Acts to be unhistorical, on the assumption that the Letters, or some of them, are genuine. But I venture to think the true conclusion is that for a couple of generations after his death the memory of S. Paul the theologian faded away with the special set of circumstances that called his theology to the point of expression, and that what was remembered was S. Paul the missionary. What we find in the Acts is re-echoed by Clement of Rome, writing at the end of the first century AD, at the very time when I think the Acts was being published. It is the unwearied patience and steadfastness of S. Paul's missionary journeys that calls forth the mention of his name.[1]

The practical result effected by S. Paul's labours upon the development of Christianity lay, in a word, not in the adoption of Paulinism, but in the presence of his converts. The Church did not embrace S. Paul's theories as a whole. What one man could do he did, but it is not given to ordinary folk to stand against the world, and the Churches which he founded slipped back into more or less ordinary Jewish and Heathen notions about virtue and morals. S. Paul's strange and penetrating criticism of the true nature of Law and Grace, and his doctrine of that trust in God which can alone set a man in the right, is alien from the thought of second-century Church theology. We hear little about 'Justification by Faith' from the Fathers of the second century. But what remained was the steady pressure of the rank and file of the Church, now almost wholly Gentile and Levantine by race and by tradition.

Through S. Paul Christianity became distinct in fact as well as in theory from Judaism, and with the change of race came a change in the

[1] Clem. *ad Cor.* v. In chap. xlvii S. Clement refers very appositely to 1 Cor i 12, and it is evident that he had read the Epistle to the Romans. But there is no sign in S. Clement of a collection of Pauline Letters.

character of the popular belief. Christianity lost its racial colouring and atmosphere, and became more and more Greek, or rather, Greco-Roman. The Christians accepted, indeed, the Hebrew Scriptures in their Greek dress, but the Old Testament was no longer to them a national literature. It was a strange foreign book, full of riddles and mysteries. And, what is still more important for us now, the Messiah and the Kingdom of God ceased to be natural ideas. To say that Jesus was the Christ, the Anointed of God, ceased to have any real meaning except that of a profession of devotion. To the children of S. Paul's converts at Corinth and Ephesus the scenes of the life of our Lord, whether in Galilee or in Jerusalem, were events in a foreign world.

A picture of normal Church life about the end of the first century is to be found in the *Didache*. The 'Teaching of the Lord by the Twelve Apostles to the Gentiles,' as the document calls itself, was first printed in 1883. But the greater part had been, in one form or another, already known to scholars. In fact, a great part of the interest of the *Didache* lies in this, that it was so often altered and adapted to suit the changing requirements of the Church in different ages. It is extant in Latin as well as Greek, and a peculiar recension of parts of it is found in

Syriac and Ethiopic. Even in the earliest extant form it may be a second or third edition, revised to date and perhaps modified in some details to suit a particular community. But the general plan appears to be unaltered.

The 'Teaching' is a short manual designed to instruct the disciple how to lead the Christian Life. The Christian Life is grouped under three heads: Christian morality, Christian worship and organisation, and the Christian hope. It begins with morality, with instruction taken from the *Two Ways*, a Jewish ethical handbook adapted for Christian usage. The Christian is here taught to love God and his neighbour, to live uprightly and to abstain from vices and from the service of idols. Christian worship and ritual includes Baptism, Fasting, Prayer—the Lord's Prayer thrice daily,—and the Eucharist. After giving Eucharistic Blessings to be said over the Cup and the Bread and after the Meal,[1] the Teaching goes on to prescribe rules for the reception and treatment of the wandering 'prophets' and for the maintenance of the regular ministry. Finally, we have a chapter on the Second Coming of the Lord, which is still the consummation instantly to be expected. There are no directions given for the burial of the dead.

[1] *Did.* § 10, μετὰ τὸ ἐμπλησθῆναι.

Thus the *Didache* runs through the whole gamut of Christian economy: conduct, worship, organisation, all is provided for. Short as it is, the book is meant to be sufficient and comprehensive, at least in essentials; we can ascertain from it the main ideas of the compiler and of the community for which he wrote. We see that all prayer was offered to God through Christ;[1] life and immortality had been given to man through Christ;[2] the true prophet was to be received as Christ;[3] the Christian's conduct was to be what Christ had commanded.[4] But biographical interest in Christ is completely absent, even more completely absent than it is from the letters of S. Paul; for aught that appears in the *Didache*, Jesus of Nazareth might never have been crucified.

Naturally we must remember that the *Didache* is a formal handbook of Christian praxis, and as such represents the low-water mark of Christian feeling and speculation. But it shews us better than any other document the aspect of Christ's work which was most prominent to the average gentile Christian in the first century of the Church's existence. To such a one Christ was the παῖς θεοῦ, the messenger from God who had come down to earth with tidings of immortality

[1] *Did.* §§ 9, 10. [2] §§ 9, 10. [3] § 11. [4] §§ 8, 15.

and now was waiting till the appointed Day when He should appear in glory on the clouds of heaven. It is not surprising that to many a believer the melancholy story of Jesus of Nazareth was a stumblingblock, and that His sufferings were incredible.

All the more was this the case among those who had attempted to find an appropriate place for Jesus Christ in the various philosophical theories of the Universe, which thoughtful men had devised and were devising. In proportion as the idea of Monotheism had become widely spread, the gulf between God and man grew. God and man, the ultimate Divine Essence and the common matter of which we and the earth are composed, seemed increasingly incongruous. The people of Lycaonia might have been willing to believe that the Gods themselves should come down in the likeness of men, but they were old-fashioned folk in a country town. And even the Lycaonians in the story did not think that the Gods stood before them with human feelings and natures.[1]

Christian sentiment and learned speculation were thus alike ready to welcome what we call the Docetic heresy. Docetism is not the name

[1] Acts xiv 11, 15. There is an intentional contrast between *ὁμοιωθέντες ἀνθρώποις* and *ὁμοιοπαθεῖς ἐσμὲν ὑμῖν*.

of a sect. It is a theory of the person of Christ which takes many forms and which has entered into the theology of many schools of thought. The essential thing is that Jesus Christ was man only in appearance. Some, like the writer of the *Acts of John*, denied that our Lord had any material existence; He could be seen and heard, but the form and the voice differed on different occasions. Others were content to deny that He felt the pains of crucifixion; others, like Marcion, denied His birth. But all were alike in this, that they regarded Jesus as having been in no sense a real human being. It is a theory incredible, almost inconceivable, to us; but we have learnt to know Jesus Christ through the written Gospels.

The part played by Docetic theories of our Lord's nature and person had a determining influence upon the official preservation of the Gospel History. In the foregoing Lectures I have attempted to sketch what I conceive to be the literary origins of the several Gospels. The point that I wish here to re-emphasise is the private, individual, and unofficial character of the earlier documents. That S. Luke's Gospel was a private venture is sufficiently indicated by the Preface. That S. Mark's Gospel was so is sufficiently indicated by the narrow escape it ran of being lost altogether. The Gospel we call S. Matthew's has a more formal, authoritative tone, and it bears marks of a Palestinian origin; in other words, it comes from the one region where we have a right to expect independent reminiscences of the Master to have survived. It would have been no surprise if the Gospel according to Matthew had been different altogether from the others. Yet, as a matter of fact, it is in structure and in much of its wording and material based on Mark. Thus we learn that even in Palestine no regular effort had been made to hand down a summary of the outward events of our Lord's Ministry.[1]

To some pious Christians biographical accounts of the life and words of the Lord may very likely have seemed unnecessary and unspiritual. But the rise of Docetic theories gave these "memoirs of the Apostles" a new and theological value. This new condition of things is mirrored in the Ignatian Epistles. S. Ignatius was Bishop of Antioch, and his Epistles were written on his way to martyrdom in Rome at some date between 110 and 117 AD. To him the Gospel history was immensely important, because it

[1] The lost 'Gospel according to the Hebrews' seems to have been very similar in general plan to our Matthew, so that it also must have had its ultimate basis in our Second Gospel.

furnished the proof of the real humanity of Christ. If Christ were not really human, His sufferings were not real, really akin to human suffering; and if His sufferings were not real, why should Ignatius be willing to endure martyrdom (*Trall.* § 10)? An acquaintance with the human side of Jesus Christ was therefore necessary to Christianity. But to make the acquaintance of this human side a biography was indispensable.

S. Ignatius was "fully persuaded, as touching our Lord, that He is truly of the race of David according to the flesh, but Son of God by the Divine will and power, truly born of a virgin and baptized by John that 'all righteousness might be fulfilled' by Him, truly nailed up in the flesh for our sakes under Pontius Pilate and Herod the tetrarch"; and, further, that "after His resurrection He both ate with them and drank with them [the Apostles] as one in the flesh, though spiritually He was united with the Father" (*Smyrn.* §§ 1, 3). Even this short summary of Christological doctrine goes, as you will perceive, beyond any known *Credo* in its literary dependence on a biographical Gospel; for that Jesus was baptized by John, that all righteousness might be fulfilled by Him, is thoroughly characteristic of 'Matthew,' and, so far as we know, it is found in 'Matthew' alone of all the Gospels that ever were written.[1] With this agrees the circumstance that S. Ignatius uses several phrases, such as φυτεία πατρός, 'the Father's planting,' which indicate the literary use of the Gospel according to Matthew. It seems likely also that he had read the Fourth Gospel, and it is almost certain that he once quotes from an 'apocryphal' work called the Preaching of Peter (Κήρυγμα Πέτρου), a document which appears to have been a very early rival of the canonical Acts of the Apostles.

But we are not now concerned with the reconstruction of S. Ignatius's library: the important thing is that the most characteristic representative of the Catholic theology of the beginning of the second century tends to base his Doctrine of Christ on a Gospel which is biographical in form. This point of view was not at first accepted by all. The Law and the Prophets, as interpreted in the new light, seemed sufficient to some. "If I find it not in the charter (τὰ ἀρχεῖα, the 'archives,' *i.e.* the Old Testament), I believe it not in the Gospel," said the opponents of Ignatius, and when he said, "It is written," they answered, "That is the question" (*Smyrn.* § 8). But Ignatius had no doubt, and the Church was with him, that the Gospel record was necessary, as

[1] Matt iii 15.

the guarantee of the real humanity of Jesus Christ.

One point deserves special notice in passing. S. Ignatius is the earliest express witness to the belief that Jesus was born of a virgin. He is most emphatic in asserting this; but the importance of the doctrine for him is not that the miracle assures us that the man Jesus was Divine, but that the Christian's God was really born of woman (*Eph.* § 18).

The Church of Antioch, if we may judge from the Ignatian writings, took its knowledge of the Gospel history from our 'Matthew.' The Church in Pontus a little later, if we may judge from the heretic Marcion, who left it in AD 138, used our 'Luke.' When and where our Four Gospels were gathered together into a single *Corpus Evangelicum*, we do not know. Traces of this Corpus are first found in Rome about the middle of the second century, and indeed the conservative character of the early Roman Church makes it a little easier to understand how so ancient a document as the Gospel of Mark came to be included in the Canon. The process seems to have been very nearly complete in the time of Justin Martyr (*Apol.* i 67; *Tryph.* 106), who wrote in the decade following 150, and it is certain that Justin's disciple Tatian constructed his Gospel Harmony out of the canonical Four.

Thus our Gospels fell into their place as the charter of the Christian Religion, a fixed standard open to the inspection of friend and foe. We need hardly follow their literary history further at this point, for in essentials they have remained unchanged from the time of Justin to this day, both in text (apart from minor corruptions and alterations) and in their nominal estimation by the Church. Before the end of the second century the Gospel Canon was absolutely established. The rivals of the Four, which here and there were still read, were being rooted out by authority, and S. Irenæus was able to say that there could not be more or less than four Gospels, that they corresponded to the four Regions of the world and the four Winds, and, above all, to the four mystic Beasts of the Apocalypse.[1] Secure in his acceptance of all four Gospels on the authority of Church tradition, Irenæus had an easy task to shew that the various speculative hypotheses as to the nature of Jesus Christ, which had been put forward by the eager theorists of the second

[1] *Iren.* iii 11: contrast *Iren.* ii 24, where S. Irenæus shews how foolish it is to argue from numbers, by collecting the instances of Fives in the Bible and Nature.

century, were inconsistent with the statements of the Gospels themselves. But there is a great gap between Irenæus and Justin. We cannot but feel it to be only too true that Irenæus accepts the Gospels on the authority of a previous age: it is, I think, almost impossible to imagine him accepting them as authorities for his theology if they had been novelties. In fact, though not in name, they belonged to an age already antiquated. The Church declared itself to be founded on the Four immoveable Columns of the Gospel, and in token of homage its members stood, as they stand to this day, when the Gospel was read out to them in their assemblies. But though the Church was still nearer to the Gospel than the heretics, it was now parted by the ever-increasing differences of conditions and the ever-lengthening stretch of years between its present state and Palestine during our Lord's Ministry. In the next generation to S. Irenæus, the Catholics themselves began to allegorize the Gospels, just as the Alexandrian Jews had taken refuge in allegorizing the Law.

To us, who are trying to understand what the Gospels really mean, more interest attaches to an earlier criticism on the Gospel, perhaps the earliest piece of criticism from outside that has come down to us. It hits the mark from more than one point of view. "I well know," says Trypho, the Jewish opponent of Justin Martyr, "that your Christian precepts out of what is called the *Gospel* are great and admirable, so admirable, indeed, that I doubt if any one can keep them—and I speak from personal knowledge of these writings. Moreover, we non-Christians specially wonder why you expect to get any favour from God, when you set your hope on a man who was crucified" (*Tryph.* § 10).

This simple and obvious piece of criticism touches the essential point. The real humanity of Jesus who was crucified in Judæa, and the soaring ethical principles that He taught,—these are the obvious characteristics of the Gospels, and it is the Gospels which secure these things as an inalienable possession of the Christian Church. Moreover, Trypho's criticism is unanswerable, if the Gospels be regarded as mere law-books, as a code of morals. The Pentateuch *is* a law-book; it is possible to obey it to the letter, and those who compiled it intended it to be obeyed to the letter. But he who exchanges the Pentateuch for the Gospel does not exchange one code for another, as actually happens in the case of a Jew turning Muslim. He who reads the Gospel finds, on the one hand, that eternal life is promised for the observance of the Decalogue (Mk x 17, 19);

on the other, that the renunciation of every earthly tie is demanded (Lk xiv 26, 27), and that except the righteousness of the Christian exceed the legal requirements he cannot enter the Kingdom of Heaven (Matt v 20). This discrepancy is more than an affair of divergent 'sources' or of rival schools of Christian ethics: it is essentially characteristic. The Gospel as a whole is not intended to introduce us to a code by which all men alike should regulate their conduct; it is intended to introduce us to Jesus Christ, whose commands differ for each age and for each individual, because He dealt with principles and not with rules. The love of God and the love of our neighbour was what Jesus Christ taught; but to turn these principles into a fixed Code of rules might easily produce a course of life harmful to our neighbour and unpleasing to God. We do not get rid of the real difficulties of the Gospel, though we make jettison of all the miracles, if we leave the Sermon on the Mount.

The Gospel Ethics need criticism more, not less, than the Gospel miracles; and for this reason, that it is more for the ethics than the miracles that the Gospels are permanently valuable. We need to put the Gospel morality into its due relation to time and place. If Christ said, 'Give to every one that asketh thee,' and, 'Unto him that smiteth thee on the one cheek, offer also the other,' we need to understand the social conditions of Christ's day, and those of our own also, before we can turn these maxims into a rational command for fellow-believers. This is not explaining away Christian morality. Many as have been the abuses of casuistry, it is a necessary study for the practical moralist. In one sense it is particularly suited to Christianity, a religion founded on the attitude of the inner man towards God, not upon the outward observance of particular acts or customs. If principles remain constant, the significance of particular acts must inevitably suffer change. It was not the practice of casuistry, but the simple fact that the Jesuits of the 17th century had systematically practised it to condone what they and their penitents knew to be wrong, that gibbeted these men for ever in the pages of the *Provincial Letters.* It is impossible to doubt that the particular type of casuistry condemned by Pascal was designed to make things easy for the evil-doer at the expense of the spirit of the Gospel, not to find an appropriate course for the spirit of the Gospel to express itself in altered conditions; and it was because this was really so, that the mordant satire gained its triumphant success. For after making all necessary deductions the common sense both of Christendom and of the world outside knows very well what is meant by 'the spirit of the Sermon on the Mount' and similar phrases. And it has ever been a mark of true Christianity to seek to apply the words of the Gospel to the changing needs of the time, a task which is none the less incumbent upon the Church for being always difficult.

But the Gospel morality is not the Gospel, any more than the *Didache* is the Gospel. Christianity stands or falls, lives or dies, with the personality of Jesus Christ; and the Gospel is our introduction to Jesus Christ. From the Gospel according to Mark we may learn who Jesus Christ was, and what part He played on earth in human history. From the Gospels according to Luke and Matthew we may learn something of what Jesus Christ taught. From the Gospel according to John we may learn what His followers declare to be the real significance of His Life. It is the great charm of Christianity that its innermost doctrine is incarnate in the person of its Founder, rather than crystallized into a set of propositions or ordinances. The propositions and the ordinances may be necessary deductions; one of them, as we have seen, forms the ground idea of the Fourth Gospel. But they are exhibited in action; like the Laws of Nature themselves, the doctrines of Christianity are human deductions from the course of events.

Let me give one instance, perhaps all the more instructive for being concerned with the practical sentiment of the Christian community than with high theological speculation. Apart from the Gospels, I cannot find that early Christian literature exhibits the slightest sympathy towards the young. S. Paul tells children to obey their parents in the Lord, and commands fathers not to provoke their children. Further, in the Epistle to Titus, the young women are to be trained to love their husbands and love their children. But this is all, and it seems rather inadequate. Outside the New Testament matters are not much better. Clement of Rome (xxi) speaks of 'reverencing the elders and instructing the young in the instruction of the fear of God,' a passage which is re-echoed by Polycarp. 'Thou shalt not take away thy hand from thy son or from thy daughter, but from youth up thou shalt teach the fear of God' is all that the *Didache* has to say (§ 4).[1]

These extracts are, in fact, characteristic of the official Christian view. In the words and actions of Jesus alone, as recorded in the Synoptic Gospels, and especially by Mark, do we find love

[1] Compare also (for a later period) *Didascalia*, xxii.

and sympathy for children. He taught His disciples that it was as honourable to receive even a child in His name as to receive the chief of all of them; and on another occasion, that he who would enter the Kingdom of God must himself become in some sense like a little child. But even Luke and Matthew leave out what Mark tells us, that our Lord took the children in His arms,[1] and that He was moved with indignation when the disciples wished to keep the children away from troubling Him. The young folk did well to shout, 'Hosanna to the Son of David!' in the Temple, for His voice is almost the only one for centuries that spoke of them with love and sympathy in the things of religion. The bereaved parents whose pathetic utterances are preserved not in Christian literature, but in the buried inscriptions of the Catacombs, had little religious countenance for their affection except from the Saviour Himself.[2]

This illustration shews as clearly as any that can be drawn the difference of atmosphere which separates the Gospels from the rest of early Christian theological literature, both orthodox and heterodox. And thus it brings us back to

[1] Mk ix 36, x 16.

[2] The memory of her little brother Dinocrates came back to S. Perpetua in prison. He had died of a cancer at the age of seven, and Perpetua ultimately saw him in a vision well and happy.

the main point which I have wished to bring before you in this Lecture, that the Gospels we have would never have become the official charters of the Church, but for the theological necessity of insisting upon the true human nature of our Lord.

The Church of the second century was content to wait until the time was ripe for formulating a Christology. Then, as ever, it was those who lived on the borderland of the Church who were in a hurry to precipitate a solution. The leaders of the main body of the Christians were for the most part merely critical of Gnostic speculation; their positive doctrine was mainly developed in controversy against the conservative Jews, the essence of this doctrine being that the Word which spoke in the Gospel message was the same Word of God that spoke to men of old time through the Prophets. But, in addition, it was an essential part of their theory that this Word of God had become incarnate as a real human being in the person of Jesus Christ. It was this part of their theory which led them to hold firmly by a set of narratives telling the story of Jesus, which had been drawn up by various writers towards the end of the first century of the Christian era, before the memory of what had really happened in Judæa had quite faded into legend. We have every reason to be grateful for the rash speculations of the Gnostic heresiarchs, for it was by reaction against their too elaborate theorizings that the Church took refuge in records of past events. It was through the premature efforts of heretics to crystallize Christian theology, that the history of the Ministry and Crucifixion of our Lord, to the Jews as ever a stumblingblock, and to the Gnostic philosophers a fable for the common people, became enshrined as the palladium of the Catholic Church.

IX.

MARCION, OR CHRISTIANITY WITHOUT HISTORY.

IN the first prospectus of the *Hibbert Journal* the editors announced that they intended to open their pages to all varieties of religious thought, but that it was not part of their design to occupy their readers with the discussion of 'dead religions.' The heretic Marcion has been dead for more than seventeen centuries, and the Church which he established has utterly perished. The religion of Marcion is on the face of it a dead religion, and having decided to speak to you about it in this Lecture, I feel it will be part of my duty to attempt to explain why Marcion still may have some living interest for us. The main object that I have in view is to shew you what form Christianity took in the mind of an earnest Christian of the second century, to whom the historical element in the Gospel meant little or nothing, a thinker who desired to give up everything in order to have his Christianity purged from all defilements of nationalistic and materialistic elements.

Let me begin by putting before you the outline of Marcion's career. I cannot claim to have any new light on the subject, which you will find admirably treated in the article on Marcion, in the *Dictionary of Christian Biography*, by the late Provost of Trinity College, Dublin. There is, indeed, little dispute as to the essential facts. Marcion was born about 100 AD in Pontus, apparently at the well-known Black Sea port of Sinope, and his life occupies the first sixty years or so of the second century. His father was a Christian; our authorities tell us that he was 'Bishop' of the Church there, and according to some accounts Marcion himself had been made his suffragan. Here we have the first point of interest. We cannot tell, of course, what was the exact state of the development of the Christian Ministry in Pontus during the first quarter of the second century. At a later period, when Marcion had become an excommunicated heretic and had founded his own heretical Society, he was regarded as their bishop, and he transmitted his 'Orders' to a succession of Marcionite bishops who came after him. The Marcionite 'orders' were not recognised at Rome any more than Anglican orders are at the present day, but that naturally did not affect their legitimacy in the eyes of the Marcionites. This matter, however, hardly concerns us now. The real point of interest is that Marcion came of orthodox Christian stock, and that the Marcionites, however much they were mistaken, and however much they were to be condemned, were definitely a sect of Christians. This is not true of most of the early heretics, or not true to anything like the same extent. For the most part, the Gnostic heretics—Valentinus, Marcus, Hermogenes, and the rest—were products of the mixture of Greek speculation with Christianity. Their systems were only half-Christian. But Marcion's ideas were Christian through and through. Two centuries later, S. Ephraim in his Hymns against Heretics avers that Bardaisan the Gnostic (who was, in fact, a distinguished Astronomer and Astrologer as well as a Theologian) wasted his time in reading heathen books about the signs of the Zodiac instead of studying the Bible. Ephraim has many hard things to say about Marcion, but he does not make that kind of accusation against him. Whatever we may think of Marcion's theories, we must acknowledge that they proceeded from the study of the Gospel.

The story of Marcion's life is for the most part unknown. According to the Edessene Chronicle he left the Church in AD 138. He then appears to have proceeded to Rome, where he hoped that his doctrine would be accepted, or that it would at least receive toleration; but in this he was disappointed. He seems to have led a wandering life, but he was established in Rome as a teacher of his peculiar doctrines during the episcopate of Anicetus (154–166), and for aught we know to the contrary he may have died there.

The importance of Marcion does not lie in the outward events of his life, but in the doctrines which he taught. They can be expressed in very few words. His teaching was the exact converse of those discourses in the Acts with which we are all so familiar, in which the speaker, S. Peter or S. Paul, seeks to prove to those who believe Moses and the Prophets that Jesus of Nazareth was the Christ of God. Marcion's teaching was very different. Believing fervently that Jesus was the Son of God, come down from the highest Heaven to reveal the Divine will to man, he took the Gospel message and asked how it was possible to believe that the Author of the Gospel could have been the God of the Old Testament.

Marcion started, in fact, from the Gospel. The God, he said, whom Jesus preached was ἀγαθός, 'Good,' or rather, 'Kind.' He is *le Bon Dieu*, a God who is able and willing to forgive. The

God of the Old Testament is Just, keeping His promise for ever. He loves them which love Him, and those that sought Him early found Him. He was kind to His friends, terrible to His foes, visiting the sins of the fathers upon the children to the third and fourth generation of them that hate Him. Those that left His service learned to their cost that He is a jealous God. He taught His worshippers that He was God, and that there was none beside Him, and His glory He would not give to another. How different, said Marcion, is the Most High whom Jesus preached; for He is kind to the unthankful and evil, and He commands His servants to be in like manner kind to their enemies and to forgive.

Here you have in a few words the essence of Marcion's religion and Marcion's philosophy. All the rest follows from it, or is the result of mere accidental co-ordination with it. What the master cause was that compelled him to be a Christian, that attracted him to the Gospel, that constrained him to believe in the Divine Message of Jesus, we do not know with precision. No Marcionite work has survived, and we have to pick up our information from opponents more eager to refute the great heretic than to expound his beliefs. That which Marcion shared with his fellow-Christians his refuters pass over for the most part in silence. But we may guess to some extent the forces that influenced him. In the first place, as we have seen, he was born a Christian. The general Christian tradition, the life of the Christian Society, had doubtless a firm hold on Marcion, as also had the belief that the same Jesus who had taught in Palestine had proved Himself the Lord of Death. But Marcion was something far deeper than a mere Christian by inheritance. The mere fact that he felt so acutely the difference between the Old Law and the New is a proof of the profound impression which the teaching of Jesus, the Gospel morality, continued to exercise upon him.

In all this we cannot fail to recognise the parallel between the second-century heresiarch and those thinkers of the present day who are attracted to the Gospel partly from ancestral association, partly from a genuine conviction that the message of the Gospel is the highest teaching which they know, who nevertheless cannot identify the Power that has evolved the visible universe of Nature and produced secular history—in a word, the God of this world—with the Father whom our Lord revealed. Our modern ideas about the early history of man and Nature are widely different from those current in the second century, whether among heretics or orthodox;

but this should not blind us to our ethical kinship with some of Marcion's leading principles of religion. As nearly as any one of whom we have knowledge, he preached the Gospel morality without external sanctions. The essence of the orthodox polemic against him was that in doing this he became involved in contradictions with his own doctrines.

Sometimes it is stated that Marcion rejected the Old Testament. That is not quite true. Marcion rejected the God of Israel as his God; but, as was the case with all early Christian thinkers, the cosmogony of the Pentateuch and its interpretation played an important part in his speculations. Nothing more clearly illustrates the great gap between modern and ancient speculation about the cosmos than the use made by Marcion of the Book of Genesis. In point of fact, the Book of Genesis had no serious rivals until the modern sciences of Geology and Archæology taught us something of the actual march of events on this planet before ordinary history began.

It is rather difficult to do justice to Marcion's speculations on the Fall of Man. To go into details in a lecture like this would be misleading. What we most need is not antiquarian lore about ancient heretics; we need to try to translate Marcion's beliefs into a form which is now intelligible, to attempt to realise what attitude he took up with regard to the problems which are still unsolved, or of which we only now are approaching the solution. The chief point is that Marcion believed that man is governed or influenced by three Principles or Forces. There is *Matter*, out of which his body was made; there is Justice, or, as we now call it, *Law*, by means of which he came into being and emerged from mere inanimate material; and there is *Grace*, a principle distinct from and superior to Law, by which man may be redeemed from the dominion of Law, and by which in the end the better and eternal part of man will escape from the defiling contamination of Matter. According to Marcion, Matter, Law, and Grace are distinct entities in the cosmos, each dwelling in its own sphere. This world we live in was made by the action of Law upon Matter. Man, the noblest product of Law and Matter, is distracted between the two principles of his being. He alone among created things consciously tries to obey Law, *i.e.* Justice, and to forsake the degrading service of Matter; but through his imperfect constitution he fails to find the true Law and becomes involved in the worship of Idols. Justice neither forgives nor makes allowances, and for the sin of worshipping Idols, false ideals which do not exist, Man goes to hell—that is to say, the spirit of Man goes to conscious torment, for the body perishes at death.

This miserable state of things went on for many centuries. At last the principle of Grace who dwells in the highest heaven—in other words, *le Bon Dieu*—took pity on Man and sent His Son down to earth to redeem them from their slavery. Hitherto He had been a stranger to Man, He had been neither the origin of Man's life nor the object of his worship. It was out of mere compassion that Grace came down and interposed—we may almost say, interfered—to save mankind from their hopeless condition.

So Jesus, the Son of God, appeared on earth, doing good without reward, and healing those who for their sins were sick, until at last the God of the Law was jealous; and the God of the Law stirred up his servants and they took Jesus and crucified Him, and He became like the dead, so that Hell opened her mouth and received Him. But Death could have no dominion over Jesus, nor could Hell retain One who was alive within its bounds. Jesus therefore burst the bonds of Hell and ascended to His Father, carrying with Him the spirits that lay there in prison. Then Jesus came down in His glory and appeared before the God of the Law, who was obliged to confess that he was guilty according to his own

Law; for Jesus had only done good to the race of men, and yet He had been crucified. "I was ignorant," said the God of the Law to Jesus, "and because I sinned and killed Thee in ignorance, there shall be given to Thee in revenge all those who shall be willing to believe in Thee, to carry away wherever Thou wilt." Then Jesus left the God of the Law and betook Himself to Paul, and revealed this to him, and sent him to preach that we have been bought with a price. All who believe in Jesus were then and there sold from the dominion of the Just Power to the Good and Kind One.

Eznik the Armenian, from whose account of the Marcionites the details recounted in the last paragraph have been taken, goes on to say: "Not all the Marcionites know all this, but only a few of them, who hand down the doctrine one to the other by word of mouth. What the Marcionites usually say is simply, 'The Good Stranger—with a price He bought us from the Lord of the Creation,' but how or with what He bought them,—that not all of them know." Most modern scholars suppose that this detailed theory of how the price was paid for man belongs to a later development of Marcionism, but there is nothing in it inconsistent with the leading idea of the Marcionite doctrine. This idea is the essential antithesis between Law and Grace. 'Mercy rejoiceth against Judgement,' and Marcion saw in the God of the Old Testament the God of Judgement, and in the God of the New Testament the God of Mercy.

It should be here pointed out that this story of how the World-Power caused our Lord to be killed, not knowing who He was, and how as a consequence He descended into Hell and harrowed it, was not confined to the Marcionites. It has dropped out from the modern presentation of Christianity, but it is always meeting us in pre-Reformation theology, from the Acts of Judas Thomas and the Nisebene Hymns of S. Ephraim to the Gospel of Nicodemus and the windows of King's College Chapel. The only real difference between the Marcionite and the orthodox forms of the story is that where the Marcionites speak of the God of the Old Testament, the orthodox speak of Satan. In either case, it is the Adversary of Jesus. The Marcionites taught that by the sacrifice of the Cross our Lord bought us from the dominion of the God of the Law, the orthodox taught that by the sacrifice of the Cross our Lord bought us from the dominion of the Devil. And I cannot help feeling that there is a definite reason why the Marcionite form of the doctrine may be the more original, and that the story which enshrines the doctrine may have originated among the Marcionites, if it does not come from Marcion himself. For Marcion was constrained to explain how the Good God came to have any concern at all with mankind. The orthodox Christian might believe that Jesus Christ came in the fulness of time, in accordance with the eternal purpose of God for His Creation. But, according to Marcion, man originally owed no allegiance to the Good God. Man was the handiwork of the Just God, and owed Him allegiance; it was necessary therefore to explain how man's allegiance was transferred to the Good Stranger.

But the most curious part of the story, from the point of view of the history of ideas, has yet to be told. The belief that the Redemption was essentially an act by which Man was bought by God from the Devil prevailed among theologians during the first ten centuries of Christianity. It was accepted by S. Irenæus, by Origen, by S. Augustine. But at last it fell into discredit, and a new theory took its place. The author of the new theory was as far removed from heresy as it is possible to be. Anselm was a prince of the Church in his lifetime, and now he is a canonized Saint. This great philosophical thinker was profoundly dissatisfied with the current view of the Atonement. He felt it unworthy to represent

God as giving the Devil his due: the redemption of man must be something wholly accomplished and transacted by the Divine Personality, not something paid away by God to some one else. And so Anselm elaborated the famous theory by which the sacrifice of Christ was represented as a debt paid by God's Mercy to God's Justice.

This thought is very near akin to the leading idea of Marcion. In Anselm's system, which was accepted by the mediæval Church, and is very commonly held even now among Protestants, God's Justice and God's Mercy are eternal principles which play separate and opposing parts. They are, in fact, if not in name, distinct Persons in the Divine Essence. The world is governed by Justice, and Mercy can only interfere by paying the price to Justice. Justice cannot and will not forgive, and it is distinct from Mercy and Grace. But this is what Marcion taught eight centuries before Anselm. The difference is only in nomenclature. S. Anselm speaks of the eternal Justice of God, and, on the other hand, of the eternal Mercy of God at last manifested in Christ; Marcion spoke of the God of the Law, and of the Good and Kind Stranger who sent His Son. I cannot see that there is any real difference.[1]

[1] 'If we searched all space,' says Luthardt, 'we should discover only the gospel of power; if we surveyed all time, only the gospel

I have not attempted to set before you to-day a complete and ordered exposition of Marcion's doctrines. In the first place, the materials are insufficient; and, in the second place, you can easily read up for yourselves all that is known about him. What I have tried to do is to shew how fundamental and vital were the questions which he raised, and how closely the solution which he proposed, strange and repellent as it sounds, is in touch with the thought of various ages, when it is stripped of mere accidents of second-century phraseology. And, indeed, the controversy between Marcion and the Church was no mere academic discussion.

We are told by Epiphanius that when Marcion first came to Rome he asked to be admitted to Communion, and when he was refused communion he went on to ask the Roman Presbyters what was meant when our Lord spoke of the new wine and the old bottles and of the folly of putting a new patch on a worn-out garment. It was a great and serious question. Christianity, we believe, is both old and new; in this saying of Jesus it is for the moment represented as a thing

of righteousness. Only in Jesus Christ do we learn the gospel of grace.' This characteristic sentence from an orthodox Lutheran theologian, quoted with approval by Canon Ottley in his article on the Incarnation in Hastings' *Dictionary of the Bible*, ii 465*b*, seems to me a piece of unadulterated Marcionite doctrine.

essentially new, and the problem of how to combine the old and the new still besets the constructive reformer of every age. But Marcion was told that the worn-out garment signified Judas Iscariot, who was worn out with covetousness, so that he was unable fitly to receive the new and heavenly hope of the Gospel; and though he was joined on to the eleven Apostles by the Lord, a worse rent came through him, and, moreover, his mind and thought did not agree with the others! Nothing more clearly shews than this answer how incompetent the heads of the Church about 140 AD were to resolve the doubts of a keen and earnest thinker like Marcion. What wonder that Marcion replied by identifying himself with the new piece of cloth and regarding the Church as the worn-out Jewish gabardine! "I will tear your Church," said he to the Roman Presbyters, "I will tear your Church and make a rent in it for ever."

The Marcionite schism was a very serious rent, and one that was not mended for many a long day. In spite of persecution, at first from the heathen, and afterwards from fellow-Christians, in spite of a severely ascetic mode of life, in spite of 'refutation' by almost every prominent orthodox theologian, one after the other, the followers of Marcion organised themselves into a

Church and maintained their corporate existence until after the 5th century. An inscribed stone is still preserved which had stood over the lintel of the Marcionite chapel of a village near Damascus.[1] It is the oldest dated inscription from any Christian place of worship, and it is melancholy to think that in all probability this building was destroyed at the instigation of Christians a few years after it was dedicated. For 318 AD, the date of the dedication of this Marcionite Chapel, occurs in the interval of toleration between the end of the great Diocletian Persecution (313) and the definite triumph of Christianity under Constantine (324), after which the Marcionites were forbidden to meet for worship either in public or private, and the buildings they had already erected for meeting-places were to be confiscated. The Marcionites had proved their devotion to our Lord by many a martyrdom, their discipline was strict, their lives were pure; but the Catholic Church waged war upon them to the death.

I do not intend to take you step by step over the detailed refutations of Marcion by Tertullian and Epiphanius. The detailed refutation of a

[1] The inscription runs: 'Synagogue of Marcionites of Lebab village of the Lord and Saviour Jesus Christ (Χρηστοῦ), at the expense of the priest Paul in the year 630'—*i.e.* 318 AD. The place-name in the Greek is *κώμης λεβάβων*, *Le Bas* iii 583 (2558).

lost cause generally arouses sympathy rather than conviction, for we ourselves are obliged to supply the arguments on the heretic's side. Moreover, the orthodox champions do much less than justice to Marcion. Tertullian is epigrammatic, harsh, and wholly without the sympathy which alone can comprehend; while Epiphanius, for all his erudition,—well, think of the narrowest clergyman of your acquaintance and what *he* thinks and says of the Dissenters in his parish—that (only much worse) is the attitude of Saint Epiphanius toward heretics. We shall do better to leave Tertullian and Epiphanius alone, until we have a better idea of the principles underlying both parties.

For, after all, the formal refutations do not supply us with the principal reasons why the Church rejected Marcion. As in all great questions, the two parties ranged themselves on opposing sides not so much from the objections which could be raised against the other's views as from allegiance to positive principles. And it is comparatively easy to pick holes in your opponent's case, to point out the weaknesses and inconsistencies into which he has fallen; but for the most part triumphant demonstrations of this kind only serve to encourage fellow-believers. For us, after the lapse of seventeen centuries, it is more interesting and more profitable to try and get at the positive ideals which underlay the controversial tactics of the two camps. We have seen what were some of the main principles of Marcion: the eternal antithesis of Law and Gospel, of Justice and Mercy, of Nature and Grace. Now let us see why the Church refused the dilemma. What were the principles to which the Church clung when Marcion was swept away?

The answer to this query lies implicitly, as I venture to think, in a piece of literary borrowing, which surprised me much when I first came across it, but which I now see to have a real appropriateness. Tertullian, as you have heard, wrote a long and elaborate refutation of Marcion. He also wrote, or (as some think) a Carthaginian contemporary wrote, a treatise against the Jews. Whether this treatise against the Jews was actually compiled by Tertullian, or not, does not greatly matter; the important point for us is undisputed, viz. that it was published a very few years after the publication of Tertullian's work against Marcion. The two works appeared at the same place, and belong to the same school of thought; they are, in fact, practically designed for the same public. Now the surprising thing is that about half the treatise against the Jews is simply copied out of the Third Book against

Marcion. Paragraph after paragraph agrees verbally, or only with the omission of a contemptuous reference to Marcion's Pontic birth.[1]

It does not matter whether the writer of the treatise against the Jews was Tertullian plagiarising from himself, or some one else plagiarising from Tertullian. The important thing is that the same arguments that were thought appropriate to use against the Jews were thought appropriate to use against Marcion the anti-Jew. Surprising as it seems at first sight, the Church had to a great extent the same controversy with both opponents. The Church was determined to maintain its claim to be the true heir of the promises of the Old Testament, the promises made of old to the Fathers. The Jews and Marcion had this in common, that they disputed the claim of the Christian Church to be the legitimate successor of the Patriarchs and the Prophets, and this was a claim that it was vital for the Church to make.

The claim was made good. Of course the price had to be paid. We sometimes hear that there is too much of the Old Testament in the Christian Religion; that may have been, and may be still, true of certain forms which

[1] Cf. Aliud est si penes Ponticos barbariae gentis infantes in proelium erumpunt (*adv. Marc.* iii 13)=Aliud est si penes uos infantes in proelium erumpunt (*adv. Iud.* § 9).

Christianity has taken. But, on the whole, there can be no doubt that the Church was right and that Marcion was wrong. The Church was right both as a matter of history and as a matter of religious theory. As a matter of history, there can be no doubt that Jesus Christ Himself believed that He came not to destroy but to fulfil, and that He believed that the Father whom He preached was the God of Abraham and of Isaac and of Jacob, the God of the Prophets and the Psalmists. No one had known the Father but the Son; yes, but that was because men were blind and crass, not because God was a stranger. Our Lord was not the kind of Messiah that the Jews were expecting, but none the less He was a Branch out of the root of Jesse. He was a Jew by birth, by training, by His whole environment; and to forget or deny this, as Marcion denied it, and to regard Him as something wholly new, come down from the Absolute, is to make Christ and Christianity incomprehensible and unreal.

And as a matter of religious theory Marcionism is inferior to its rival. In fact, we can see this now much clearer than it could be seen in the second century. Neither Tertullian nor Marcion had much idea of the orderly development of Religion from crude and childish notions about

God and the world to thoughts adequate for a maturer stage in human history. But while Development occupies only a small space in the Catholic theory, in Marcion's theory there was no room for it at all. It is a theory of catastrophe: a New God comes down from nowhere, and proclaims true religion for the first time. And closely allied with Marcion's rejection of the Old Testament history as being in any sense the history of true religion was his denial of the reality of our Lord's body as being in any sense true flesh and blood. Marcion's Christ condescends to treat with the God of the Law, but He will have nothing to do with Matter, which in Marcion's view was a thing altogether unclean and outside the Christ's beneficent operations.

The refusal of the Catholic Church to give up the real humanity of our Lord, or to regard our material life as essentially unclean and impure,—the two refusals are most intimately connected—is one of the highest claims it has upon the gratitude of the modern world. That what is Divine is degraded by becoming really human carries with it the corollary that the things which really make up human life, eating and drinking, marrying and giving in marriage, the trivial round, the common task, have no part in the service of God. They are not things to be consecrated: they have nothing to do with religion. Consequently we find those that hold this theory either regard mere morality as a thing indifferent; or, as more often happens with those in whom the religious feeling, the devotion to the Divine, is strong, they fall into the opposite error of asceticism.

Among these was Marcion, and he impressed his beliefs on his followers. According to Marcion, the procreation of children was a doing the works of the Creator of this world, an act unworthy of a member of Christ. And so no Marcionite was admitted to baptism, unless the candidate was prepared to live a life of absolute continence from that day forward. Holy Matrimony to the Marcionite meant marriage to Christ, and for man and wife to live together meant divorce from Christ.[1]

Tertullian's strictures on Marcion about this very important point are both vigorous and sensible. Gluttony, he says, is bad, but that is no reason for proscribing food; what is needed is temperance. Marriage may be the cause of many evils, but it is not to blame for those evils. In common with almost all Church writers, Tertullian believes that 'holiness,' *i.e.* a life of continence, is better than the married

[1] Tert. *adv. Marc.* i 29, iv 34

state, but (he says) we hold up this ideal not as good as opposed to bad, but as a better as opposed to good. And, he adds, when marriage is attacked as unlawful for Christians, the Church expressly defends it.

We shall all be ready to side with Tertullian here, rather than with his opponent. But we must be careful about the terms we use in reprobating the Marcionite theory and practice. Marcion was not alone in his rejection of marriage. Nor was the actual practice of his adherents quite so revolutionary as it sounds to our ears. The mere fact that the Marcionites continued to exist for more than three centuries, enjoying all the while a reputation not for licence, but for puritanical austerity, is enough to shew that they were not a sect of 'race-suicides.' It was in their Sacramental theory rather than in their social life that the Marcionites differed from their Catholic cousins. No doubt there were many young folk among them who volunteered early for baptism and actual participation in the Holy Communion, just as there were, and are still, young Catholics who volunteer to become monks and nuns, and remain so. But these, I venture to think, did not form the majority of the sectaries. The majority lived like their neighbours in the world, attending their 'Church' (in which they were allowed to witness the celebration of the Eucharist without partaking of the sacramental meal), and no doubt distributing towards the necessities of the Saints. Such persons, of course had not yet been through the ceremony of baptism. No doubt most of them were married like their Pagan neighbours: the Wedding Feast, and for aught I know the Wedding Ring itself, is a good deal older than Christianity. But a Marcionite marriage was not recognised by the Marcionite Church, and neither man nor woman was admitted to baptism and communion until he or she was ready to live apart for the future. The general result, therefore, was that the sacramental life was deferred; it became a preparation for entering the life after death rather than a régime for the present.

This view of the Sacraments was by no means confined to the followers of Marcion. I have attempted elsewhere to shew that it prevailed in the Syriac-speaking Church down to the fourth century. It is at least certain that candidates for Baptism in this branch of the Church were warned that if their hearts were set on marriage they had better turn back from Baptism[1] and go away and be married. Yet these folk were in communion with the rest of the

[1] Aphraates, *Hom.* vii 20.

Catholic Church, and their Bishops sat with the rest in the Council of Nicæa. And we may remember that the Council of Nicæa was summoned by Constantine the Great, a Christian Emperor who thought it well and seemly to delay his own baptism until a few months before his death.

The reservation of the Sacraments for those who had withdrawn themselves from the world by celibacy and freedom from worldly cares is not therefore a special feature of Marcionism. None the less we cannot doubt that the Church was right to reject it. Both the Catholics and the Marcionites believed that the reception of the Eucharist involved the real presence of God in the recipient. But while the Marcionites thought that so holy a Presence ought not to be mingled with the elements of everyday human life, the Catholic theory, however haltingly and however imperfectly, declared that the elements of everyday life are not essentially unclean, and that the highest union with the Divine Nature of which man is capable will consecrate these elements, not destroy them.

All this was involved in the Church's controversy with Marcion. The issues at stake were really great and always new and vital. When we remember this, we may be more able to understand and partly to excuse the bitterness with which Church writers speak of an ardent and earnest Christian thinker.

I must now say a few words upon Marcion's Bible, that is to say, his Gospel, and his edition of S. Paul's Epistles. Thirty or forty years ago this would have been the centre of interest in a Lecture on Marcion. A very general belief was then current in critical circles that the Gospel accepted by Marcion was not, as Tertullian and Epiphanius asserted, a mutilated edition of S. Luke, cut about to suit the heretic's notions. It was thought that Marcion's Gospel might be the original and our S. Luke a later interpolated version used by the orthodox. But this theory has been entirely given up on closer study of the question from various points of view. The assertions of Tertullian and Epiphanius have been fully vindicated, and Marcion's Gospel has sunk into a mere curiosity of literature.

In the first place, the numerous omissions, by which Marcion's Gospel chiefly differs from the canonical S. Luke, are all, or almost all, easily explicable. Most of them, indeed, could not have been retained by one who held Marcion's views. The birth of Jesus Christ from a human parent and the baptism of Jesus Christ by a prophet of the old order were inconsistent with what Marcion taught. Marcion did not believe that Jesus could have said that God had clothed the grass of this material world, or that He could have declared the old Prophets to have spoken of Him. So all these passages are absent from the Marcionite Gospel. But no one doubts that they form a genuine portion of the Third Gospel.

Again, the linguistic evidence is fatal to the priority of the Marcionite edition. If the parts rejected by Marcion did not really belong to the Third Gospel, but were later accretions, there should be some difference of style between these portions and the rest. But as a matter of fact there is none. The characteristic style of the Lucan writings equally pervades the passages rejected and the passages retained by Marcion; in fact, there is nothing to separate the two classes except that what Marcion rejected does not fit his peculiar theory.[1]

The trend of modern Synoptic criticism is also adverse to the priority of Marcion's Gospel. The Gospel according to S. Luke is a composite work, compiled by the Evangelist from two main sources, one identical with, or at all events nearly resembling, our Gospel according to S. Mark, the other mostly consisting of our Lord's Discourses.

[1] The linguistic evidence is admirably marshalled in Dr. Sanday's *Gospels in the Second Century*, pp. 222–230.

But Marcion's omissions are spread over both documents. Some of the passages omitted, such as 'Go and tell that fox' (Lk xiii 32), are peculiar to S. Luke; others, such as the Parable of the Wicked Husbandmen (xx 9–18) and the Widow's Mite (xxi 1–4), are found also in S. Mark. It is, I firmly believe, impossible to invent a hypothesis which will account for the actual facts, except the hypothesis advanced by the Church Fathers, that Marcion himself abridged S. Luke's Gospel. Of course, he believed himself to be restoring the pure Gospel, purged of foreign accretions, but from a purely literary and historical point of view we can scarcely agree with him.

One thing, however, we may note in passing. Marcion is, in a sense, the last of the Evangelists. He is the last to produce a book, professing to give the Gospel Story, which is not a mere Harmony of the Four Gospels. The Christian of a later age, however heretical, did not feel himself free to select and to reject; Marcion's method of treating S. Luke does not differ in kind, only in result, from S. Luke's very free treatment of S. Mark's Gospel.

A copy of the Marcionite edition of S. Paul's Epistles would be, on the whole, a more valuable discovery than a copy of the Marcionite Gospel.

The Marcionite Gospel is merely an abridged and altered edition of what we already possess, but Marcion's edition of the Pauline Epistles very possibly represents an earlier stage of the collection of S. Paul's letters than the canonical. The history of the collection of these letters is distinct from the question of the genuineness of any or either of them. That the longer letters ascribed to S. Paul are really his, is the verdict of most scholars, whether they belong to the critical school or otherwise; and further, it seems probable that several of these letters, notably 1 Corinthians and Galatians, have come down to us practically in their original form. But there is no great probability that S. Paul himself made a collected edition of his letters, or even that he kept copies of those that he sent. He may have done so, but there is no evidence. It is indeed wholly uncertain how or when these letters were first brought together into a *Corpus*. I think we may fairly consider our present collection to be at least a second edition, revised and enlarged; and there is something to be said for supposing that the previous edition was due to Marcion's reverence for the great Apostle. As I said before, this question is distinct from the question of the genuineness of the several letters. There is clear evidence that some of the letters, especially

1 Corinthians, were known and held in great respect by writers earlier than or contemporary with Marcion. But there is no tangible evidence for an *Apostolicon*, a collection of the Epistles. Thus S. Clement of Rome, writing to the Church at Corinth, quotes 1 Corinthians by name, and most appropriately: "Take up the letter of the blessed Paul the apostle, how . . . he spiritually charged you concerning himself and Cephas and Apollos."[1] But it is more than doubtful whether S. Clement had ever heard of the letter which we call the Second Epistle to the Corinthians, and it is very likely that the genuine letters of Paul, out of which our Epistle is composed, were at that time lying unknown to the rest of the Christian world in Corinth itself. Again, there is very little to suggest that S. Ignatius knew the letter to the Galatians, though he certainly knew 1 Corinthians, and probably knew Ephesians. When, therefore, we consider Marcion's special interest in S. Paul, he being, according to Marcion, the only one who understood the doctrine that Jesus came to deliver to mankind; and when, further, we remember that Marcion was perhaps more of a traveller than any other Christian in the second century, and therefore had opportunities for collection above most of his contemporaries; when we consider these

[1] 1 Clem. xlvii 1.

things, we may be permitted to wonder whether Marcion may not have been the first to make a regular collection of the Pauline Epistles. At the same time, I should be sorry to leave you with the impression that this hypothesis is an assured result of criticism. It is not so; it is no more than a guess, and the evidence is not sufficient to enable us to reach anything like certainty in the matter.[1]

Marcion's share in the collection of the Pauline Epistles must remain doubtful. But there can be little doubt that he was the first to canonise the New Testament. The Bible of the earliest generations of Christians was the Bible of the Jewish Church. The Law and the Prophets and the Psalms, together with the still undefined limits of the rest of the Books, were to them the recorded Word of God. The idea of a new volume, to be added to what had been written aforetime, was strange and foreign to their thought. No one can read S. Luke's Preface to his great work and not feel that the author could never have imagined that his work would be sacred, otherwise than by

[1] Marcion's collection consisted of ten letters, which he arranged as follows :—Galatians, 1 Corinthians, 2 Corinthians, Romans, 1 and 2 Thessalonians, Ephesians (called by Marcion, 'To the Laodicæans'), Colossians, Philemon, Philippians. He did not receive the Epistles to Timothy and to Titus.

the fact that words of the Lord Jesus were recorded in it. S. Paul writes to his spiritual children with natural authority, but the Gospel which he enforces is a living, floating belief, not a written record. And this remained the point of view of the early Church. They remembered the words of the Lord Jesus, they repeated the prayer He had taught His disciples to use, but the Scripture, the written Word of God, remained what it had been. To such an extent is this the case, that when we find in a very early Christian writing, the so-called Epistle of Barnabas, the words, 'Many called, but few chosen,' with *as it is written* prefixed, we feel that we are confronted with a real difficulty.[1] It is probable that 'Barnabas' really had the words of Jesus in his mind, whether he knew of them through our Gospel according to Matthew or from some earlier collection of sayings; but it is very improbable that he intentionally quoted them with the regular Scripture formula. It has therefore been supposed, with a good deal of reason, that he had forgotten the reference, and consequently has employed the formula 'as it is written' by inadvertence for the more appropriate 'as the Lord said to His disciples,' or something of that kind.

The Church felt in no need of a new Bible; as

[1] *Barn.* iv 14.

we have seen, the preoccupation of Church theologians was to vindicate the Church's claim to be the Heir of the Covenants, to prove that the Law and the Prophets rightfully belonged to the Christian Church rather than to the unfaithful Jewish Synagogue. But Marcion rejected the Law and the Prophets. He was left without a Bible. For him true Religion began with the descent of the Son of God to preach in Galilee. The record of this preaching was for him what the mystical lives of the Patriarchs were to Jewish and orthodox Christians, and the writings of the true theologian Paul were the true prophecy. Thus for Marcion the Gospel and the Epistles made up a New Testament, replacing the Old.

The Catholic Church complained, not without reason, that Marcion's Gospel was nothing more than a mutilated version of a thoroughly orthodox and trustworthy work, and it was not to be expected that Marcion's edition of S. Paul's letters would be accepted without scrutiny as complete or accurate in text. But the fact remains that Marcion is the first to come before us with a collection of Christian writings which are treated as Scripture, that is, as works out of the words of which doctrine can be proved. Before Marcion's time, in the works of what are commonly called the Apostolic Fathers, we can find traces of the literary use of certain of S. Paul's Epistles and (less certainly) traces of the use of some of our Gospels. But though the Old Testament is often quoted, no formal quotation is found from the books which comprise the New Testament, with the exception of the quotation of 1 Corinthians by Clement and the passage from the Epistle of Barnabas to which I have just now referred. Marcion then appears on the scene with a collection of books, which, though rudimentary and incomplete, is recognisably our New Testament. A generation later we find the idea of a written record by Evangelists and Apostles firmly rooted in Catholic theology. When we remember that this same Marcion, in whose hands a New Testament is first found, had far greater need than his Catholic brethren of an authoritative New Testament, it is impossible to avoid the inference that to Marcion himself is due the introduction of Christian books into the sacred Canon. The books were not new; they were used and venerated before, but they did not occupy the same rank as the Old Law.

A New Testament Canon of some kind would doubtless have been formed, if Marcion had never appeared, and, as a matter of fact, the Church rejected Marcion's Gospel in favour of earlier documents. What we really owe to Marcion, as

I venture to think, is the enormous preponderance of the writings of S. Paul in our New Testament. To Marcion, as afterwards to the Reformers of the 16th century, S. Paul was the great Theologian, the leader and fashioner of theological thought. But it was not so to the early Catholic Church. The antithesis of Law and Grace, Justification by Faith, the Church regarded as the Body of Christ,—on all these points the ancient baptismal Creeds are silent. I think it would surprise any one who knew the writings of the early Fathers from Clement of Rome to the Nicene Age, but was unacquainted with the New Testament, to learn that even though the Gospel was included four times over, letters of Paul occupied a quarter of the official Canon. It is the great service which Marcion rendered to the Church, that he recognised and emphasised with a fervour, that was none the less effective for being narrow and one-sided, the unique position of the great Apostle of the Gentiles.

[For the Marcionite Prologues to S. Paul's Epistles, see the separate Note, p. 353.]

X.

THE RIVALS OF THE CANONICAL GOSPELS.

BEFORE I bring this set of Lectures to a close you will naturally expect me to say something about Apocryphal Gospels, the unsuccessful rivals of the Canonical Four. It will be impossible, of course, to do more than touch upon this great subject, so full of difficulties and unsolved problems in almost all its branches. Some parts of the subject, indeed, are not only difficult but dull, except to the specialist investigator.

For there is little doubt what constitutes the main interest of the Apocryphal Gospels, at least for most minds. It is, in one word, a reflexion of the surpassing interest of the Canonical Gospels. From the Canonical Gospels the world has learnt the story of Jesus Christ, and even those to whom the tale means little or nothing cannot fail to note the immense influence that His Personality has exercised upon human society. We know His Portrait from the official Church Canon, and we cannot but ask whether something new and yet true may not lie hidden in the rejected accounts of His sayings and doings on earth. The Church's chosen documents may only tell us what the Church wants us to learn: is it not possible to get another and a different glimpse of Jesus from what the Church has rejected?

It is well to say at the outset that I do not think these expectations can be gratified from what has come down to us. Of all the communities and schools of thought to whom the personality of Jesus presented any interest, the Church itself was the one most concerned to portray His human Nature. There were sects and thinkers to whom He was raised altogether above humanity: from these we cannot expect to learn new facts of His history. There was, of course, the indifferent heathen world outside, and the unconverted world of Judaism, but these had neither the time nor the inclination to investigate the tale of the Nazarenes' Prophet, at least, not until independent sources of historical information had ceased to be available. Josephus, if the famous passage about our Lord be his, as I believe it to be, must have been indebted to some Christian acquaintance for his information. The heathen Celsus is practically dependent on our Gospels. Thus we have no source of information about our Lord except from believers.

Nevertheless, the study of non-canonical Gospels presents many features of great interest. If they do not give us direct historical information about our Lord, they yet tell us much about the way in which some of His early followers thought of Him. They shew us the intellectual atmosphere through which men looked back at the wonderful Figure which stood at the beginning of the new dispensation.

Let us begin with a class of writings which lie altogether outside the domain of history in the strict sense, viz. those Gospels which profess to deal wholly or mainly with what happened after the Crucifixion. We shall find these books united by a common characteristic: they all profess to give out a secret revelation on the authority of the Risen Christ. According to S. Luke in the Acts, when our Lord appeared to the disciples after the Resurrection, He was 'speaking the things concerning the Kingdom of God,' but beyond a command not to depart for the present from Jerusalem, nothing is given of these conversations except a rebuke for overmuch curiosity about the time of the restoration of the Kingdom to Israel. Later writers had more to tell. Take, for example, the work which calls itself 'The Testament, or Words which our Lord, when He rose from the dead, spake to the Holy Apostles.

To us the historical setting of the *Testamentum Domini* is a transparent literary device, but we cannot allege this with regard to the public for which it was intended, and it is impossible to separate it from other earlier books which make use of the same device. The 'Testament' begins thus:

"It came to pass, after our Lord rose from the dead and appeared unto us, and was handled by Thomas and Matthew and John, and we were persuaded that our Master was truly risen from the dead, that falling on our faces we blessed the Father of the new world, even God, who saved us through Jesus Christ our Lord, and being held in very great fear we waited prostrate. . . . But Jesus our Lord, putting His hand on each one of us separately, lifted us up, saying, 'Why hath your heart thus fallen, and are ye stricken with great astonishment? . . . As children of light, ask of My Father which is in heaven the Spirit of counsel and might, and He will fill you with the Holy Spirit, and grant you to be with Me for ever.'" Then the disciples ask for the Holy Spirit, and Jesus breathes on them, and they receive the Holy Spirit. Peter and John then ask what are the signs of the End. There is a long answer: the usual calamities are foretold, signs in heaven and ragings of the sea and monstrous prodigies; then come exhortations to endure patiently unto the end, then the coming of Antichrist is foretold, and the Eastern wars that he will inaugurate, with which is incorporated a curious description of his personal appearance. Meanwhile the faithful are to watch and pray without ceasing. The disciples receive the revelation with reverent thankfulness, and ask how it is fitting that they should arrange the 'mysteries of the Church,' *i.e.* the order of Church services. This, of course, is the real purpose of the 'Testament.' So our Lord replies: "Because that ye also have asked Me concerning the rule ecclesiastical, I deliver and make known to you how ye ought to order and command him who standeth at the head of the Church, and to keep the perfect and just and most excellent rule, in which My Father who hath sent Me is well pleased. . . . But because in the midst of the assembly of the people there are, more and more, many carnal desires, and the labourers are feeble and few, only My perfect labourers shall know the multitude of My words, all also which I spake to you in private before I suffered, and which ye know; ye both have them and understand them. For 'My mysteries are given to those who are Mine' (Isaiah xxiv 6), with whom I shall rejoice and be glad with My Father. . . . But from the day that My faithful ones also have the desire to know, that they may do the things of the Father, even whatsoever is in this My Testament, I will be with them and will be praised among them, and I will make My habitation with them, by power informing them of the will of My Father. See that ye give not My holy things to the dogs, and cast not pearls before swine, as I have often commanded you. Give not My holy things to defiled and wicked men who do not bear My cross, and are not subject to Me, and My commandments be for derision among them. . . . I tell you therefore how the sanctuary ought to be; then I will make known the holy rule of the priests of the Church. Let the church, then, be thus: let it have three entrances, etc."

Here follows a Church law-book, giving directions for the due performance of all ecclesiastical functions. It is a sister document to the so-called Apostolical Constitutions and akin to what is known as the Canons of Hippolytus. No doubt it borrows something from the *Didache*, that early Christian manual which we considered in Lecture VIII. But I have made these rather extensive quotations from it only to exhibit the method of composition. The author's intentions are quite plain. He has something new, viz. his Church legislation, and he uses the evangelical history to legitimatise and sanction this new material.

I have spoken of the *Testamentum Domini* at perhaps excessive length, because in this case the literary procedure is particularly clear. But it is only one of a series of works somewhat similarly planned. The *Testamentum* is chiefly concerned with Church regulations and the Liturgy. Another work, of a wholly different age and character, is concerned with the esoteric teaching of Gnosticism. This is the *Pistis Sophia*, an exposition of the mystical and cosmological doctrine of an Egyptian thinker or school of thinkers. In its present form it may date from the 3rd or 4th century, but no doubt it contains very ancient, partly pre-Christian, speculations. The main object of the *Pistis Sophia* is to expound the Gnostic theory of the world as received by the writer, and at the same time to inculcate the doctrine that this theory is the real esoteric Christianity. To do this he employs the same machinery as is employed by the compiler of the *Testamentum Domini*, that is to say, it is all given as a post-Resurrection Revelation by our Lord to the inner circle of disciples. As in the *Testamentum*, so in the *Pistis Sophia*, the justification for this to us unwarrantable playing with the Gospel History is that to the authors of these books the test of truth was dogmatic, not historical. The authors believed that the Church Order or the Gnostic Doctrine was the right Order or the right Doctrine, as the case might be; whether what they wrote was in accordance with the course of past events did not really matter.

It is important for us to realise this point of view when we attempt to make a study of early Christian Literature, because it was the view of so many Christian writers of historical or quasi-historical books. It is, in fact, the point of view of the whole mass of writers who wrote in other folk's names from, let us say, the compiler of the Book of Enoch to the writer of the Second Epistle of Peter. Indeed, as I have had occasion to point out to you more than once in the course of these Lectures, the main reason why the Canonical Gospels themselves contain so much that is actually historical is not the interest of the Catholic Church in accurate history as an excellent thing in itself, but the dogmatic necessity of maintaining the true humanity of Jesus Christ and the reality of His Passion against various forms of Docetic philosophizing. The struggle with premature systems of theology drove the Church back into what, compared with Gnostic thought, is authentic and historical tradition.

Some perhaps would refuse to count the *Testa-*

mentum Domini and the *Pistis Sophia* among the Gospels, even among 'Apocryphal' Gospels. In the case of these works the historical framework is almost obviously a mere pretence, and the whole interest of the author lies in the doctrine put in our Lord's mouth. But I have called attention to them here because it seems to me that with these works in our minds we can better attack the criticism of the 'Gospel' and 'Apocalypse' of Peter.

Before 1892 little was known of the 'Gospel of Peter' beyond what Eusebius told us in his History.[1] There we read that this Gospel was accustomed to be read in the Church of Rhossus, near Antioch, but that it was suppressed by Serapion, bishop of Antioch, when he found, on examination, that it really taught the Docetic heresy. The 'Apocalypse of Peter' had left more trace in Christian literature. We knew that it dealt with the Last Judgement, and with the torments meted out to various classes of sinners. It is quoted once or twice as Scripture by Clement of Alexandria, and used by several Christian writers of the 3rd century. It formed, in fact, one of the ultimate sources from which mediæval authors derived their descriptions of Hell. In 1892 large fragments of these lost

[1] *HE* vi 12.

works were published from a vellum book found in a Christian grave in the ancient cemetery of Akhmim in Egypt. The book, which also contained fragments of the ancient apocryphal work called the Book of Enoch, was entire, but the text which it contained of the Gospel and Apocalypse of Peter consisted of fragments merely. Evidently the MS from which they had been copied was itself mutilated, so that what has come down to us begins and ends in the middle of sentences.

Incomplete, however, as the fragments are, they are enough, and more than enough, to identify them and to give a very fair idea of the character of the documents when perfect. I suppose you are all more or less familiar with the contents of the 'Gospel of Peter.' You know that our fragment begins just after Pilate has washed his hands of the guilt of condemning our Lord, which is wholly borne, according to this document, by Herod and the Jews. These drag away our Lord to crown Him with the crown of thorns and to crucify Him. He all the while keeps silence, 'as having no pain,' but one of the malefactors reproaches the crucifiers, saying, 'We have suffered thus for the evils that we have done, but this man having become a saviour of men, how hath He wronged you?' Then comes the darkness at noon, and the Jews are alarmed, not at the portent, but lest the sun should have really set, and so the Law should have been broken. Then 'the Lord cried out, saying, "My Power, my Power, thou hast forsaken Me"; and having said it, He was taken up.' Here we may remark in passing not only that our Lord's cry on the Cross has been given a turn whereby it attests the non-catholic belief that His Divine nature departed from Him just before the death on the Cross, but also that this new turn has been given to the cry through a misunderstanding of the Aramaic words preserved in Mark and Matthew, *Eli* being understood to mean 'My Power,' and not 'My God.' Thus we see in the Gospel of Peter at this point an interpretation of Mark (or Matthew) rather than real independent historical reminiscence. The style of paraphrase is after all not unlike that which is put into the mouth of Pistis Sophia in her 'repentances.'

The Gospel of Peter goes on to narrate the deposition and burial of the Lord and the Guard at the Tomb, and then describes the Resurrection in detail, as seen by the Soldiers and the Elders who were keeping watch with them. It is very well told, and there is an impressive dignity in the Voice from Heaven which speaks to our Lord as He emerges from the Tomb, saying, 'Hast thou preached to them that sleep?' But however much or however little the writer may have used the Canonical Gospels, we do not feel that he is any nearer the historical facts.

The visit of the women to the Tomb on the Easter morning is narrated in our fragment very much as in Mark, and it goes on to tell what occurred afterwards, when Simon Peter (in whose mouth the whole story is put) went away fishing with Andrew and Levi the son of Alphæus. At this point our fragment comes to an end: evidently the Gospel of Peter went on to narrate an appearance of the Risen Lord in Galilee.

The fragment of the Apocalypse of Peter which is preserved in the same MS shews us the Lord in the midst of the disciples predicting the false prophets and the oppression that was to precede the final Judgement, exactly as in the *Testamentum Domini*, but instead of going on to draw up rules for Church government, the revelation that He gives is about the state of the righteous dead, who live in a land of brightness and never-fading flowers, and about the state of the wicked, who are tormented according to the nature of their sins. Here, of course, we pass beyond the region of the Canonical Gospels. But the question I wish to raise is whether, in passing from the 'Gospel of Peter' to the 'Apocalypse of

Peter,' we have really passed from one work to another? Is it not possible that our two fragments are really parts of the same work?

In the MS from Akhmim there are no running titles, no indication of the name by which the fragments were known. But both fragments profess to be the work of Simon Peter,[1] who writes partly in his own name, partly in the name of the Twelve: the phrase 'we, the Twelve Disciples,' occurs both in the Gospel and in the Apocalypse. I cannot help thinking that both Gospel and Apocalypse form only one work, and that its main object was to commend the description of Paradise and Hell by setting it in a quasi-historical framework.[2]

It is very likely that the writer did not draw entirely on his imagination for his theories about the state of men after death. Dr. Montague James has suggested that their ultimate origin is

[1] Ἐγὼ δὲ Σίμων Πέτρος, *Ev. Pet.* § 14, *ad fin.*; ἐγὼ δὲ μετὰ τῶν ἑταίρων μου, § 7. The expression ἡμεῖς οἱ δώδεκα μαθηταὶ occurs *Ev. Pet.* § 14, and also *Apoc. Pet.* § 2. The transition in *Apoc. Pet.* § 4, is made thus ἰδόντες οὖν ... ἔκθαμβοι γεγόναμεν ... καὶ προσελθὼν τῷ Κυρίῳ εἶπόν ... λέγει μοι κ.τ.λ.

[2] The main objection to regarding the Gospel and Apocalypse of Peter as parts of a single work is that some authorities reckon the length of this Apocalypse at 270 or 300 *stichi*. According to this, very little would now be lost. More probably, however, the Revelation may have been separated off at a later time after the whole work fell into disrepute as heretical, just as 'Paul and Thecla' was separated off from the 'Acts of Paul.'

to be found in Egyptian beliefs and the cycle of ideas that underlie the *Ritual of the Dead*, and this is very likely to be the case. No doubt Pseudo-Peter altered what he took, just as he freely altered the Gospel narratives of the Passion. And perhaps the Egyptian priests would be as ready to charge him with heresy from their point of view, as Serapion was from the point of view of Christological doctrine. The fault of which I would accuse Pseudo-Peter is not his use of S. Peter's name or his Docetism. I venture to think his main fault is that which he shares with the compilers of the *Testamentum Domini* and of the *Pistis Sophia*. It is this, that he has used the Gospel to bring us to his doctrines, and that he has forgotten his Hero in the events which he describes and the doctrines which he makes Him teach. It is hardly a mere trick of style that the 'Gospel of Peter' always speaks of 'the Lord': the memory of Jesus was merged into that of the wholly supernatural Being, the mere touch of whose dead body caused the earth to shudder.[1]

The Apocryphal Gospels we have hitherto been considering have dealt with the Passion and the period after the Resurrection. A few words must now be said in passing on the group that deal with the early history of our Lord. These

[1] *Ev. Pet.* § 6.

are all of very small historical and ethical value. Some, like the '*Protevangelium* of James,' narrate the birth and childhood of the Virgin Mary, as well as the birth of our Lord; others, like the 'Gospel of Thomas the Israelite,' tell stories about the childhood of Jesus. These documents are of unknown age. No doubt the comparatively orthodox forms in which they have survived to our time are not the earliest forms in which they were circulated, but at any rate the silly story about the child Jesus refusing to learn the Alphabet from His teacher was used by the Marcosians whom Irenæus refutes.[1] No one can suppose that any of these Gospels of the Infancy rests on anything which has a right to be called Tradition. Their genesis is rather to be sought in the same circumstances that gave rise to the Christian and Pseudo-Christian Gnostic speculations. They represent what in the imagination of some thinkers must have occurred, if the Christ on whom they believed was really the Son of God sent down from Heaven. But the attempt to glorify the infancy of Jesus does not succeed. The 'Gospel of Thomas' is a record of miracles performed by Jesus from five to twelve years old, ending with the visit to Jerusalem which is narrated in the Gospel of

[1] Iren. *Haer.* i 20; cf. *Ev. Thomae*, § 6.

Luke. To us who have learnt to know our Lord through the Canonical Gospels the tales are only a painful exhibition of the bad taste of the writer. Perhaps the least offensive is the story of how Jesus made clay sparrows on the Sabbath, and when rebuked for breaking the Law He clapped His hands and the sparrows flew away. As I said just now, some at least of these stories are very ancient, and that the Catholic Church rejected them shews that the Church required more from those who wished to honour her Lord than the mere ascription of miracles to Him. The Jesus of these tales is not really Human, and although the orthodox Church writers of the second century repudiated most strongly the accusation of worshipping a mere man, they nevertheless held fast to the true humanity of Jesus Christ.

One point I wish especially to bring forward, a point which shews, I think, more clearly than any other that the tales about Christ which were circulated were ultimately inspired by theological and philosophical considerations, not by historical and biographical interest. It is this—the absolute silence concerning the whole period between the boyhood of our Lord and His Baptism. The Gospel of Thomas and the *Protevangelium* shew us that mere lack of historical material did not hinder the development of tales about the doings of our Lord on earth. The coming of the Son of God into the world of humanity appeared to the thinkers of the second century a difficult and mysterious process. Their thoughts dwelt on it, as to how and in what manner it could be, and the result of these thoughts shew themselves both in the speculations of Valentinus and his companions, and in the puerilities of 'Thomas the Israelite.' But it was agreed that the Son of God, in whatever manner and with whatever nature He had been born into the world, passed the long years between His boyhood and His Baptism without any outward manifestation or assumption of special Powers or Authority. It was a period of mere natural growth: consequently it excited no interest at all in the second century. Had the men of that time the same sort of biographical interest in Jesus Christ that we have, this period would not have been left in unbroken silence.

The most interesting of all the lost Gospels is doubtless that which is known as the 'Gospel according to the Hebrews,' and it is a little discouraging to have to record that recent modern discovery and criticism have added practically nothing to our knowledge of it. The greater part of the fragments that are preserved have come down to us through quotations made by S. Jerome, who found the Gospel used by the Nazarean Christians of Aleppo. These 'Nazareans' allowed S. Jerome to examine their book. The Greek and Latin rendering which S. Jerome made has unluckily perished, but he quotes the Gospel here and there, as Origen also had done before him.[1]

Those who quote the Gospel according to the Hebrews naturally quote it for something which differs from the Canonical Gospels. Where that Gospel agreed with the Canonical Gospels it was not worth quoting specially. Consequently what we have is a bundle of strange-looking fragments, representing the peculiarities of the Gospel. If it had been preserved as a whole we should doubtless find much which is already represented in Matthew, Mark, and Luke. In fact, the general impression produced by most of the fragments is that the document is a first cousin, if not a sister document, to the Canonical Gospel according to Matthew. For instance, Jerome quotes from the Gospel according to the Hebrews as follows :—[2]

[1] The fragments have often been collected together: my references are to Preuschen's *Antilegomena*, a very useful collection of all the non-canonical Gospel fragments.

[2] *Contra Pelag.* iii 2 (*Preuschen*, 6).

"'If thy brother have sinned in word and have done thee amends, seven times in the day receive him.' Simon His disciple said to Him, 'Seven times in the day?' The Lord answered and said to him, 'Yea, I say to thee, unto seventy times seven. For even in the Prophets, after they were anointed with the Holy Spirit, there was found matter of sin.'"

The latter part of this saying is found as a marginal note to Matt xviii 21, 22, in a Greek minuscule MS,[1] in which the Hebrew Gospel is called *τὸ Ἰουδαϊκόν.* The last clause is, as Dr. Westcott says, obscure: it seems to mean that since even the inspired prophets were not sinless, it is unreasonable to expect our neighbours to be without fault. But I did not quote the passage for exegetical reasons. I quoted it, because it definitely states that the Saying of our Lord about forgiving 'unto seventy times seven' had a place in the Nazarean Gospel, and that in a form which bears all the marks of superior originality to the parallels in Matt xviii 21, 22, and Lk xvii 3, 4. With Matthew it speaks of seventy times seven and brings Simon Peter into the story; with Luke it definitely supposes that the offender has asked for pardon, and speaks of forgiving seven times in the day. So far as this passage is concerned we might even regard the Nazarean extract as giving us the text of the lost document common to Matthew and Luke, which I have

[1] Cod. ev. 566.

called Q; but since the Nazarean Gospel has parallels elsewhere with Matthew, where Luke has none, it is better to regard the Nazarean form as simply giving another text of the Matthean type. For example, the same minuscule which has the note at Matt xviii 22, says, at Matt xvi 17, that *τὸ Ἰουδαϊκόν* has 'Son of John' instead of 'Bar-jona': this can only mean that the Gospel according to the Hebrews contained the Saying of our Lord to S. Peter about the Gates of Hell, which begins in the Canonical text, 'Blessed art thou, Simon Bar-jona'; and this is a saying which is definitely Matthean.

Similarly, S. Jerome tells us, in commenting upon Matt xxiii 35, that in the Nazarean Gospel it is written 'Zacharias, son of Jehoiada,' instead of 'Zacharias, son of Barachias.' The parallel in Lk xi 51 has 'Zacharias' only, without any patronymic. Here it is pretty certain that the Nazarean Gospel does not present the primitive text. No doubt by the 'son of Barachias' is meant that unfortunate Zacharias whose murder in the Temple is related by Josephus; and if this be so, the saying as reported in Matt xxiii 35 cannot be a verbally correct report of words of Jesus. But it is very unlikely that He should have referred to the murder of the son of Jehoiada mentioned in 2 Chron xxiv 20, 21. The general meaning of the phrase, if we read 'son of Jehoiada' with the Nazarean Gospel, is, "all the murders done in the name of religion from Genesis to Malachi"; the general meaning of the phrase, if we read 'son of Barachias' with the Canonical Matthew, is, "all the murders done in the name of religion from the beginning of human history to the present day." This last is the true meaning: the reading of the Nazarean Gospel implies a study of the Bible rather than that of the human heart.

There are two other passages of the Gospel according to the Hebrews which I must mention here, as I think they bring out very well the considerable, but not supreme, value of this lost monument of early Christianity. The first, preserved by Eusebius,[1] tells us that in this Gospel there was a different form of the Parable of the Talents, in which three servants were mentioned —the virtuous one who multiplied his Lord's talent, the slothful one who hid the talent, and a prodigal who wasted it; and that the one was welcomed, the second only blamed, while punishment was reserved for the prodigal. Thus the whole point of the Parable was changed, in order to drag in a piece of what may be called Sunday School morality. Had the prodigal servant stood

[1] Mai, *Nov. Patr. Bibl.* iv 1, p. 155 (*Preuschen*, 7).

in the original form of the Parable, I cannot think so obviously edifying a judgement would have been suppressed both by Matthew and by Luke.

The second passage is very similar. In Origen's Commentary on Matt xix 16 ff, as preserved in the ancient Latin version, we read:

"It is written in a certain Gospel called 'According to the Hebrews,' if any one will receive it, not as an authority, but as an illustration of the subject before us:—The other of the rich men said to him, 'Master, what good thing shall I do to live?' He said to him, 'O man, do the Law and the Prophets.' He answered unto him, 'I have done them.' He said to him, 'Go, sell all that thou hast and distribute to the poor, and come, follow me.' But the rich man began to scratch his head, and it did not please him. And the Lord said to him, 'How sayest thou, I have done the Law and the Prophets? Because it is written in the Law, *Thou shalt love thy neighbour as thyself*, and lo, many of thy brethren, sons of Abraham, are clothed in filth, dying of hunger; and thy house is full of many good things, and nothing at all goes out of it to them.' And He turned and said to Simon His disciple, who was sitting by Him, 'Simon, son of John, it is easier for a camel to go through the eye of a needle, than a rich man into the Kingdom of Heaven.'"

This well-known passage raises many questions, but I think there can be little doubt about the most important point. There can be little doubt that this form of the story is in the end derived from what we read in Mark, and that it is of inferior historical value. This second rich man was doubtless introduced by the same hand that introduced the prodigal into the Parable of the Talents, and for the same reason, viz. the supposed interests of ordinary ethical teaching.

The condemnation of the Rich Young Man in the Gospels seemed too severe, unless it could be asserted that he had *not* fulfilled the Law, as he claimed to have done. But in the story as we have it in Mark (and in Luke) the man is not blamed for being niggardly or for not having told the truth. He is blamed for lack of real enthusiasm. In the historical setting, as he spoke with our Lord on the way to the Passion at Jerusalem, he is simply found to be unfit to volunteer. The Lord did not tell him to distribute his property to the poor because they were in need; He told him to get rid of his property, because at that crisis the ties of respectability would be an encumbrance to those who wished to follow Him. But in the story as told in the Gospel according to the Hebrews the historical situation is forgotten, and the writer is anxious to emphasise the claims of the poor rather than the call to follow Jesus to the death.

In one noteworthy point the Gospel according to the Hebrews and the Canonical Matthew agree in an alteration of the Marcan story which is certainly not primitive. 'Master, what good thing shall I do?' is certainly less primitive than 'Good Master, what shall I do?' followed as the latter is by the answer, 'Why callest thou Me Good?' The fragments of the Gospel according to the Hebrews are not extensive enough for us accurately to determine its literary relation to the Canonical Gospel according to Matthew, but that they form a special group of the Synoptic documents derived from and historically inferior to our Gospel according to Mark, this passage alone is enough to demonstrate.

The most curious point about this Hebrew Gospel, and one that is at present unexplained, is that it is said to be shorter than our Matthew. Wherever its readings are preserved it gives an extended and fuller text. We have seen there is a second Rich Man and a third Servant in the Parable. There is also the impressive story of the appearance of the Risen Christ to S. James the Just, which is not represented at all in the Canonical Gospels. If, therefore, the Hebrew Gospel and our Matthew were nearly akin, and yet the Hebrew Gospel had all this extra matter, there must have been great omissions somewhere in the course of the narrative. It cannot, I think, be quite certainly discovered whether there was anything in it corresponding to the Nativity Story of our Matthew,[1] but that would only account for some 100 lines of the ancient reckoning, and if the figures of Nicephorus's

[1] Jerome, *De Viris Illustr.* 3, may be referring to the Canonical text.

Stichometry be correct, the Hebrew Gospel had only 2000 lines to 2500 in Matthew. It is difficult not to think that the figures must be wrong, and that the Gospel contained nearly all that we find in the Canonical Matthew, with other matter beside.

I do not propose to give here a detailed criticism of the fragments which commonly go by the name of the 'Oxyrhynchus Logia.' Very valuable and interesting they are—who would question it?—but I venture to think they add very little to our knowledge of the Gospel History. In the first place, it is almost impossible to work with mere fragments. The fragments of the Gospel and Apocalypse of Peter contain 16 rather closely written pages of text, but the fragments of the document published by Dr. Grenfell and Dr. Hunt in 1897 and 1904 only consist of two leaves, and one of these is torn across, so that half of every line is lost. It is obvious that any conclusions based upon such materials must be beset with much uncertainty. But besides this, I am not at all sure that the Sayings of Jesus in the Oxyrhynchus Papyri would commend themselves as historically authentic, if the whole document were preserved. I find it a little difficult to believe that a document which puts 'The Kingdom of Heaven is within you' side by side with the Greek maxim 'Know yourselves' can be regarded as a faithful report of the words of Jesus of Nazareth. Perhaps the Oxyrhynchus documents may have preserved genuine Sayings of Jesus which were otherwise unknown, but the collection must have been mixed with non-Semitic elements. I feel sure that its main value is apprehended, when it is regarded as a monument of the influence of Christianity upon Greek thought.

It is the special merit of the Synoptic Gospels, and, above all, of the Gospel according to S. Mark, that they are so little influenced by the spirit of the Greco-Roman civilisation. The Church itself became ever more and more European. Greek and Roman ideas of Philosophy and Law became dominant in the Theology and the Organisation of Christendom. We cannot doubt that it was good that it should be so. The mission of Christianity is to influence the world, not to impose itself upon the world as an alien domination. The Kingdom of God is like unto leaven; and the use of leaven is not primarily to make more leaven, but to make good bread. It was therefore necessary that, in proportion as Christianity became a living influence upon the ages, it should take up into itself the ideas and conceptions that make the ages what they are, and that the primitive forms in which Christianity was embodied should suffer change and disappear.

But this is not all. Christianity is something more than a belief in a Divine Spirit which influences the world through the medium of a Society of men in which it works. Throughout all the multifarious varieties of Christian speculation, belief in the transcendent importance of the Life and Work of Jesus Christ remains.

The Church is conscious that it cannot afford to lose touch with Christ, with the Jesus of Nazareth who once suffered on the Cross. It was this which, in the second century, drove the Church back upon historical tradition to escape the inferences of Gnostic theorizing about Christ and His work, so that the Church's belief became enshrined in accounts of the Life of Jesus as well as in Creed and Sacrament.

I have purposely abstained in these Lectures from discussing most of those parts or features of the Gospel History which usually form the subject-matter of modern controversies. Our belief or disbelief in most of the Articles in the Apostles' Creed does not ultimately rest on historical criticism of the Gospels, but upon the general view of the universe, of the order of things, which our training and environment, or our inner experience, has led us severally to take. The Birth of our Lord from a virgin and His Resurrection from the dead—to name the most obvious Articles of the Creed—are not matters which historical criticism can establish. The exclamation in Addison's Play, "It must be so; Plato, thou reasonest well!" is not really true to life: fundamental beliefs are rarely acquired through a logical process. As I ventured to say in the Introductory Lecture, we do not get our leading ideas of religion or philosophy from historical criticism. But the Christian religion is not only a matter of imagination and philosophy. The Crucifixion under Pontius Pilate and the Death and Burial of our Lord are as much Articles of the Christian Creed as the Resurrection itself. And in these Articles, Christianity enters the arena of ordinary history. The Interpretation of the Life of Jesus Christ in Palestine is a matter of Faith; but the Tale itself, the course of events, belongs to History and is a matter for the scientific historian to scrutinise.

Meanwhile, I am sure it is the plain duty of the Christian investigator to strive to get as clear ideas as he can of the outward events of the Ministry of Jesus, and of the positions which our Lord actually took up with regard to the thought and action of the age in which He lived among men. The more we understand these things, the more we individualise the Figure of our Lord as manifested in action in that long past scene, the better we shall be able to embody the spirit of His teaching in forms appropriate to our own surroundings.

NOTE ON THE LATIN PROLOGUES TO S. PAUL'S EPISTLES.

AMONG the many contributions to Biblical and Patristic learning that have been made during the last three hundred years by members of the Benedictine Order few have been so startling as the sixteen pages communicated by Dom D. de Bruyne to the *Revue Bénédictine* for January 1907. The object of Dom de Bruyne's paper is to shew that the short 'arguments' or prologues, prefixed to S. Paul's Epistles in most MSS of the Latin Vulgate and frequently printed in Editions of the Bible, are the work of Marcion and were originally composed as headings for the Epistles in the Marcionite *Apostolicon.* This surprising theory has been accepted by Harnack (*Theologische Literaturzeitung* for March, 1907), and indeed after reading de Bruyne's paper it is difficult to understand why so many generations of scholars, from Victorinus and Ambrosiaster to those of our own day, should have been blind to the marks of Marcionite authorship. The set does not include an 'argument' to Hebrews, and those to Timothy and Titus, and to 2 Corinthians and 2 Thessalonians, are of a different construction from the others. The argument to Ephesians also is later, being merely an imitation of those to Philippians and Thessalonians. But the remainder all belong to one series, which also included an Epistle 'to the Laodiceans.' They were arranged in this order: Galatians, Corinthians, Romans, Thessalonians, [Laodiceans,] Colossians, Philippians, Philemon. At least it is certain that Galatians came before Corinthians and that Colossians came immediately after 'Laodiceans,'—and this is Marcion's order and nomenclature.

But it is the contents of these Prologues, their standpoint and theological ideas, that are definitely Marcionite. They are the work of one who was as much obsessed by the opposition of Paulinism to Judaizing Christianity as was Baur himself. All the Epistles are looked at from the point of view of the Epistle to the Galatians and the struggle between the Apostle and his opponents the Pseudo-Apostles. None but Marcionites occupied this point of view in the second and third centuries. And who but a Marcionite would have described the teaching of the 'false Apostles' as it is described in the Prologue to Romans, where it says that their converts 'had been brought into the Law and the Prophets' (*in legem et prophetas erant inducti*)? The Law might be merely Jewish in parts, but the very essence of second-century Catholic theology was that the Prophets spoke God's word about Christ and the Church. It was Marcion alone who rejected the Prophets.

As the Prologues are so short, I quote them in full that they may speak for themselves:—

'*Galatians* are Greeks. These accepted the word of truth first from the Apostle, but after his departure were tempted by false Apostles to turn to the law and circumcision. These the Apostle recalls to the faith of the truth, writing to them from Ephesus.'

'*Corinthians* are of Achaia. And these similarly heard the word of truth from the Apostle and were perverted variously by false Apostles, some by the wordy eloquence of philosophy, others brought in by the sect of the Jewish Law. These the Apostle recalls to the true Evangelical wisdom, writing to them from Ephesus by Timothy.'

'*Romans* are in the parts of Italy. These were reached beforehand by false Apostles, and under the name of our Lord Jesus Christ had been brought in to the Law and the Prophets. These the Apostle recalls to the true Evangelical faith, writing to them from Corinth.'

'*Thessalonians* are Macedonians [in Christ

Jesus], who having accepted the word of truth persevered in the faith even in persecution from their fellow-citizens. Moreover, also, they received not the things said by false Apostles. These the Apostle praises, writing to them from Athens [by Timothy].'

'*Laodiceans* . . . ' (missing).[1]

'*Colossians*—these also like the Laodiceans are of Asia, and they had been reached beforehand by Pseudo-Apostles, nor did the Apostle himself come to them. But these also by an Epistle he corrects, for they had heard the word from Archippus, who also accepted a ministry unto them. Therefore the Apostle already in custody writes to them from Ephesus.'

'*Philippians* are Macedonians. These having accepted the word of truth persevered in the faith, nor did they receive false Apostles. These the Apostle praises, writing to them from Rome [out of prison by Epaphroditus].'

'To *Philemon* he sends a private letter for Onesimus his slave, and writes to him from Rome out of prison.'

The bracketed passages are omitted in the text as read in the Freising Palimpsest, the only

[1] The extant Argument to the Ep. to the Ephesians runs as follows: 'Ephesians are of Asia. These having accepted the word of truth persevered in the faith. These the Apostle praises, writing to them from the City of Rome out of prison by Tychicus the Deacon.'

extant Old Latin MS of this part of the New Testament. The Prologues are said to be not by the first hand in this MS, but, even if this be so, they were added in the sixth or seventh century, and thus this text is one of the oldest and most independent we possess of them. It is worth remark that no prologue is given in the Freising MS to 2 Corinthians, a fact which accords with de Bruyne's view that the short Prologue to this epistle found in many MSS does not belong to the Marcionite series.

When once the key-word 'Marcion' has been uttered, the Prologues need no commentary. I cannot do better than conclude here in Harnack's words (*Theol. Ltztg.* 1907, col. 140). After pointing out that the Prologues must have been originally composed in Greek, not only because of certain expressions, but also because no one living in the West would have written *Romani sunt in partibus Italiae*, Harnack says: 'We know now, unless unexpected objections are raised, that just as the Catholic Martyrology goes back to an Arian Martyrology [*i.e.* that quoted on p. 254], so also the ancient Prologues are a monument of the Marcionite Church standing in the midst of the Catholic New Testament. Is not the canonised collection of the Pauline Epistles itself such a monument?'

GENERAL INDEX

GENERAL INDEX

GENERAL INDEX

INDEX OF BIBLICAL REFERENCES

INDEX OF BIBLICAL REFERENCES